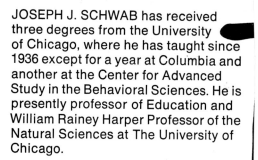

JOSEPH J. SCHWAB has received
three degrees from the University
of Chicago, where he has taught since
1936 except for a year at Columbia and
another at the Center for Advanced
Study in the Behavioral Sciences. He is
presently professor of Education and
William Rainey Harper Professor of the
Natural Sciences at The University of
Chicago.

COLLEGE
CURRICULUM
AND
STUDENT PROTEST

COLLEGE CURRICULUM AND STUDENT PROTEST

Joseph J. Schwab

THE UNIVERSITY OF CHICAGO PRESS
CHICAGO AND LONDON

Library of Congress Catalog Card Number: 69-15416

The University of Chicago Press, Chicago 60637
The University of Chicago Press, Ltd., London W.C. 1

CONTENTS

ACKNOWLEDGMENT

My institution, the University of Chicago, has long enjoyed an unusual degree of community, so much, indeed, that I would have great difficulty in tracing particular ideas in this book to particular individuals. This community, moreover, has shown an astonishing capacity for survival: the habits of lending ears and ideas not only endure, they also are contagious. This is so much the case that with each new generation my debt to colleagues increases. Among those currently present, I can surely identify as contributors, witting or not:

Wayne Booth	Norman Maclean
James Charbonnet	Richard McKeon
Marc Cogan	Gerhard Meyer
Harold Dunkel	William O'Meara
Jerome Frese	James Redfield
Knox Hill	Charles Wegener
Edward Levi	Gilbert White
Donald Levine	Warner Wick

Of course, I will have clarified, simplified, vulgarized, distorted or otherwise altered many of their contributions. The reader is therefore given the customary warning: what he approves may be credited to my colleagues; what he disapproves may be laid to me.

I am also much indebted to the Ford Foundation for a grant which made it possible to complete the book with reasonable dispatch.

College Curriculum and
Student Protest

INTRODUCTION

This book, is, in a sense, medical. It is, first, an examination of the style, the expression, and some of the content of student protest as presenting symptoms of evils of their education; student ineptitudes and ignorances indicating neglects by the curriculum; perversities indicating distortions and mistreatments. It is, second, a survey of resources available for treatment of these curricular ills. Third, it is a series of specific prescriptions drawing on these resources and aiming to ameliorate the ills identified.

The prescriptions are not intended to abolish or quiet student protest but they may improve it by two avenues. On the one hand, they should make instigators and purveyors of student protest better able to see and discriminate facts and more competent at using them well. This might change considerably some of the content and tactics of student protest. On the other hand, since the ills diagnosed are ills of the curriculum (not of the protesting student alone), and the prescriptions are addressed to the curriculum, the beneficiaries should be most students. They should become a more demanding and discriminating clientele, better able to distinguish the better and worse among alternative actions and proffered arguments.

The promise of such gains will not move some administrators and faculty, especially those who subscribe to the supermarket view of universities. In this view, the central fact is that protestors are few and the silent, many. Ergo, "Since the large majority of students tolerate what we are doing now, why change?" If we take the argument as stated, there can be no reply. If the first principle of education is to expend the minimum energy necessary to satisfy the ignorant client, so be it. It would be a mistake, however, to assume that "to tolerate" means "to be satisfied with, to be pleased by." On the contrary, the current of dissatisfaction and uneasiness about college curriculums runs deep, and well beyond the borders of the highly audible protest group. There are very good students who note and formulate weaknesses of the curriculum quietly instead of disruptively (so far). There are many more who note uneasily but are silent by virtue of conditioning to conformity or because of the anxiety roused by the risks of protest. It is in the light of such facts that protest becomes an extremely useful body of presenting symptoms. It is the "silent" coronary thrombosis which kills.

There is one unpleasant but necessary consequence of this treatment of student protest and curriculum. As one student put it, "You aren't being fair! You don't say what's good about student protest." I don't. I am not "fair" to either side; what is good about protest, protesters, curriculums, and professors, what is already in a healthful state, would become relevant to present purposes only if there were so little of it as to constitute a hopeless case, rendering any prescription useless. I do not think this is true. Some aspects of student protest are contemptible, some laughable, some boring. Some aspects of American education are contemptible, some laughable, and many boring. But some aspects of student protest are admirable; so too, some aspects of American education.

In one respect, the book *is* "fair." It is not a recipe for giving student protest what it wants, a sedative program with which to quiet student protest, or a demonstration that what students want should be denied them. Some things students want are, in fact, recommended here, but not simply because they want them. Some things that protesters ask for are here denied or ignored, but not because they ask for them.

There are also omissions entailed in a treatment of protest as symptomatic. It will not provide a solution to the moral-legal-administrative problem of handling the disruptions, "civil disobediences," and violations of civil rights often involved in student activism, though such a solution, especially one which is not itself a violation of defensible rights or a capitulation to threat, is sorely needed. It will not provide an acceptable psychosocial explanation for the rise of activism. It will not provide a satisfyingly direct response to the content of student protest.

DIAGNOSES I

Diagnosis 1   Conditioned paranoids

There can be no doubt that some student activists are sick. A very few are very sick: incipient schizophrenics, psychopathic personalities, free-floating haters, and depressives. Such cases are beyond the competence of a university or college as such. They are the business of admissions officers and psychiatrists. Equally clearly, however, such persons are a tiny percentage of student activists.

A larger percentage of the sick ones are mild paranoids and anxiety states. These *are* the business of college and university as such. It takes very little scrutiny to see that the style and severity of their symptoms closely resemble those of many assistant professors approaching the up or out point of their contractual tenures. It takes no more to see that the symptoms in the two groups arise from much the same sources. Student activists, like many assistant professors, do not know who makes decisions. They do not know how decisions are made well. They have only foggy and incomplete knowledge of the number and variety of considerations which go into the making of good decisions.

They do not know because, on the one hand, we have not taught them and because, on the other hand, we have mistaught them by making them on occasion both witness and victim of bad decisions badly made.

That we have mistaught them is patent enough.

The "constitutional" student government whose actions are subject to review and reversal at whim by a dean or other administrative officer is one case in point. Another, and worse, consists of the nearly universal existence of large numbers of elective courses with names cryptic and catalog descriptions opaque, as far as students are concerned. A third, even more vicious in its side effects, consists in our widespread insistence on early commitment by students to a "major" or field of concentration. A fourth and significant one: the neatness and air of inevitability with which we invest our accounts in science textbooks and lectures of the evidences which lead to current theory.

Through operations like the first of these—student government—we mock students. In effect, we tell them that they may play at decision-making as long as the outcomes agree with ours. The original reason for such a policy is clear enough: students, as treated currently, are put in no position to maintain a respectable frequency of good decisions, and on good decisions the prosperity of the institution obviously rests. Indeed, students lack at least three crucial components of such competence. (1) They are unaware of the bodies of fact which link almost all decisions on student life to the surrounding community. They are almost equally unaware of the facts of *diversity* of interest and attitude among students and professors which constitutes an additional part of the problem of decision. (2) They are unskilled, because untrained, in ways of dealing with the numerous, concrete facts of actual situations, even where they know of them. (3) Perhaps most important, their "involvement" with the institution is inadequate: that is, their felt sense of its life expectancy does not exceed the four years of their tenure; their

sense of the threat of having to undergo the consequences of a bad decision is pale and dilute by virtue
of their merely peripheral membership in the community and remote connection with those among the
faculties whose membership is intimate and durable.

Students need not, however, be forever treated as
they now are. Their ignorance of the facts of institutional life, their lack of prudential skill, their inadequate
affective involvement in the ongoing life of the college
or university are conditions which can be remedied
in some, perhaps considerable, degree by means which
can be defended as legitimate parts of their education.
I shall presently suggest such means.

Through the second of these misteachings—the prof-
fering of opaque electives—we positively *celebrate* nonrationality of decision. Where electives exist for the
earlier years of student tenure, nearly all are opaque
and almost entirely so. Not even the names of subject
fields convey much; course descriptions convey still
less. Even in later years, the student has little more
by which to judge. He may have some idea of what
he will learn *about* in a given course, but not much of
what he will learn about it. He cannot know what disciplines are required by the problems of the course.
("Prerequisite: Economics 207" merely pushes the
problem back to Economics 207.) He has no way to
know what disciplines he will acquire—or forever miss.
He does not know whether he wants them, whether
he ought to want them, or what they will do to him.
Yet there the electives are, and elect he must. The
election thus becomes a repeated exercise in blind
choice, submission to scuttlebutt, or control by the
equivalent of brokers' tips.

It is clear, I hope, that the problem is not the exis-

tence of electives but their opaqueness as described and
proffered to students. It is not, morever, an opaqueness
to be overcome merely by more elaborate printed descriptions, for the appropriate language of description
is itself opaque to the extent that the electives—as
they should—lead away from what the student knows
best. What is required, especially on the subjective side,
the side of knowing what it *feels* like to submit to and
to be master of the disciplines of a course, is some form
of anticipatory experience of it—immediate or by a still
vivid one remove. A way to provide such experience
will be described.

The third of these misteachings—insistence on early
commitment to a major—is obviously damaging, in
direct effect as well as side effect. Very few students—
mainly those with a conspicuous bent in one direction
only—know enough about their tastes, their talents,
and the character of the academic fields to have the
raw materials for a good decision.

Consider, first, our failure to test talents and exhibit
the character of a field. Most high school and first-year
collegiate courses (especially surveys and general
courses) systematically convey a false impression of the
fields they represent and the talents they require. They
do so by almost universal use of a single device. Instead
of giving experience of the kinds of problems and modes
of enquiry characteristic of the field, they provide the
student with the experience of assimilating, applying,
or otherwise using the *fruits* of enquiry in the field.
Yet these two—assimilation and use as against pursuit
of a body of knowledge—are often radically different
in the competences they require and the satisfactions
they afford. Consider, as a crude but telling example,
the difference between solving a textbook problem in

genetics as against charting the breeding pattern which would discern an unknown mode of inheritance, carrying out the indicated experiments, and processing the resulting data. Consider, again, the vast difference between glib use of a historical generalization to "throw light" on a current problem as against the processes by which a kind of fact appropriate to a kind of history is discriminated among the welter of kinds, the facts in their particularity sought for and found, and the generalizations constructed with some responsibility.

Tragically enough, in courses deliberately designed as a conspectus of fields leading to student choice, the situation is worse. The faculties involved in such courses often engage in competitive seduction, each taking pains to make the "hard" easy and the complex simple, to replace mathematical equation with spool model, to emphasize the "practical" applications and the economic value of the knowledge it purveys, and to trot out for brief exposure its Famous Name and most winning personalities. Through such devices we eliminate the possibility of a realistic appraisal by the student of his talents and their appropriateness to the available alternatives. We make the whole thing a matter of taste, of likes and dislikes; and even in regard to this factor we are remiss, since we do nothing curricular to rectify students' prevailing false beliefs about the nature and use of felt wants and likes.

Thus the student is misled and discovers he is misled when he comes to the later courses in the field. At this point, effect and side effect become the same. The student comes to a realization of lost time, is haunted by a sense of failure and futility, is unable to determine how far he is at fault, how far the institution.

These are remediable curricular sins. It is entirely

possible to construct and locate in the curriculum the kinds of courses which will represent the activities characteristic of a field and give students a chance to test the talents they require.

The third factor involved in defensible choice of what to do with one's time and energy—the factor of likes and dislikes—poses a vastly more tangled problem. Not the simplest of its tangles arises from the frequency with which we professors take the view that tastes and other such "personal" and "subjective" conditions of students are none of our business. For at the same time we have to live with the consequences of students' tastes (real and fancied) in the shape of the energies mobilized and the energies not mobilized by students and the directions in which they bend these energies. If this unexamined distaste of ours for meddling with the "subjective" is set aside for the moment, three facets of student beliefs and ignorances about tastes emerge (one monstrously absurd, the other two not so obvious) which lend themselves to curricular correction.

First, many students believe that tastes are unalterable, even at age seventeen or eighteen, and that these "unalterable" tastes are the first defenses of the citadel of "self," to be asserted and defended at all costs. Much of this view is assimilated from the vulgarity of the parental community ("I've got as much right to my opinion as anybody else": "I don't like the violin"—or asparagus or Jews), but much of it is confirmed by our professorial smugness. We betray to students our own unexamined tastes and biases. By inflection and grimace some of us boast about them. We do little or nothing to offer models of examination and self-correction of tastes and prejudices. The smugness could be altered only by education of professors, a difficult task. The lack of models can be rectified by curricular devices to be described.

Second, students are almost unanimously ignorant of the extent to which tastes derive from and are changed by discovery, development, and recognizable use of competences. I shall examine this point in a later diagnosis.

Third, students are largely ignorant of the nature of "wants" and the extent to which "wants" misrepresent themselves. Like the progressive educators before them, they confuse "want" in the sense of a deprivation with "want" in the sense of "I want—." Further, they are unaware of the extent to which the immediate representations to consciousness of wantings and not wantings are unreliable: that the midnight "wanting" of a peanut butter sandwich can go unappeased by the eating of the sandwich; that our impulses are often dark and obscure; that they are often seen only in the mask with which our inexperience clothes them; that they require, if life is not to be entirely short and brutish, enough of suspense, of temporary check, to permit examination of them and reflection about them.

This unawareness, this ignorance about want and wanting, is having grave consequences and will continue to have them unless corrected, entirely apart from the problem of choice of major field. Combined with the belief that wants are the first defense of the citadel of self, it constitutes one of the principles of many protest arguments, not only those directed toward anti-institutionalism generally. It underlies student demands that they control curriculum and determine the content of courses. "I'm educating myself the way *they* want.

—I'm not learning what I want to learn—I don't care about the feudal system. I want to learn about life.[1]

It is one of the bases for justifying forcible rebellion: "The institutions *our* resistance has desanctified and delegitimatized, as a result of *our* action AGAINST THEIR OPPRESSIONS OF OTHERS, have lost all authority and, hence, all respect. As such, they have only raw, coercive power. *Since they are without legitimacy in our eyes,* they are without rights."[2]

There is need, then, and also *possibility*, of curricular treatment of this matter. This suggestion will appear absurd to many professors, for many professors are party to the naïvetés which suppose a divorce of thought and action, which subscribe to the self-indulgences of a curbstone Freudianism in which the rational ego can relate to the demanding id only as pander to its appetites, which conceive of "curriculum" only as "courses" and a "course" as a lecture series. Yet it is quite possible to use resources of philosophy and resources of literature in a context of discussion which juxtaposes and interrelates the particular with the general, the immediate with the remote, the affective with the cognitive, and which moves as well as explores and excogitates by drawing its particulars, its immediates, its affects, and its accounts of affects from the experiences of the participants. It is possible to do so, furthermore, without alarums and excursions and without

1. From a letter by a young woman student to the *New York Times,* November 29, 1964, as quoted with approval by Carl Davidson in a document titled "The Multiversity: Crucible of the new working class: Long-range strategies for student power movements" (n.d.).

2. "Toward Institutional Resistance," a mimeographed paper given away at a meeting of the Students for a Democratic Society, November 1967, bearing the name of Carl Davidson, Interorganizational Secretary. The italics are mine.

raising the eyebrows of anyone other than Mrs. Grundy. I despair of providing an adequately vivid description of such a "course" but I shall return to the task as part of the section on articulations.

The fourth example of misteaching with respect to decision—the neatness and air of inevitability with which we invest our accounts of science in textbooks and lectures—dignifies by explicit treatment the alienation of thought and action, theory and practice, which we purvey elsewhere by osmosis. By saying little or nothing about the data which point in directions different from currently accepted theory and by our silence on phenomena not encompassed by current formulations, we give the impression that in science all is unequivocal, all rational, sure, and matter of fact. Typical textbook rhetoric omits the uncertainties of scientific evidence and is silent about the expediencies and prudential considerations which enter into decisions on evidence and preferments among theories. In this way, it reinforces the popular view (popular among academics too) that the reasonable and rational estimation of better and worse among alternatives is a property of science, of the theoretical realm, and hence that choice in the realm of the practical is to be identified only with the nonrational—with whim, unexamined preference, conformity or reaction to existing mores, or unarguable taste.

Through operations like student government, then, we make fools of students. Through opaque electives we demand and celebrate nonrationality of decision. Through the demand for ungrounded early commitment to specialization we mislead and encourage the student to mislead himself. Through textbook rhetoric in the sciences and through our silences we identify the practical with the nonrational.

Little wonder that anxieties, persecution feelings, and a wearisome spate of intemperate, stereotyped protest should flood from students' mouths. Still less should we wonder that they so often cite their unexamined impulsions as sufficient ground for choice and, indeed, confuse the one with the other.

Diagnosis 2   A poverty of models

Two to three percent[3] of student activists are vicious junior demagogues and cornbelt stormtroopers bent on attaining a following by kicking their father surrogates in the teeth and trying to usurp their functions. They are the counterparts of Joseph Conrad's secret agent. They combine ignorance of worldly conditions, handicaps of appearance and manner, considerable native ability and equally considerable interpersonal incompetences in such a fashion as to produce an enormous greed for power and prestige, an infinite capacity for generating righteous indignation and the entirely correct conviction that only the destruction of public faith in legality and the shattering of social order will produce the success to which they are sure they are entitled. These student activists constitute primarily a threat to the very existence of colleges and universities, by way of force and violence, of course, but also by virtue of the administrative and faculty time and energy which are thereby diverted from their proper use. As such, they are beyond the scope of this book. They also constitute symptoms, however, which are very much

3. These and other percentages are crude estimates based on anecdotal data only.

our business. They raise the question of how and why they succeed as well as they do in persuading other students to fight their battles for them—what needs they fill and what kinds of appeals they find effective.

In some institutions, their implosive success suggests a nearly complete vacuum. In others, where the success of the junior demagogue is less spectacular, the character of the demogoguery is seen to be of a similar and curiously significant kind: the demagogue creates not followers but imitators. His hearers tend to go out from his exhortations and recriminations not to do what he exhorts or to become backers, constituencies, cohorts, but to become leaders of their own constituencies, exhorters on a smaller scale, and seekers of lesser targets for their own lesser attacks. The erstwhile listener who finds himself a member of a committee of six attacks three of them in a style appropriate to an absent enemy of hundreds—the style of last night's model demagogue. The chairman of a meeting of twenty amicable persons uses Roberts' Rules in ways appropriate to a large, unruly meeting of dissidents—the problem effectively met by last night's chairlady. The student who meets a five-cent rise in the price of a college cafeteria hamburger sees the increase as one more exploitation of downtrodden labor (namely, middle-class students), compares it with the exploitation of itinerant farm workers, and finds the forces at work just as sinister.

This enthusiastic tendency toward imitation, this absence in a revolutionary movement of "party discipline," as it would have been called thirty years ago, leaves little doubt about one vacuum the demagogues fill. It is an absence of maturer and better models, of adults visibly and palpably exemplifying styles of life, uses of talents and competences, preoccupations, cultivated tastes and concerns which are sources of enduring satisfaction to them and of useful outcomes to others.

The scarcity of models is of two kinds. In some small colleges it is a literal poverty, a poverty of models as such. The faculty have no professional lives apart from their teaching. They make no music. They write no books. They uncover no new knowledge. They forge no policies. They are not conspicuously engaged in honorable public service. They administer little apart from their homes and classrooms. They teach, to be sure, but their teaching is the full-time service they perform, not a flowering or a sharing of expertise or scholarship. In consequence, the teaching, after a first few years, becomes dull for the students and by them seen to be unsatisfying to the teacher.

In some multiversities, it is a literal poverty of another sort. The visible bulk of the faculty is very busy indeed but not at their own business. They are not doing what flows from their talents but what is marketable. Here, as in the occasional small college, the intrinsic satisfactions are visibly low. The pay (in fame and power as well as money) is high but so is the visible level of harassment, the intensity of competition, and the professorial consumption of amphetamines, barbiturates, and ethanol.

In many other institutions, the scarcity of accessible models is not a poverty of models but of visibility. Men of research or scholarly bent are plentiful. They lead lives of sensibility or intellectual pursuit or both, and do so with durable satisfaction. Unfortunately, these lives and their satisfactions are not visible to the undergraduate. The life of sense and sensibility is led in one place and at one time of the day. The life of teaching undergraduates is led in another. Administrative structure, curriculum structure, the system of rewards and approvals, precedent, and sheer numbers each contribute their share to this separation. The idea that undergraduate teaching might be a sharing of the fruits of scholarship and sensibility and an induction into the competences of thoughtful and responsible intellectual work is not rejected. It is not debated. It is simply that nobody brings it up.

There is an intellectual community of sorts, but the students don't belong to it, not even as second-class citizens. No wonder that they try to forge an emulative community of their own, one whose model—the civil rights movement—is far less relevant to curricular revision than its origin: students' exclusion from the intellectual community.

There is exclusion from the possibility of a role in the intellectual community. An undergraduate curriculum which is a mere inculcation of what I have elsewhere called a rhetoric of conclusions and of a body of rote methods for solving rote problems is its excluding wall, and the exclusion has an objective as well as a subjective consequence in relation to student demagoguery. It not only leads to protest and resentment, it results in noneducation. The student demagogue employs logic chopping instead of logic, and the difference passes unnoticed by his student audience. He cites facts that are not factual and omits facts that are facts and his student audience again does not notice. The student demagogue uses magic words like "alienation," "power structure," and "commitment" without thought for their meanings, and the student audience responds to the words as does the subject of a tyranny to its flag.

This confusion of word, fact, and idea may on occasion be knowingly and viciously used by the demagogue. Often, however, he is almost as innocent in his confusion as his audience. He does not know a fact when he sees one. He does not even know how to look. How could he when his education has usually been professorial recital, memorization, and re-recital? His professor of chemistry, biology, even physics, has expounded inference, interpretation, and theory as if they were facts, and has exhibited facts, even laboratory facts, in such fashion that they appear to have presented themselves to the scientist wearing their meanings on their sleeves. His teacher of literature has imposed a critical doctrine and recited interpretations of literary works. Often he has not even revealed the existence of other doctrines, other interpretations, much less afforded students adequate occasions for the testing of doctrines and interpretations; still less has he been concerned that students develop their own measure of the competences of interpretation and criticism. Some social science teachers have recited the plausibilities of sociological and political speculation without reference to the richness of social fact which permits alternative plausibilities, while others, the self-styled hard-nosed, recite allegedly hard facts without reference to the overriding fact that the relevance and meaning of hard facts is conferred by ideas.

Little wonder then that many students are ready dupes of student demagogues. Little wonder that meetings and student protests are Towers of Babel. Students are irresponsible about facts and what they mean, about words and their reference, about ideas and their relationship to facts, because we have left them ignorant of the complex structure of knowledge, innocent of the exacting work involved in a responsible concern for truth, and undisciplined in the discrimination of meaning and the estimation of probability. We now reap the consequences of our failures, and I hope that we continue to be harassed to the extent necessary to rouse us from our bad habits.

There is a second, possibly significant, facet of this emulation of student demagogues—that the models are models of political-executive-administrative action. This feature may, of course, be entirely accidental, the enthusiastic emulation being due wholly to the scarcity of other models and not at all to what is modeled. It is the case, however, that the obscurity of models of theoretical intellect and sensibility is accompanied in our time by an unparalleled conspicuousness and public approval of executive-political-administrative models: our empire-building bureaucrats, such as the heads of NASA, NSF, Defense, NIH, and FBI, our corporate executives, and our political executives, especially those who are sons of wealth. It is also the case that the academic administrator and not the professor is the more attractive campus target of student activists.

These items suggest that the behavior of students in response to their demagogues may indicate an unfilled need for models of a particular kind as well as for models generally, that is, constructive workers whose materials and outcomes are people and institutions, as well as those who work with ideas and things. I shall return to this point later.

There is a third significant aspect of the enthusiastic emulation of student demagogues by students—that the demagogues are *accessible* models. The model is only a little older (if any) than the emulator, only a little more experienced, a bit more knowledgeable. The gap of facility, competence, or know-how, is, or appears to the emulator to be, small enough to bridge in an imaginable duration by expenditure of a possible effort. And the model himself is, or appears to be, willing and able to serve as mentor. These particulars, too, have bearing on our problem and will be examined further.

It is also doubtless true that the enthusiastic emulation of student demagogues is due partly to the fact that they *are* demagogues, that they include conspicuous models of defiance, of maniac self-approval, of easy answers to hard questions. But the lesson I can see in this is too general to be usefully diagnostic: merely that the young are young, that many of them are badly brought up (an antique phrase), and most not very well educated.

Diagnosis 3   *Privations of competence*

If a few student activists are sick and another 2 or 3 percent demagogues, some 10 percent are in it for kicks. A few of these are incorrigibly frivolous, pursuing the hostile or destructive act "for fun," for its own sake. Most of these represent accidents of childhood or simple emptiness of resources. There is little we can learn from this contingent and less that we can do for them.

The rest of them, by far the larger proportion, are another matter. They are not hostile or destructive per se; they show evidence of possessed resources, untapped and undeveloped, but present. They protest for kicks because they possess only a few alternative sources of durable satisfaction. (In this respect they are exemplars of a privation which characterizes a large proportion of students generally.)

Their sources of satisfaction are mainly these: sex of course; certain forms of bodily control and use (dance, and often subtle controls of posture, voice, walk, and facial expression used as media of communication and provocation); direction of others' behavior and expressed attitudes; and an intense and extensive orality—speech which is predominantly eristic, recriminative and provocative, or seductive.[4]

---

4. There is one deliberate deployment of body control which should interest administrators and teachers. Imagine a meeting of faculty and students at which a faculty member has just completed a statement not wholly sympathetic to the protest position. A student rises to respond. (He is usually the third to respond, rarely the first.) Once risen, he loosens shoulders, legs, torso, and inclines his head, though not to the point where it hangs. If a chair is nearby, he rests his hands on it in an effect of mild support. His face is "quiet"; eyes are focused on a distance. He opens his mouth, hesitates, then begins to speak. The voice is characterized by two qualities. It is much lower in volume than that of the previous speaker, low enough to demand (and get) a profounder silence in the room; it is "breathy," with little change of volume, pitch, rhythm, tempo—except for a drop toward inaudibility at the end of each sentence. Sentence structure is awkward and simple. The effect is disarming. Hearers tend to perceive the speaker as unaggressive, even unassertive, certainly not hostile. The awkward sentence structure and dying voice convey innocence, humility, and the absence of calculation.

In a variation on this technique, torso and legs are kept relaxed but the head is held level, eyes meet those of the audience, and voicing is maintained to the end of sentences. Voice timbre is firmer and sentences are well constructed. The effect is, again, disarming, but this time with respect to the content of the statement rather than emphasizing the innocence of the speaker. The manner announces that the speaker is well informed, reasonably confident, and anxious to get at the truth of the matter. It suggests a competent professional

These satisfactions (apart from sex) are among those which would derive from the developed competences discovered and exercised in quite early childhood by way of the sparse models, approvals, and successful transactions afforded by middle-class parents. The sources of satisfaction which normally would be instigated by models, approvals, and successful transactions at a later age with persons in other than parental relations and developed by way of the school curriculum are (except for the political-executive) conspicuous

speaking to respected peers, aware of his competence but also aware of youth and inexperience.

A third version is, to put it bluntly, seductive. A note of sweetness is added by way of facial expression and a degree of added vulnerability by way of posture. The appeal is to fatherly (or motherly) protectiveness and to latent homosexuality.

The tactical uses of these devices tend to run between two poles. On the one hand, if the disarming and seduction work sufficiently well, the affected persons are then taken on as allies, appealed to as defenders when circumstances require it, or exploited for particular resources at their command. At the other pole, the tactic is diversionary. The speaker embarks on his disarming or seductive procedure and sustains it until significant members of the audience are more than half-persuaded of the reasonableness, the innocence, the relative helplessness of the speaker, or at least substantially diverted from their original caution. Then, without warning, the speaker snarls, his voice crescendos to a roar or shriek, a few obscenities and abusives are flung at the targets. The effect in many cases is to reduce the targets to relative helplessness and, in a few cases, is devastating. The victims become captives of, say, a mixed student-faculty committee or withdraw entirely, leaving the students able to claim that the faculty refused to cooperate.

What I have described here is not merely a guess or interpretation. One student (West Coast) boasted of the techniques before a mixed student-faculty audience, gave names to the tactical uses, described some of their results. Three students (Midwest) each independently described the devices to me, one attributing the techniques to revolutionary manuals, one to reading and experience with group dynamical methods. One student (turncoat activist East) gave me a demonstration. Meanwhile, I saw the techniques used on three occasions.

by their scarcity. Music is listened to but is heard only to be moved by. (Indeed, a number of this group are under the impression that their generation invented the protest song.) Reading is largely for reassurance—for vivid expression of the already believed and arguments in its favor. Thinking is devoted to the marshaling of reasons for and expressions of these same beliefs. "Making" in all its aspects—crafts, constructions, manual competences of all sorts, not merely the fine arts—is virtually absent. Listening, looking, and reading for the discovery of form, structure, and coherence, accompanied by satisfaction in both the process and the outcome, are rare. Reading and thinking concerned with the dispassionate examination of beliefs and for evidences against as well as for them are denigrated arts. In general, then, listening, looking, reading and thinking are taken as merely tedious means required by urgent ends, and not as sources of satisfaction.

Even the arts which define student activism, the political-executive arts, are exercised in only truncated form. There is exhortation and debate of the affirmative-negative-rebuttal variety. There is executive assignment of labors and reasonably assiduous execution of assignments. There is mass action. But missing are the genuinely practical arts—deliberation and calculation—by which agreement on proximate ends is found, means evaluated, and cooperation effected without need for threat, coercion, or force. Since these practical arts are often as scarce among professors as among students, a word of explanation is in order.

The practical arts in their political aspect begin in two premises: (1) that institutions are normally to be preserved and changed, not destroyed, since it is only through institutions that political life can go on and action be effected; (2) that *legitimate* differences of interest exist among men, since institutions imply differences of members' roles and each role generates its peculiar needs. Given these premises, it follows that practical reason operating within an institution must find its goals and select its actual strategies in ways which preserve the institution by honoring and taking fullest possible account of the diversities of interest, talent, experience, and habits of thought which constitute its human resources. If it does otherwise, it must either lose the unhonored resources or try to reduce the persons exemplifying them to slavery. Neither of these alternatives appears to be practicable in the long run. (The same rules on a larger scale apply also to the practical operation of reasonableness *among* institutions.)

With respect to goals, this means that proximate goals are hit upon by searching out and rehearsing a wide variety of possible goals to find the one or ones that yield to the greatest degree the *diverse* goods needed and sought by the diverse interests represented. Since each party to the search knows and honors his need for the other talents present, this useful process is a workable one.

With respect to means, the process proceeds analogously. Means are hit upon by assaying each of the practicably largest number of alternatives for two components: (1) its effectiveness in reaching the agreed-upon proximate goal, (2) the ratio of effort and cost to the probable advantages accruing from it for each participating interest. And, as in the search for proximate goals, the *known* dependence of all parties on one another means that the "right" ratio need not be a simple one to one. The good of each is involved in the good of the institution as a whole. Consequently, a means which promises much for the common goal promises much for me as a member of that commonality in addition to what it promises me in my specific role. Further, the life of an institution is a *succession* of selected means and proximate goals, and the history of these means and ends is well-preserved. Hence, I can anticipate that the much which may this time be demanded from me will be returned on another occasion from the much expended by another.

Three further points. First, the assay of means and judgment of proximate goals must take place inter-linearly, in tandem, for, on the one hand, the cost in expenditure of means to a possible goal is a factor in the estimate of the value of the goal; on the other hand, the value of a possible goal helps determine the appropriate expenditure. Second, the practical emphasis on proximate goals does not take place at the expense of remote ("ideal" or "larger") goals. It is by way of proximate goals that larger ones are achieved, for it is only as proximate goals are achieved that remote ones become understood as goals at all—that is, as possibly achievable and desirable. Third, these processes exist not only to *serve* the diversities of interest which constitute an institution, they also require and consolidate the diversities. The processes require the widest possible variety of alternatives for consideration, and variety of alternatives arises from variety of experience and varied habits of mind. The processes consolidate variety in affording one of the most intimate meetings

of diverse minds to be found among human coopera-
tions: they involve immediate experiences of the effectiveness of others' minds on the enjoyed operation of
one's own and have outcomes of extraordinary benefit
to all concerned. The processes of deliberation, in short,
are not only necessities of cooperation but the crucible
in which coaction is formed and discovered to be a satisfying activity not simply as a means but in its own
right.

Student activists know that there are such things as
arts of the practical but they lack knowledge about
them. They know so little about them, indeed, that they
are inclined to give them invidious names—logrolling,
backscratching, compromise. They lack competence in
the exercise of these arts and consequently take no satisfaction in their use. Yet the students are engaged in
political-executive action, and this union of inclination
and incapacity constitutes one of the most alarming
aspects of student activism: that despite its studied
disavowal of the doctrinaire it has been taken in by the
apparatus of doctrinalism. Instead of deliberation, there
is debate. Strategic and tactical positions are arrayed
against one another in the fashion appropriate to doctrines—one to win as true, the others to lose as false-
hoods. Instead of cherishing diversities of interest and
talent, proponents of various positions are also arrayed
against one another, good guy and bad guys, the bad
to be dispensed with or, where they must be used,
"used" in the worst sense of the word—exploited as long
as useful, disarmed or immobilized, and then discarded.

One student to another: "Let's talk this over somewhere else, where we won't be interrupted by people
who disagree with us." It is this apparatus of doctri-

nalism that leads to the wholly impractical situation among the student activists themselves, as well as between students and others, in which he who is not with us is against us, and one or another species of warfare is the only recourse.

Most of these competence deficiencies and satisfaction deficiencies point unmistakably and in the most conventional sense to deficiencies of curriculum. If most species of listening, looking, reading, and thinking are tedious to students who are potentially competent at listening, looking, reading, and thinking, it is because we have not discovered to them the existence of their competences or contributed to their sufficient development. If, as appears to be the case, students do not even know (even unformulatedly) that the discovery and exercise of well-developed competences is a major source of human satisfaction, the case is even worse, for one must conclude that the experience of discovery of a new potential and of its development has been too infrequent to have left an effective memory trace.

The practical competences of deliberation are not, of course, traditional obligations of the academic curriculum. I have tried to indicate, however, that there is every reason why they should become so. The apparatus of doctrinalism, which leads inevitably to the warfare of who-is-not-with-us-is-against-us, like the belief in felt wants as first defense of the self, is an error we cannot afford not to correct in students and in ourselves. Our systems of lectures, lecture notes, prescribed readings, and examinations must make room for some experience of deliberation and reasonable choice, of mutual criticism, of a pooling of diversities of experience and insights—and do so frequently enough and effectively enough to constitute them as sources of durable satisfaction.

Diagnosis 4 Community

The majority of student activists (85 percent on some campuses—rarely less than 50 percent, judging by newspaper stories, membership claims of SDS, and word-of-mouth estimates from students and faculty members) are not sick, not demagogues or imitators of demagogues, and not members of the new left. They are, to put it inaccurately for the moment, *occasional* protesters. Some are moved to first participation by a particular issue. Many are originally moved by the ordinary impulse of any late adolescent to use an opportunity to thumb a nose at (*not* kick in the teeth) the parental generation. Another substantial group are first moved by a sense of generational loyalty. And some, of course, are mere sheep, afraid of what they are being led to do but following anyway, through greater fear of being left out.

What is important about this large group of occasional protesters (the sheep excepted) is what makes the name inaccurate: they do not remain occasional. Many of them discover something or are affected by something in the course of their first participation, or their first few, which makes them readier for further participation. For some, the discovered impulse is obscure and probably various. For most it is one thing and very clear: they discover community.

Dozens of this group (from different campuses) have said, in effect, "The sit-in was one of the deepest experiences of my life. We were packed in those rooms and corridors with hardly room to breathe, talking the whole night through. We came to no agreement but it was a great experience just the same."

Said others, "It was a *religious* experience." "I will remember it all my life." "It was the greatest thing that ever happened to me." "I didn't know you could feel that way."

The lesson of these memories is very clear. To the question, "What did you talk about?" the answer (from highly capable young people) was a vague and lordly "Oh, everything," or "It doesn't matter" or "I don't remember" or "The administration." Such vague responses as these, together with the emphases on "experience," "feeling," "happening," as well as clearer descriptions of what was felt, make it very clear that the appeal was not particularly cognitive, not to explicit value biases, not to resentments, not to latent symptoms, not even to generational loyalty, but to community pure and simple. So starved of community are these young people that they saw nothing comic, even a week later, in a "deep experience" which was mainly a sharing of stinks, of verbal exchanges with little or no memorable content, and with little consequence apart from the wish for more.

Hopefully this euphoric nostalgia is not permanent. Many of the affected students turn out to be bright enough, even affectively sophisticated enough, to realize after a few weeks that their experience of community had something wrong with it, that it lacked a history and a future, that there were missing components as well as missing relations. (I do not mean to suggest that students know what is missing—only that they know something is. I shall return shortly to the question of what is missing, why community is much more than a warm, crowded nest with lots of cheeping.) They realize that its repetition would be unsatisfactory at best and eventually cloying. The experience has revealed to them, however, the importance of community, and discovery of the inadequacy of this particular experience of community only confirms them in their appetite for a more complete one.

That many students have this hunger, even that it is a legitimate hunger, constitutes no necessary reason why we should assuage it. That the university is Alma Mater is no reason for her becoming Omna Mater.

TABLE 1

DISTRIBUTION OF SCHOLASTIC APTITUDE SCORES

SCORES	VERBAL		QUANTITATIVE	
	Activists	All	Activists	All
750–800	11%	13 %	15%	13%
700–749	33	26	22	24
650–699	30	25	28	24
600–649	13	18	22	19
550–599	11	12	4	12
500–549	2	4.5	9	5
Below 500	0%	1.5%	0%	3%

NOTE: For the entire group (All), $N = 700$; for Activists, $N = 46$.

The university is only one of many agencies that affect students' lives; it has a character derived from its special functions; and this character can unsuit it to some other functions. I shall indicate presently, however, that it is appropriate for a university to be a community in certain specific respects and to afford students a member's role in the community.

It is worth emphasizing that this diagnosis of a hunger for community applies to a majority of students generally, not merely to a majority of activists. This means that we are talking about a student group that for many of us includes our own children and the children of our friends. They are, on the whole, ignorant, misinformed, and confused; but they are also intelligent, serious, and of decent, primitive habits (toilet-trained and habituated to control of other impulses as well).

Diagnosis 5 *Student activists as students*

It has been stated or suggested by some that the differentiation of student activists and other students is a differentiation of the best or better students from the poor and average. I do not find this to be the case. On the contrary, student activists appear to be drawn from, and to represent well, almost the entire spectrum of student competence. Consider the data from one university summarized in Table 1. (The small number of activists [forty-six] arises from the difficulty of identifying activists as such: the forty-six are indubitables.) In short, student activists are *students*. They are drawn from the ranks neither of superior students nor of inferior, but from the whole range of students generally. The group of forty-six is about as representative of the entire group of scores as any such sample is likely to be.

But an exceedingly important fact is implicated in this one. Included among student activists are some of our best students, best, moreover, with respect to mathematical as well as verbal competence.

Additional characteristics of this group are identifiable. It does not include the highly audible "leadership" of student activism or, to judge from a very small sample, the doctrinal theorists who claim to speak for the "movement." (Leaders seem to be drawn mainly from the 600–699 group.[5]) Neurosis, unfortunately, is no respecter of intellectual potential; the superior group has its full share of serious symptoms, generalized hostility, and difficulty in establishing effective relations with over-thirties. But, even if we stretch the meaning of "hostility" and "difficulty in establishing relations" about as far as they will go, make no allowance for the possibility of recovery from the evils of mid-adolescence, and subtract all such as well as the seriously ill, a substantial proportion of the superior group remains: highly intelligent, flexible, potentially capable of effective relations with a variety of people.

Of special importance is their possession of a quality which arises from the union of their high intelligence with the bents that lead them to protest: what is mere alienation in the less capable and less stable is here at least partially transformed into cultural freedom. They are able to see some of the personal and institutional values of our generation from a clarifying distance. The same distance provides them with refreshed standards by which to evaluate what they see. (The evaluation tends, of course, to emphasize vices rather than virtues, but this is a relatively small and reparable matter except to stuffed shirts.) Further, and perhaps

5. There are some who believe that at the bottom of the pile, well-disguised "real" leaders are aiming, not at any kind of "reform" of colleges and universities but at violent revolution in the nation at large, using college students much as the Chinese communists use children. They have been variously identified as Trotskyites, Maoists, anarchists, or something new. I have no firsthand evidence on this point. The recent (1967) New Left convention at the Palmer House in Chicago is witness to the fact that these and other leftist groups are trying to use students. Whether, in fact, one or more of them has succeeded remains unknown.

of greater significance, precisely because they are to a degree different from—alien to—the surrounding culture, they are forced to examine *themselves*. They are neither willing nor able to assume that they are like the parental prototypes, chips off the old block; hence they must try to see afresh what their potentials are, what their needs are, and the extent to which existing institutions are and are not appropriate.

The fruits of this examination are rotten in some cases, green in many others, ripe in relatively few. In the first place, such evaluative processes are among the most difficult of enquiries, and in the second place, these young people have been systematically mistaught (or not taught) the methods and principles appropriate to such enquiries. Nevertheless, the potential for such enquiries exists in the group to an extent vastly greater than existed in our generation.

If members of the group could (a) be inducted into a curriculum with intellectual content which (b) included a substantial and mature practical component, which (c) existed in a community with a place for students in it, and which (d) possessed a culture identifiable with the lives of its faculty and potentially sharable by students, this small portion of the activist body might well become a saving part. They could become some of our finest allies in the continued development of such a community and culture and in the work of bringing it effectively to bear on an increasing proportion of the student body, activist and nonactivist.

The superior activists, however, are not capable, even with appropriate education, of alone fulfilling such a role, for the very alienation that confers their peculiar advantage also confers the disadvantage of crippling their readiness to collaborate with elders and those firmly established. But consider what might emerge if the superior, adequately controlled, and decently educated activist students were indiscriminately combined with the substantially larger number of equally superior, better controlled, and decently educated not-so-activist members of the student body, the combined group to play a distinguishable, needed, and honorable role in the collegiate community vis-à-vis both their fellow students and the faculty. The smaller, activist constituency would supply a much needed yeast of challenge to set ways and those set in their ways; the larger constituency would supply needed discipline, needed resistance to easy change, and criticism uncolored by the impulse toward change for the sake of difference; the members of the combined group would constitute a potent and uniquely competent force for learning, for teaching, and for the establishment and maintenance of a collegiate community. Their unique competence would arise from the conspicuous ambiguity of the role they would play: constituted of both studenthood and facultyhood and acting as a link between the two.

I shall indicate in Community Prescription 9 (p. 292) the character of this role, how we might recruit students to it and work with them.

Summary Diagnosis

Our diagnoses show six classes of radical privation requiring curricular attention.

1. Though student activists boast of their morality in contrast to others' and demand a part in the making

of decisions, they (and students generally) are almost empty of what is required by either morality or decision-making. Seven distinct privations are involved. I list them briefly here pending their further explication in the Practical Prescriptions.

1.1 Students are ignorant of defensible grounds of morality, using, instead, three platitudes: "sincerity," "self-integrity," and "service to others."

Two of these are good platitudes (integrity and service), but until the complexities and interconnections of "self," "other," "integrity," and "service" are understood, they can only dazzle and mislead.

1.2 They are ignorant of what is involved in the processes of decision and choice.

Most students are under the impression that good decisions are immediately derivable by simple matching of "principles" and cases; that decisions otherwise constructed are products of compromise out of cowardice and self-interest—all these terms, including "compromise," being used invidiously. They are unaware of the complexity of actual cases: the conflict of principle which exists in almost all cases and inevitably requires compromise; the difficulty of bringing even one principle to bear on the ambiguities of real cases.

1.3 They are ignorant, a fortiori, of the considerations pertinent to decision on the three matters that concern them as students: curriculum, collegiate institutions, and their own educational potentialities, needs, and interests.

1.4 They lack competence in the arts by which the facts of real cases are dealt with—deliberation, calculation, and "rehearsal."

Since they are ignorant of the roles of fact, of the ultimate particularities involved in practical choice, they are without experience in dealing with them —experience in the identification and discrimination of relevants, the balancing of each against and with the other, the envisaging of alternatives, and their test by forecast and rehearsal of consequences.

1.5 They lack experience in collaboration toward *proximate* goals. They believe that cooperation is possible only among persons who agree in all respects (doctrinalism). They are self-conditioned to behave accordingly, feeling uneasiness and distraction among persons whom they suspect of differing from themselves in "values," commitments, and ultimate goals. They have had little conscious experience of the fruitful collaboration that can result from discovery of common proximate goals among persons otherwise differing.

1.6 Their decisions are irresponsible, both habitually and (especially) with respect to decisions affecting the collegiate institution.

Choice is responsible when it is made in full expectation of having to undergo the consequences of the choice for better or for worse (unless deflected by our own further choices and actions). Most students, in virtue of having lived most of their lives as children, are, in this sense, irresponsible, for the consequences of childish choice are normally deflected by the intervention of others if the consequences threaten to be painful. Students continue to expect such interventions.

Students are especially irresponsible with respect to decisions that may affect the life of the college or university, for they are inadequately involved in its life. It is another country; they are temporary (four-year) visitors at best and can leave at any time if the country is threatened or weakened.

1.7 Students are largely lacking in two habits indispensable to good decision-making; suspense of impulse, especially of impulsive wants and partisanships, and the cherishing of diversity—diverse habits of mind, diverse interests, diverse opinions. (See also 1.5.)

2. Our students have little idea of the variety of lives that can be led and of the range of satisfactions they can afford.

One psychosociological plausibility traces a large part of protest behavior to the witnessed incoherence and poverty of their parents' lives taken as models. Whether this is the case or not, it is clear that most colleges and universities afford little by way of alternative models. Only by accident are students witnesses to the satisfactions of developed competences and cultivated tastes, of lives of research and scholarship, artistic and institutional creation, thoughtful public service and administration.

3. Our students lack resources of durable satisfaction and pleasure.

They are untrained in the arts and disciplines of looking, listening, and reading with respect to form and structure, coherence and cogency. Hence they find little satisfaction in these acts and no impetus toward further development of the competences involved. This indicates a special obligation of the humane disciplines.

4. Our students lack knowledge of the character and location of meaning and are consequently irresponsible in their use and reception of language. They are ignorant of canons of evidence and argument, and hence poorly equipped to judge solutions to problems.

5. Our students are almost entirely deprived of proper curricular occasions, especially sufficiently early occasions, for discovery, assay, and exercise of their competences with respect to form and structure, coherence and cogency, evidence and argument, recovery and formulation of meaning.

The occasions which result from the uniformly assigned curricular task (the routine apparatus of the inadequate curriculum) are *not* proper to this purpose. They permit professorial assay but not the student's; they use but do not exercise the competences required; they do not constitute acceptable discovery. A generation enjoying close linkage with its predecessor generation and through such linkage assured of the benevolence and good judgment of its members might find such routine

occasions satisfactory. It could not only accept professorial assay as competent but internalize it.
Professorial praise might suffice as impetus toward
further development of the competences involved.
Not so for many of our students.

6. Our students are men and women without a country. They are tolerated aliens in the collegiate
community and, to use the word correctly for
once, feel deeply and resent their alienation. Their
substitute for this withheld membership—a group
of peers only, desperately seeking reasons for existence ("We're meeting tomorrow to figure out
what our purposes are") and subsisting mainly on
aggressions against the rejecting community—is
rickety and unsatisfactory.

CURRICULAR
RESOURCES

2

THE NEEDS

Some of the needs implied by student privation are obvious enough. Some are not, especially if they are to be, as they must be, conceived in curricular terms. Consequently, we list them here.

1.1 With respect to the platitudes of integrity of self and service.

The need is for a "theoretical" treatment of ethics and personality. By "theoretical treatment," I mean a curricular segment which conforms in large part to the conventional view of a "course," that is, one in which the focus is on written and spoken embodiments of *systematic* treatments of a problem or a subject matter. In this case, our treatment should involve at least three doctrines concerning choice in relation to human personality, its health, "goodness," or "completeness," and the ways in which health may be lost or completeness fail to develop. The treatment, however, would not be wholly conventional, since materials would not merely be recited or read. They would be "discussed"; that is, their radical differences (and similarities) clarified, then traced to the differences of conceptual frame which dictate what facts they choose as relevant, what interpretations they make of the facts so chosen, and what emphases and subordinations are thus imposed. The same program of discussion would be concerned as much with the relations of the doctrines to the persons undertaking discussion—their powers, habits, actions, and undergoings—as with the relations of the doctrines to one another.

1.2 With respect to ignorance of what is involved in decision and choice.

The need is for knowledge of actual cases exemplifying the problem of practical decision. Ideally, the cases would be of two kinds and seen in two modes. There would be cases of corporate decision—decisions forged through the interaction and collaboration of several parties to the process and eventuating in institutional policy. There would also be cases of personal decision—decisions by single persons concerned primarily with their own good. Both kinds of cases would be seen historically (after the fact of decision, hence susceptible of informed afterthought) and currently (in course, when consequences can only be anticipated, anxiously and hopefully, that is, "rehearsed").

Only the historical mode is easily susceptible to conventional curricular treatment and, in this mode, the cases of corporate decision are easier to come by and to give responsible treatment. The others must be done by indirection or omitted.

1.3 With respect to students' ignorance of the particulars of curriculum, of colleges, and of their own educational possibilities.

The need, obviously, is for the particular facts of particular cases as these facts are seen in their unorganized complexity *before* disposition of the case. This is virtually impossible to supply to any number of students and especially difficult with respect to cases involving the college (institutional rules and policies) and the curriculum. It is possible, however, to introduce some students to the diverse genera of facts involved, and a few students to the particular facts of some cases. I have in mind the possibility of establishing watching briefs, apprentice memberships, and limited participations in deliberations concerned with institutional and curricular plans.

With respect to individual needs and interests relevant to curricular choice, the way is easier. The first need is for courses whose materials and methods discover to the student the activities and competences required by academic fields, what it feels like to operate within their disciplines, and the extent to which he possesses the required potentials. The second need is for correction of the prevailing pattern of demand for early commitment to specialization and our prevailing habit with respect to the offering of electives.

1.4 With respect to student incompetence in the arts of decision and choice.

The need, obviously, is for experience: experience

with the manifold ambiguities and complexities of real situations which make even the formulation of the problem difficult; experience in the resolution of the further difficulties involved in solving the problem; experience of undergoing and dealing with the consequences that flow from decisions made.

It is impossible to provide such experience in the quantities requisite for developed competence. This takes a good part of a lifetime—the one fact for which the young cannot forgive the older (especially the relatively few older who, in fact, have had and profited from such experience). It is not impossible, however, to provide sufficient foretaste to initiate in some students a habit of seeking further experience and trying to profit from it. Whether the numbers of students so initiated and the effectiveness of their search will constitute a degree of educational success roughly equal to that of conventional curricular efforts remains to be discovered.

I need hardly add that if the style and content of the institution's administration are exhibitions of the slick, the arbitrary, the high-handed, or the invariably "safe," this too will teach—and effectively. Very little we may do by way of filling needs 1.2, 1.3, and 1.4 is likely to compete successfully with this administrative model.

1.5 With respect to student incompetence in collaboration.

The need, again, is for experience, experience of

the effectiveness and satisfaction of discovering among divers other persons the existence of common proximate goals and of working with others toward these goals. This can, and should, take place within the framework of the curriculum, as means toward mastery of disciplines necessitated by curricular materials and demands.

1.6 With respect to the irresponsibility, habitual and circumstantial, of students' decisions.

The needs are two. With respect to habitual irresponsibility, the need is for an overhaul of regulations, usages, and administrative procedures, to the end of ensuring that students shall, indeed, not only undergo the consequences of decisions made or defaulted, but know that they will, that the consequences are extremely unlikely to be deflected by administrative or faculty intervention. This includes, of course, the widely urged overhaul of our traditional role *in loco parentis.*

There is need, second, to make a place for sufficient membership, sufficient involvement, in the continuing life of the institution. This involves two species of membership: membership in the continuity of students older and students younger; and *felt* relationship with representatives of the more enduring class of university citizens, the faculty.

1.7 With respect to susceptibility to impulse and rejection of diversities of habit and value.

The need is for curricular materials (especially

humane materials and materials in the social sciences) which can evoke (when properly treated) and reward the suspense of impulse. The need is for curricular occasions and demands which require and reward the conjunction of differing competences and of differing competences housed in persons of differing habits, values, social class, and ideological origins.

2. With respect to the poverty of models of the variety of lives that can be led and of the range of satisfactions they afford.

The need is for constructing, as part of the curriculum, a visibility of models. In some institutions this will require reorganization and change in the character of faculties so that models may, indeed, be present. In almost all institutions it will require a sweeping reorganization and change in the character of undergraduate courses so that models present on the campus will become accessible as such.

3. With respect to lack of resources of durable satisfaction and pleasure.

The need here imposes a special obligation on the humanities, but the other subject fields are not exempt. The need is for a curriculum which, through and through, requires competences of looking, listening, and reading with respect to form and structure, coherence and cogency; which provides adequate occasions for the development of these competences; which rewards their development. This will require such a sweeping shift of emphasis that the traditional preoccupation with *what* the student knows will be at least coordinate with concern for how critically he knows and how well he can master the new.

This, in turn, will mean a shift from the merely lectorial to the discussional, a shift from merely knowing what is said to knowing how it came to be said—that is, the ground in principle and method (evidence and argument) for conclusions reached and doctrines expounded; and, in the case of the arts, especially the literary arts, a shift toward emphasis on discerning the character of the manifold connections of parts to parts that constitute the unity of a work and, in turn, discerning in the light of that unity, the propriety and the functions of the parts which constitute it.

A parallel shift in the character of examinations is also required—not merely review of what has been learned but occasions for the exercise of competences.

This will also mean the institution of numerous and early occasions in the curriculum for selection or election by students of work to be done, choice of how to do it, and attempts, with solicited help, to do it.

4. With respect to ignorance of the character and location of meaning.

5. With respect to appropriate occasions for the discovery and assay of competence.

See (3) above.

6. With respect to the lack of community felt by students.

The need, in the first place, is for a community to exist; in the second, for a place in it for students; and in the third, for ways by which to induct them into that community. Let it be understood at once that I mean the academic community, not the domestic community on its periphery. Neither paternal nor buddy-buddy relations with professors are relevant here, nor intimate glimpses of their family life. (The student needs some witness of a style of life which offers a contrast to the convention-bound, competition-directed, indulgent, tasteless, or vacant styles, one or more of which is likely to characterize most students' homes. Unfortunately, these adjectives apply more and more to professors' homes, too.)

A first step toward academic community will be taken if models are present, visible, and accessible. A second step will be taken if what they model, their competences and sensibilities, are accessible in the curriculum. Curricular materials must be good enough to evoke in professor as well as student—and to reward—the exercise of these competences and sensibilities. Curricular intentions must include a degree of student mastery of them. A major component of classroom activities must consist of exemplification and practice of these competences and sensibilities.

These factors, though desirable in themselves and indicative of the locus of the relevant community, do not yet constitute community. More is required to bring the whole to communal life, especially (*a*) procedures through which the entering student discovers the existence of this intellectually centered community, and (*b*) establishment of a linking class of persons between faculty on the one hand and young students on the other, through whom the young students can be drawn toward membership. More on this later, in Community Prescription 9.[1]

Curricular Resources

There are two glaringly questionable characteristics of this budget of needs, if a practicable curriculum is envisaged. We shall deal with one of them only at the end of chapter 2. The other was well put by one who interrupted an early discussion of these matters to say, "It can't be done. You can't change people by making them read a book." I agree. Curriculum includes much more. It includes books read and lectures heard. It also includes, however, what can be done to the books and lectures and what they can be made to do to those who read and hear them. It can also include experience of what the books are talking about.

Resource 1:   Arts of Recovery

In the first place, the substance and soundness of books read and lectures heard can be made to constitute a challenge to the competences and judgments of students. In the ordinary curriculum, they are

1. P. 292.

"assignments," not challenges. That is, they are designed to be "learned," and they are presented as official doctrine to be submitted to. Their design as "assignments" involves two factors. Their vocabulary, sentence structure, and logical structure (if any) are hopefully chosen to be within the already existing competence of the student. Second, the story they have to tell is "written down," simplified, to fit prevailing belief about what the student is already able to comprehend. They are presented as official doctrine by way of two additional characteristics. Their content is a rhetoric of conclusions, a body of positive and often unqualified assertions about a subject matter, conclusions unsupported by evidence or argument. Second, the body of positive assertions appears alone, without critic or competitor.

Materials appropriate to challenge require substantially the contrary of each of these characteristics. Their vocabulary, syntax, and organization will be the syntax, vocabulary, and organization appropriate to the meaning they are to convey. The meaning they convey will be the meaning determined by a subject matter of enquiry and the pattern of enquiry used upon it. Third, they will convey an enquiry—a problem conceived, a plan for attack upon it, the data or argument involved —as well as the fruits, the conclusions, of the enquiry. Finally, they will not appear alone and unchallenged. In many instances, they will be members of a pair or a trio of enquiries, treating a similar subject matter in different terms, posing different problems, seeking different data and argument. In other instances, they will be in the company of critics. Where they are alone, they will be presented to the student as essays *toward* truth rather than as the truth itself, hence to be examined as trials, their sources of weakness as well as their sources of strength to be sought for and assayed.

This means that the appropriate materials are not only history textbooks but histories, not only science textbooks but reports, syntheses, and criticisms of research, not books about philosophy but philosophical works, not only expounded analyses and interpretations of literary works but the works themselves submitted to analysis and interpretation.

With such materials, the classroom can be proportionately transformed. It ceases to be the place where the student is mainly tested to determine what he has understood from his "homework" and where the ununderstood official doctrine is re-explained by the instructor. It becomes, instead, the place where the sense and soundness of materials are dealt with by students and instructor in concert.

The flavor of such an enterprise is best indicated by an example. Let us take as a case in point a discussion among first-year college students in the second quarter of a year's introductory biology course. (The previous quarter has dealt conventionally with conventional textbook materials. Hence the students have some familiarity with biological vocabulary but little experience of scientific work as such.) They are assembled to discuss a group of scientific papers read the night before. One of them is an early clinical report, titled, "On a Cretinoid State Supervening in Adult Life in Women." It is excerpted below.

Case I

Miss B., after the cessation of the catamenial period, became insensibly more and more languid, with general increase of bulk. The change went on from year to year, her face altering from oval to round, much like the full moon at rising. With a complexion soft and fair, the skin presenting a peculiarly smooth and fine texture was almost porcelainous in aspect, the cheeks tinted of a delicate rose-purple, the cellular tissue under the eyes being loose and folded, and that under the jaws and in the neck becoming heavy, thickened, and folded. The lips large and of a rose-purple, alae nasi thick, cornea and pupil of the eye normal, but the distance between the eyes appearing disproportionately wide, and the rest of the nose depressed, giving the whole face a flattened broad character. The hair flaxen and soft, the whole expression of the face remarkably placid. The tongue broad and thick, voice gutteral, and the pronunciation as if the tongue were too large for the mouth (cretinoid). The hands peculiarly broad and thick, spade-like, as if the whole texture were infiltrated. The integuments of the chest and abdomen loaded with subcutaneous fat. The upper and lower extremities also large and fat, with slight traces of edema over the tibiae, but this not distinct, and pitting doubtfully on pressure. Urine normal. Heart's action and sounds normal. Pulse 72; breathing 18.

Such is a general outline of the state to which I wish to call attention.

On the first aspect of such a case, without any previous experience of its peculiarity, one would expect to find some disease of the heart leading to venous obstruction, or a morbid state of the urine favouring edema. But a further inquiry would show that neither condition was present; nor, when minutely studied, is the change in the body which I have described to be accounted for from either of these points of view.

Had one not proof that such a patient had been previously fine-featured, well-formed, and active, it would be natural to suppose that it was an original defect such as is common in mild cretinism. In the patient whose condition I have given above, there had been a distinct change in mental state. The mind, which had previously been active and inquisitive, assumed a gentle, placid indifference, corresponding to the muscular languor, but the intellect was unimpaired. Although there was no doubt a large deposit of subcutaneous fat on the extremities, chest and abdomen, the mere condition of corpulency, obesity, or fatness, would not in any way comprehend the entire pathology.

It is common to see patients with a very superabundant accumulation of fat in the subcutaneous adipose tissues, and on that ground more inactive, without the change in the texture of the skin, in the lips and nose, increased thickness of tongue and hands, etc., which I have enumerated. The change in the skin is remarkable. The texture being peculiarly smooth and fine, and the complexion fair, at a first hasty glance there might be supposed to be a general slight edema of it, but this is not confirmed by a future examination, whilst the beautiful delicate rose-purple tint on the cheek is entirely different to what one sees in the bloated face of renal anasarca. This suspicion of renal disease failing, anyone who should see a case for the first time might suppose that the heart was the faulty organ, due to venous congestion. But neither would this be confirmed by an exact inquiry into the cardiac condition.

I am not able to give any explanation of the cause which leads to the state I have described. It is unassociated with any visceral disease, and having begun appears to continue uninfluenced by the remedies. . . .

In an interesting Paper on sporadic cretinism occurring in England, my friend Dr. Fagge has given a case which began as late as the eighth year, in a subject previously healthy and well developed; and he states that in this case the physical configuration was alone manifested, or at any rate that any change in the mental powers was doubtful; and he adds it may therefore be interesting to speculate as to what character would be present should the disease, if that be possible, arise still later in the course of adult life.

. . . In the cretinoid condition in adults which I have seen, the thyroid was not enlarged; but from the general fulness of the cutaneous tissues, and from the folds of skin about the neck, I am not able to state what the exact condition of it was. The supra-clavicular masses of fat first described by Mr. Curling, and specially drawn attention to by Dr. Fagge as occurring in cases of sporadic cretinism in children, did not attract my attention in adults. The masses of supra-clavicular fat are not infrequent in the adult, without any associated morbid change whatever.

The instructor and the students have the paper before them. The instructor puts the opening question: "What is the problem dealt with by the paper?" There are a few moments of silence. One student then suggests in a tentative tone, "He is trying to find the cause of myxedema." The instructor receives this answer without indication of approval or disapproval and looks enquiringly at other students. Several indicate agreement. The instructor's attention returns to the first student, "What sort of evidence of causation does the author look for?" The student is startled. It has not occurred to him to look for the "kind" of evidence. In the second place, he cannot recall any such evidences (since there are none in the paper). He then turns to the paper and defensively asks, "Isn't he talking about the heart as a possible cause in the third paragraph?" "Is he?" asks the instructor. "Take a second to read that paragraph and see whether you agree with yourself." The student reads and insists that he is right. He also says that surely the fourth and fifth paragraphs are considering possible causes.

The instructor now probes this additional ground for the student's interpretation: "What causes is the author considering?"

The student promptly and pleasedly answers, "Heart trouble, kidney trouble, and cretinism."

The instructor now has a small decision before him. He can appeal to common language usage to cast doubt on these factors as "causes" (that is, they are commonly used as names, not for causes, but for diseases). He can raise the same question at the level of ideas by enquiring whether such a factor as "heart trouble" can be considered a cause and, if so, what notion of "cause" is involved. As a third alternative, he can try, first, to make precise what "effect" would be entailed if heart trouble, kidney trouble, and so on, were considered to be "causes." He chooses to combine the first and second possibilities by asking, "Suppose that a patient came to the doctor with symptoms clearly identified as pointing to cretinism, heart trouble, or kidney trouble. In such a case, what would be one of the first questions asked?"

The student answers, "What the cause of the cretinism is." He then stops abruptly, showing by facial expression that he thinks he has confessed an error, that the matter about which a cause is sought could not itself be a cause. The instructor, however, does not take this line at all (since, of course, an indefinitely long chain of antecedent-consequent events can be pursued). Instead, he asks, "In that case, what *exactly* is the effect whose cause is being pursued?"

The student heeds the emphasis on *exactly*, takes time to consider, and replies, "The symptoms displayed by Miss B."

"Right you are," says the instructor. "And if we treat the abnormal organ (kidney, heart) as a *cause* of disease, then what is the disease?"

"The set of symptoms."

"Are you happy with that distinction? Before you answer, consider a patient who comes to the office with a set of symptoms such as pain and bleeding clearly 'caused by' an abnormality of the stomach lining, an ulcer."

Before the student can respond, another, silent until

now, asks recognition, receives it, and says, "It looks to me as if the author were comparing the case of Miss B with other diseases rather than looking for a cause."

Now an issue is joined: there are two "readings" of the text. The instructor asks the first respondent to entertain the second respondent's view, the hypothesis of "comparison." He does so, with some hesitation, and finally agrees that the paragraphs can be so interpreted.

The instructor now turns to the student who suggested comparison and invites him to entertain the view held by the first student. Additional students enter the discussion as each paragraph is scrutinized for its meaning and relevance to the debate in hand. It is agreed, after some minutes, that the paper is, in fact, concerned to determine whether the case of Miss B constitutes a hitherto unidentified disease or is only a deviant instance of familiar ones. It is also agreed, however, that "cause" in a narrow sense (and this sense is spelled out) could cover such a search for identity.

The discussion moves on to closely related further questions: what conclusion the author reaches; on what kind of evidence; what further evidence would provide a satisfactory solution to the problem of myxedema; how that evidence might be obtained. With these questions resolved, the discussion shifts from the paper itself to broader problems suggested by it: what the agenda for further research on myxedema might be; and, in a quite different direction, questions about the general problem of disease taxonomy—what the component notions of "disease" are, what alternative modes of disease classification are suggested by each such note.

Thus the paper is seen in several lights. It is seen as

one item in an ongoing enquiry into a disease, its cause
and cure. It is seen as an instance of a general problem
of enquiry: classification. It is seen as raising a question
about the nature of disease in general. This same paper
(or others) might also be seen as throwing light on the
habits of nineteenth-century clinicians or on the organization of English medicine in the nineteenth century.
(A given course or program would, naturally, use the
paper only in the ways appropriate to course purposes.)

There are two major components to such concerted
work toward the recovery of meaning. On the one hand,
questions are addressed to the work under scrutiny
and to matters extending out of it, as in the example
above. Differences of "reading" are evoked; debates
about these differences are developed. Then resolution
of these debates is sought. Differences of reading are
reduced in number and given some order. (They are
rarely resolved to a single, official reading.) With this
manageable order to hand, questions and debate then
turn to the quality of the work—the soundness of its
evidence or argument, how and the extent to which
the enquiry has taken hold of its subject matter, the
adequacy and soundness with which it has effected
connections among its parts—and the analogous questions appropriate to works which are not primarily
enquiries, artistic constructions, for example.

"Debate" here has two senses. The persistance of
nineteenth-century rhetorical forms on television "talk"
shows, the high visibility of our adversary pattern for
the conduct of trials by law, and the prevailing tendency of high school "discussion" to be only a voicing
of uninformed opinion, all tend toward an eristic form,
a kind of warfare. Early debate among students will

almost inevitably, therefore, constitute only a pattern of defense and attack. The eristic form, however, can be quickly mixed with, and eventually replaced by, irenic forms.

The key to the transformation is instanced in the example of debate described above. It is the student who thought the research paper to be concerned with causes who is asked to entertain the suggestion that it is concerned rather with a problem of taxonomy. It is the student who suggested taxonomy who is asked to entertain the possibility that the paper is concerned with causes. *Entertain*, here, means much more than a moment's silent repeating of the possibility. It means that the student is asked to take the countersuggestion very seriously indeed—by formulating it aloud, searching for evidence which supports it, reinterpreting his own favored passages in the light of it. It means too that he is asked to seek for evidences which indicate weakness in his own position.

How alien is this notion of seeking the most defensible instead of one's favored solution to a problem is seen in the frequency with which first requests of this kind are met with the injured reply, "But *I* don't believe it is true." The reply, of course, is that that is precisely why *he* is being asked to consider it—since what he believes is not of much importance unless it has been chosen from examined alternatives. Usually, this or a similar remark suffices to initiate the transformation toward the irenic. Occasionally, however, the student is so firmly wedded to the eristic or so frightened of retreat that he refuses to participate. In such a case, one passes on to another student. On another occasion, a few days later, the litigious student is again invited to "argue against himself." He almost always does—and often with a smile.

More than one important purpose is served by this transformation. It is not only the pattern of discourse appropriate to the problem, it is also the institution of collaborative community and the beginning of discovery of the existence and value of diverse habits of mind. Of the latter two, we shall have much more to say later. Meanwhile, what is of importance is that irenic forms of discourse be adopted as appropriate to the problem undertaken.

In such forms, differing views will still be voiced by partisans, but the examination, the debate, of them will not be partisan. Rather, once a number of views have been laid before the group, they will be treated as imperfect opinions, raw materials for *conjoint* scrutiny aimed at discovery and repair of their errors and omissions, and formulation of a better or best opinion by the group as a whole and not as contestants in a sparring match.

The second major component of such concerted work consists of *reflexive* scrutiny of the debate itself, with an eye to the bases of sound and unsound reading, grounded and ungrounded judgment, adequate and inadequate analyses raised and identified in the course of the debate. In such reflexive scrutiny, the questions are addressed to utterances of the student rather than to the text, and concern what he has said and done, why he has done it and whether it is the appropriate thing to do, given the materials in hand and the circumstances of its examination.

A simplified transcript will illustrate the main point. Consider that students have been given a deliberately unorganized array of facts concerning a case of espionage before a federal court. A young federal employee, female, has abstracted confidential papers from files and passed them on to a Russian agent with whom she is living. It is peacetime. She is a product of the depression 1930's and of that era of undergraduate leftism. The papers, though confidential, turn out to have dealt with matters which yielded little profit to their alien recipients. These and numerous other facts (also given the students) are admitted by both sides. The problem is one only of determining punishment.

The students are informed that the judge has wide latitude in respect of punishment, from probation of various sorts, or a suspended sentence, to a substantial prison sentence. They are asked to participate in this judgment: to decide what punishment is appropriate and to give a reason for their choice. Assume that five students have given the following replies:

1. Suspended sentence: the girl was in love with the foreign agent; had been conditioned by her adolescent opinion climate.
2. One year in prison: the act occurred in peacetime and the papers were of little importance.
3. Probation for psychiatric treatment: only this form of reeducation would constitute rehabilitation.
4. Five years in prison with wide publicity to be given to the decision: it must be widely understood that any espionage activity will be severely punished.
5. Five years in prison: the law must be enforced.

At this point, reflexive scrutiny begins. The fourth student is asked: "When you give the reason you do, to what factor in the situation are you appealing?"

He is at a loss, does not understand the question. The instructor explains: "Notice that none of the five reasons given contradicts another or denies it. Instead, each seems to deal with a different matter and each seems to be cogent."

The student sees the point. (Of course, in differing situations, different pathways, and perhaps longer ones, will be necessary to clarify the question.) He considers his earlier response. Finally, he says, "I suppose I was concerned with the effect of the punishment on others."

His manner and voice suggest that he is torn between a degree of shame for having put this factor first (perhaps an impression that the question has been addressed to him as an implied criticism of his choice) and the conviction that the factor is a relevant one and defensibly to be taken into account.

In view of his expressed doubt, another student, one who had not contributed to the list of punishment proposals, is asked whether he thinks it proper to consider this factor. He does not: the girl could hardly help what she was doing. Still another student interrupts to assert (and argue) that, of course, the use of punishment as a deterrent is an important factor to be considered. A brief debate is joined from which it emerges that (a) the previous student did not speak to the question but, instead, asserted that another relevant factor was, in his opinion, the weightier factor in this case; (b) that punishment as a deterrent is relevant in general as well as in this case.

With this clarification of the question, other students who proposed punishments identify the factor embodied in each of their reasons. Further discussion is devoted to examination of the list of factors so identified, additions are made, and some time is spent trying to find a schema which will provide an exhaustive list of the factors involved in determining punishment under law. Discussion then turns to the difficult question of how these various factors are to be weighted in arriving at a judgment in individual cases, whether there are rules for the weighting and, if not, what can take the place of rules. (Questions of this kind, calling for reflexive scrutiny, are most often asked in the course of debate about a problem or a work, but they may also be addressed in retrospect. They may be addressed to the same student whose utterances constitute their subjects; they may be addressed to another student functioning as critic of the first.)

Such activities, both the first-order debate and the reflexive scrutiny together constitute a *discipline* in two senses when properly conducted. First, they are activities imposed and undergone in order to establish a habit of intelligence. Second, the intelligent habit aimed at is the habit—the pattern of search, analysis, and articulation of meaning—appropriate to the kind of work in question and to the kind of use to which it is being put. If it is a scientific work to be treated as such, the habit is search for the precise formulation of the problem attacked in the work; for a view of the terms in which the problem is treated—that is, what data, how interpreted, would constitute solution to the problem; for the data in fact found, and how, and how far, they justify the generality and the asserted predicates of the conclusions reached. If it is a scientific work treated as a fact of history or as an expression of the beliefs and values of scientists, it is treated accordingly and the one treatment or discipline is not confused with another. In similar fashion, the short story or novel treated as such becomes a search for character, for circumstance, for action and its consequence, and for the articulations with one another given them by the author to constitute the unity of the work. The same work of art treated as illumination of human character or commentary on its vicissitudes, or as a historical or sociological resource, receives other treatments, which can be joined to but not confused with one another.

The acceptable reasons and arguments offered in the discussion and debate about "readings" are, then, the reasons and arguments appropriate to the enquiry being conducted on the work in question, and acceptable estimates of soundness depend on criteria applicable to the mode of enquiry or construction represented by the work.

The reflexive scrutiny of the debate is the principal means by which to identify and segregate the appropriate and inappropriate and to show that they are the one or the other. In this process, the student is asked to recover the tacit question he has asked himself and is answering. He is invited to note its terms and premises and hence the kind of conclusion it is leading to. He is asked to identify the kind of enquiry and kind of subject of enquiry to which these terms and premises are appropriate and to determine whether, in fact, it is this kind of enquiry and material to which the group is addressing itself.

These processes of reflexive scrutiny apply as much to simpler and more detailed levels of discipline as to kinds of enquiries and kinds of works. Three classes of detail require attention. The first is exemplified by the student who rejects a sentence in a work as "wrong." He can be asked in what word or phrase the error lies, what meaning he has assigned to the word or phrase in which the alleged error lies, whether in view of the context this assigned meaning is defensible and if not, what other meanings are possible, and which of these is most defensible. Concerning the second class of detail he may be asked what facts he is appealing to as grounds for the charge of error, whether the facts are indeed what he takes them to be, and, if they are, whether they are the kinds of facts appropriate to judging the truth or falsehood of the statement in question. With respect to the third class, he can be asked what ideas he has taken as implicated in the notion of "cause" or "social class" or "culture," used in the work in question, and whether in fact these implicated notes are coherent with the conception of cause, social class, or culture used by the work. In brief, reflexive scrutiny can be addressed to words, to things, to ideas, and to their connections with one another to constitute meaning, on a small scale as well as a large.

The role of the instructor in such operations is both dominant and demanding. It is demanding in three respects. First, he must know the work under analysis through and through. Second, he must be equally familiar with the varieties of questions and attacks which can be made on such a work, know what sorts of treatment they constitute, and be willing to acknowledge the legitimacy of each such attack within the limits of what it can do. Third, he must be alertly and sensitively mindful of what each student is saying and doing, not only in the moment but in the whole course of the discussion.

The role of the instructor is dominant since he possesses the disciplines and the students do not (or possess less of a discipline and practice it with less expertise). In consequence, he must serve in the first place as exemplar. It is his questions addressed to himself with respect to the work and answered by him which provide the first clues to what is possible and appropriate. He must also serve as guide through the questions he formulates and the order in which he chooses to present them. Finally, he must serve as critic through the questions he asks in reflexive examination of interpretations and evaluation.

It does not follow, however, from the fact that discipline is an aim and that the instructor's role is dominant, that the appropriate instructorial response to students' statements is a yelp of "Right!" or "Wrong!" or the facial equivalent of a yelp. On the contrary, the instructor's aim must be, as far as possible and especially in the beginning, to "honor" each student response. Honoring involves, in the first place, putting the best interpretation on a student's response and enquiring whether that is, indeed, what he meant. ("You meant, I assume . . . .") It means, second, testifying to whatever of soundness and effectiveness the response possesses. ("That sort of attack would be a good way to . . . ." "Not many would notice that hint." "A nice insight, especially with respect to . . . .") It also means acknowledging a student's general competence (when it exists) in the moment of identifying flagrant error. ("I wouldn't have expected that of you." "Where is your usual alertness?") Eventually, of course, honoring means clear identification of error and why it is an error. (This is still honoring, even in the affective mode, since a person honors another when he takes the trouble to reason with him. One not-honors or dishonors by rejection or indifference.)

Such honoring is indispensable to curricular development of a discipline of recovery. A discipline of recovery is, by necessity, an *intelligent* habit. It is an intelligent habit in that it is a way to operate, a pattern of enquiry or construction, possessed and used in full cognizance of what it assumes in the materials acted on and the outcomes expected. It is such by necessity because it must be adapted and modified in each application. No novel is exactly like another. One of Jane Austen's differs radically from one of John Barth's. Two of Virginia Woolf's differ significantly if more subtly from one another. No scientific work is exactly like another. Many researches in biology differ radically from physical researches. Even scientific works in the same narrow line of enquiry may differ significantly from one another. Hence, not only the order in which questions can be put to the work but what questions can be put (i.e., what questions are answerable) varies from work to work. The same variability marks the places and ways in which answers to the questions are sought and the relative importance of one answer as against another. The variability of works, then, requires adaptability of discipline and adaptation requires cognizance of the reason and effect of each element in the discipline. Hence the importance of honoring as here defined, for it is the process of giving reasons and of ensuring, in the course of reflexive scrutiny of the honored responses, that reasons are understood and found acceptable by students.

Honoring is a curricular resource in still another respect. It marks the place and way in which one vital element of community is founded and developed. But more on this later.

Recovery of meaning, then, is a curricular resource which can be used toward four outcomes. From its discursive activities comes, in the first place, mastery of the sense and soundness of the work treated. The student "really" knows it. He knows the facts or factlike materials which ground it. He knows the ideas, in the shape of terms, distinctions, and premises, which directed the choice of facts covered and the significances assigned to them. He has some idea, consequently, of what is left uncovered by the work—what other or additional facts might be encompassed, what other emphases might emerge from pursuit of the problem in other terms and with other premises.

In the second place, the student has enjoyed an increment to his command of language in the service of sense. From mastery of the complexities of the document itself has come increased competence to *receive* sense. Two increments to such competence are especially noteworthy and especially to be sought. One consists of a more sensitive, discriminating and richer set of expectations—of possibility with respect to mode of organization, argument, justification—in which a received discourse, written or spoken, can find its appropriate resonance, be recognized for what it is and what it can convey. The other concerns distinctions. It consists, on the one hand, of discovery of the force and character of distinctions and alertness to them: that they may be distinctions without a difference; if they are distinctions with a difference, that there are many sorts of difference, hence that many sets of distinctions can be brought to bear as dissectors of a subject matter; that each set so brought to bear throws its own light on the subject analyzed (e.g., the ratio of negro to white convicted criminals as against the ratio of the poor to the well-off among convicted criminals). It consists, on the other hand, of an increased alertness to the number as well as the character of distinctions: of the vulgarity, evasion, and opacity of too few ("A novel is a novel." "The five steps of scientific method are . . ."); of the preciosity, sterility, and distraction of too many ("Every novel is unique." "Each scientific investigation is a law unto itself"); of the necessity for adjusting fineness and coarseness of distinction to the purposes of analysis and to what the subject matter will bear.

From the student's efforts in the course of reflexive scrutiny to make clear and defend his interpretations has come increased competence to make sense. The facial expression and voiced comment of fellow students have told him when he has been clear, when opaque, when he has conveyed what he did not intend. The questions then addressed by the instructor to him and to his hearers have located the arrows of his discourse which missed their mark. The situation so created has invited invention and trial of alternative and (eventually) more successful conveyors of intended meaning. Instructorial comment will often then have identified the class and character of the error made and indicated how that kind of error can be avoided. Meanwhile, the expectations generated by the instructor's habit of asking the student what he has and has not understood of another student's discourse, and of requesting paraphrase or critical analysis of other students' statements, has sharpened the student's ear and enormously multiplied the effectiveness of debate by invoking numerous silent participations for each audible one.

As a third outcome of this resource, the student not only knows something more but knows *what* he knows and *that* he knows; i.e., from his adventure with a given work, he has some mastery of the tactics appropriate to such materials, some idea of why they are appropriate, by what signs to recognize another work to which similar tactics will be appropriate, and some small scope, at least, for instituting adaptive changes in the tactics.

The fourth outcome is of a different order. The student has done his work in concert with an instructor who has been part exemplar, part guide, part critic, part source of stimulus, reward, and respect. He has worked with other students, as well as with the instructor: assisting and being assisted, receiving and giving criticism, profiting from others' examples, both good and bad.

These transactions not only constitute a further internalizing link between reader and read, they also constitute links between student and student, student and instructor. Giving and receiving help from recognized persons leaves its affective marks, especially when the help involves a durable increment in competence (as it will when a discipline is being shaped) and not merely assistance over a rough place in the road. Thus person-to-person relations are established between one student and another. At the same time, students have suffered together the stresses imposed by the instructor in the course of shaping a discipline and together have profited from the discipline incorporated. Thus a sense of membership in a class, in studenthood, is initiated. But the profits (and pains) have also accrued from the efforts of an instructor, both in one-to-one relation with each student and as member of the professorial class in a relation to the students as a class. Hence these transactions also constitute an instance and a contribution of the relation of group to group (faculty and student) and of person-to-person relations between members of the two groups. In brief, this curricular resource makes four sorts of contributions to community as well as contributions to knowledge and discipline.

Resource 2: Articulations

At its very common worst, curricular treatment of discourse does not contribute to discipline (unless mere lingual memory can be called a discipline). Instead, the discourse is imparted as a body of statements. The professor or the textbook spouts and the professor and the examinations make it entirely clear that the student is expected merely to spout back. If "story problems" or similar embodiments of "application of principles" are involved, there is still no discipline, merely technique, since the problems and applications are selected and designed to fit the "principles" exactly; no embarrassing adaptation, requiring knowledge of reasons, is involved. (I recall the case of a professor who, having taught a statistical formula for years,

$$s^2 = \frac{S(d)^2}{n-1} \, ,$$

realized one day that he could ask his students to solve for n and compute the value needed for a given s.

He felt that he had a major contribution to education. He had in fact made a small one, but he withdrew it the next year by adding a lecture on the importance of an adequate n, including in the lecture the formula by which to compute its value for a desired s.)

At its best, academic treatment of discourse often involves disciplines of recovery. With respect to the discourse in hand, thought and language are articulated. (For example, s is discerned and understood as a parameter of a normal distribution. The conditions which justify its formulary calculation are disclosed. Its connections with other parameters are seen.) The discipline is further extended to involve the *kind* of discourse involved. That is, discourses on parameters of the normal distribution are seen as instances of a sort of statistical enquiry and invention, so that the student is better able to master an ensuing discourse of the same sort.

But it is the curse of the academic (to which I shall have other occasions to refer) that its articulations tend to stop here. Its first love and primary concern is with the "theoretical," with knowledge and method in their most general form. Hence, though thought and language may be articulated with clarity and distinction, articulations of thought with things, with facts as comprehended *before* they are simplified and purified by assimilation to theory, are generally neglected. (The "practical" course which appears to put great emphasis on application is not an exception to this general rule, since on the one hand, the "facts" usually involved are the purified ones to which the generality is immediately appropriate, and, on the other hand, the theoretical articulations are neglected—that is, one deals with a formula and its uses but not with its meanings and origins in enquiry, especially not with its meanings and origins in the *facts* which give rise to the enquiry.)

This preoccupation with theory, this neglect of the crude fact, is the "book" the professor had in mind which cannot make a person change. It is the self-imposed limitation of the academic which corresponds to the naive protester's protest that he does not learn about life. (Of course, the ignorant student commits, in reverse, the same error of which he accuses the academic: he has no notion of the fruitfulness which accrues to fact from its articulation with theory.)

The curriculum need not operate within this tyranny of the theoretic. It can function effectively (and cogently) with the crude facts, with "life," and do so, indeed, with respect to three different loci of facts.

In the first place, it can deal with them as the facts which *give rise to* enquiries treated. Such facts differ markedly from the facts *of* the enquiry. The latter are facts which correspond closely to the etymological sense of "fact" as something made. They are refined facts, facts stripped of the "irrelevant" and converted to data, to the shape and form dictated by the enquiry and best adapted to its instruments. The facts which give rise to the enquiry—which the enquiry often purports to encompass but does not wholly encompass— are almost always more complicated, richer, more ambiguous and diverse than the facts of the enquiry, or are contaminated by the enquiry.

In consequence of such disparities between originating facts and the facts of the enquiry, theoretical knowledge does indeed cut itself off in some degree and in certain ways from that of which it purports to be knowledge. This constitutes a gap between "life" and the academic which requires a bridge of articulations between the facts *of* and the facts which *give rise to*.

This gap is seen vividly in some of the efforts of current political science to write equations which claim to predict, say, the outcome of operations of the House Committee on Appropriations. If such an equation shows the outcome as a function of six variables, five will represent more-or-less measurable quantities. The sixth, however, is a "random variable," a pretentious name in this case, not for a factor in the operations of the House Committee, but for nothing more than what the prediction equation cannot predict—unidentified originating facts which the facts of the enquiry do not encompass. In a sense, such a "random variable" is a commendably candid admission of disparity between reality and the model of it proffered by the enquiry. In one respect it is silly—the random variable often accounts for 15 to 95 percent of the variability of the "predicted" outcome.

In this extreme case, the originating facts are inaccessible, unknown so far. In most cases, however, what happens to the originating facts in the course of conversion to facts of enquiry can be traced and articulations established. In general, facts of enquiry are (a) idealizations of the originating facts; (b) selections from them; (c) abstractions; (d) contaminations.

To take, first, a familiar case of contamination, it is a fact of the enquiry that 48 percent of persons queried in December 1967 answered, "Approve," when asked, "Do you approve or disapprove the way Johnson is handling his job as president?" But the facts which give rise to the enquiry are facts about attitude and estimate of Johnson which the facts of the enquiry imperfectly represent. Between the two lie such unknowns as the intonation with which interviewers put the question, who was with the interviewed at the time, what his mood was, the weather, the vivid events of the hour just past, his plans for the minutes ahead, the mail from his son in Vietnam. Soundly managed enquiries try, of course, to minimize this sort of disparity between the two kinds of fact—in this case, by careful training of interviewers, careful formulation of the question, attention to size of sample, times and places of sampling. It is knowledge of precisely such efforts, and experience of the originating facts which demand them, which constitute one way in which the curriculum can reach beyond the facts of the enquiry toward the facts which give rise to it.

Idealization is seen in many parts of classical physics. Thus the constantly accelerating body of classical dynamics was the acceleration of a body in free fall, a kind of fall which was scarce, to say the least, since, at the time, neither Venus probes nor efficient vacuum pumps were available. The facts of the enquiry, the rates of acceleration from moment to moment, were, in this case, idealizations from originating facts of fall within a medium and involved, moreover, the fiction of instantaneous velocity. In the same way, the law which asserts that the intensity of incident light is inversely proportional to the square of the distance from the source is a law which holds for a point source. It does not hold for sources of ordinary, "real" magnitudes—light bulbs, sunny windows—though it approximates to them.

Abstraction is exemplified when experimental designs

elicit facts which take on questionable significance by virtue of lost connection with similar facts suppressed by the experimental design. Primitive physiology, for example, may use an experimental pattern in which an organ is removed and the consequently missing aspects of the organism's behavior are identified. By such means, the researcher concludes that organ A has function x and organ B performs function y. Only if by accident or design he removes organs A and B from the same animal may he discover that the results are far different from the expected mere sum of the losses of functions x and y. Such abstractive disparities between originating facts and facts of the enquiry are particularly abundant in experimental psychology (for example, studies of learning).

"The" facts about a culture, a community or an organism differ from the originating facts in still another way: they are selected facts, depending for their selection on the conception of culture, community, or organism which grounds the enquiry and dictates what data it requires.

Thus one study of a subsociety grounds its conclusions on facts about transactions between its members —who gives and who receives, who orders and who obeys. Another looks to facts which indicate conflicting aspirations and demands for loyalty focused on the subsociety by other subsocieties. A third looks for signs of congruency and disparity between basic human needs and the facilities for their satisfaction afforded the subsociety by the encompassing society.

The facts which give rise to enquiry can be encompassed in the curriculum by relatively simple and familiar means. They can be sought symbolically, in discussion, by attention to the problem which generates the search for facts, by concern for the sense of the facts of the enquiry and attention to the methods used for obtaining them. They can be sought in field and laboratory by experience afforded by the originating materials *before* these materials are transformed to perception by familiarity with the terms of enquiry (for example, the living organism seen before instead of after anatomical diagrams and simple statements of structure and function). They can also be encompassed by a more fruitful though more complex method which will be described in the next section.

The curriculum can also deal with the facts of life as the facts to which theories are applied. The childish riddle, "Which falls faster, a pound of iron or a pound of feathers" can be used honestly instead of dishonestly, namely, it can be discovered that the pound of iron falls faster, despite the apparent sense of the laws of force. The calculated behavior of an electrical network can be compared with the measured behavior of a real network (where the pure inductances, resistances, and capacitances of calculation are replaced by real capacitors which have inductance, inductances which have resistance and capacitance, and resistors which have inductance and capacitance). Two standardized forms of a standardized psychological test can be administered to the same persons under different circumstances, circumstances supposedly irrelevant to the tested competence.

Above all, and with great cogency to the problems represented by student protest, the "facts of life" can be sought both from and within the student himself. They can be sought *from* him in the sense of instances and counterinstances which he can cite, from inferences he makes and consequences he envisages, from possible applications which he notes and is invited to rehearse.

This procedure takes on an added and special dimension when carried on with a number of diverse students. Then the contrasts are not only between theoretical object and possible real one but among theoretical object and different versions—fantasied, prejudiced, or actual—of the real, thus displaying even more vividly the limitations of theory as well as displaying the role of quasi theory in all our apprehensions of the "real."

In the case of the humanities and many parts of the social sciences, the "facts of life" can be sought not only from but within the student. After all, he is a member of a culture and a social class. He enters into relations with peers, superiors, and inferiors. He is a sib, a son or daughter, an urban or suburban, a liberal or conservative. He is a learner and a forgetter. He is assertive, aggressive, hostile, submissive. He has some experience of encounter with vicissitudes and of agonizing over alternatives. He has been befriended and betrayed. In short, however imperfect and distorted his perception of himself may be, what he perceives and how he perceives it are relevant "facts of the case," and relevant in two ways: they are instances of the subject matter under study; they also stand between the student and his ability to understand and believe. His acceptances and rejections of "fact," doctrine, theory, portrayal, can be elicited, scrutinized, discussed; his reasons for acceptance or rejection sought and examined. Variants and oppositions can be constructed and criticized. Affective responses can be contrasted to the responses of others, can be voiced, can be speculated on.

This factor can be especially poignant when the materials in question are the circumstances and characters of effective literary works. In such a case, if the works are selected with an eye to three different criteria, a thoroughgoing and affecting use can be made of them.

They are chosen, first, for the articulations which can be effected between them, on the one hand, and the characters and circumstances of the students, on the other. Second, they are chosen to exhibit sufficient complexity and subtlety of articulation of their own parts with one another (especially character to character and character to circumstance, action, outcome) to constitute an adequate challenge to students' powers of analysis. Third, they are so chosen that their "scene" (time, place) is remote from the "scene" of the student readers.

By the third criterion we ensure that the student will not immediately assimilate the work to his own feelings and experience. This is of first importance, for if such an assimilation occurs, the work cannot play the role of "theory," that is, it cannot be a treatment of its "facts" (or any others) in its own right. Consequently, it cannot lead to a reexamination of, a modified perspective on, the student and his circumstances. Instead, the work is merely assimilated to the student's own experience and feelings, and thus misread or otherwise lost.

Given sufficient remoteness, however (but not so much as to evoke no interest), attention to the parts and articulations of the work itself can be invited: who is involved, what they are like, what they are involved in, how they respond, and why. Differing responses to such queries are scrutinized, tested against the discourse of the work, clarified, as they would be in any recovery-of-meaning discussion.

Then—and only then—the screen of remoteness can be withdrawn effectively, the student invited to see what has hitherto been partly hidden—the parallel between the work and his own character and circumstance: how they are the same, how different; how the author has (by the many devices of fiction) evaluated and judged the behavior of his characters; how the students have evaluated their own behavior; what new light is thrown on each by the other.

It goes without saying, I trust, that articulations are not always to be sought in the same way and with the same emphasis. The facts of life are not always the important items; disciplines differ in the ordering they make and the connections they establish among facts, words, and ideas; indeed, articulations should be sought as much to wean students away from their indefensible estimations of the importance of facts as to satisfy their legitimate cravings for them.

This point is seen particularly in the treatment of literary work just suggested. Half its function is to give word and idea (the "meanings" of character, action, and interaction assigned to them in the work) their just due by preventing the facts of "life" as seen by the student from beclouding them. Another function, as indicated in the suggested treatment, is to preserve the literary work as "idea" and to bring this idea to bear on the facts of life as a means of interpreting them. Only in a small way does the treatment function to bring the facts of life to bear as means by which to interpret or judge the work. Further, in all these functions, there are not only the words and ideas of the literary work and the facts of life but also the facts of the literary work: Flem Snopes is not any white, rapacious, socially mobile southerner, nor is hè a photograph of some Lem Stokes of Columbus, Mississippi; he is Flem Snopes of Faulkner country.

A similar importance of factors other than the facts of life exists in other materials. In the lyric poem, the words that convey images and the images they convey are themselves inalienable parts of what the images convey. In many parts of modern physics, the substantive structures which guide enquiry, the facts of the enquiries, and the theoretical structures which encompass them have such tightly woven relations inter se that the originating facts can be intruded only by main force and at the risk of incomprehensibility. The wisest plan is probably to treat them only as they can be represented as facts to which the theory is applied.

The services to be sought from articulators as a curricular resource are those already implied. In the first place, the real and ineluctable gap between theory and practice is not only identified but admitted. The gap fancied by the naive and ignorant student (complete, unbridgeable) is shown him in two ways to be fanciful: he discovers that all discussable notice of fact involves some degree of theory or quasi theory; that these can be better and worse; and that criteria central to the making of theory discriminate the better from the worse in application. Third, some increment to the discipline of articulation, not only of theory to the facts "outside" but also to our own fancied or habitual facts, can be achieved. That is, the intelligent habit of examining inside and outside facts in the light of theory, and theory in the light of facts possessed or accessible, can be initiated and furthered. Fourth, and perhaps of equal or greater importance, the student discovers himself honored, not only as individual respondent by individual instructor, but corporately: he witnesses students as a source of content, of substance, which has its place beside the content of official theory, has relations to it, is subject to and worthy of the same kind of critical attention.[2]

Resource 3:   Principles of Enquiry

The curriculum can also deal rationally with the problem, perennial in humane and social studies, of diversities of answer to similar questions and alternate solutions to problems.

The source of this pluralism is not peculiar to the humanities and social sciences. In all fields, the "hard" sciences included, systematic enquiries begin in principles of enquiry, guiding conceptions of the subject matter which determine what questions to put to it,

2. A reflexive articulation of some of my own remarks is in order at this point. In the two sections above, I have used series of clauses or phrases, e.g.: (p. 66) ". . . in what word the error lies, . . . the meaning assigned, . . . whether defensible, . . . other meanings possible, . . . which most defensible; and, ". . . recover the tacit question, . . . note its terms and premises, . . . conclusion leading, . . . kind of work to which appropriate, . . . kind of work to which the group is addressing itself."

Each such series is intended to be systematic. Each is a set of the elements or directions of discussion or other treatment under consideration where the series appears. Each member of a set is a highly compressed, perhaps inexcusably compressed, representative of what would be, in fact, ten minutes or two hours of discussion of a given work or a sustained topical thread throughout a treatment. Similar series will be used again.

A further note which may be of interest mainly to the professional educator: these two sections constitute a radical criticism of two of the tiredest platitudes of American pedagese—"interpretation of data" and "application of principles."

what data are relevant to its solution, what these
data indicate (that is, how they are to be interpreted).
Classical dynamic investigations, for example, proceed
on a commitment to a time which is taken as everywhere the same and to a space conceived as the
wholly neutral stage on which the dramas of motion
are enacted. Another dynamic conception commits
research to a time which is a function of place and
to a conception of place or space as having effect on
the motions which occur in it. Each of these views
dictates different questions to be asked in enquiry,
requires somewhat different data, and puts different
interpretations on them. In the case of biology or
social anthropology, a community (whether of persons or plants and animals generally) can be conceived as individuals or groups in a proximity to one
another which facilitates exchange of surpluses and
needs among them. Given that view, research on communities becomes the effort to identify the materials
exchanged, the exchangers, the routes and means of
exchange. But community can also be conceived as
a state of organization definable in terms of a set
of specified functions, each of which is performed by
one or another agency in every community. Given
this view, research into a given community becomes
the search for the particular agencies it uses to carry
out each function, how the agency does its work, and
how well. Still a third conception treats community
as the locus of predator-prey, exploiter-exploited,
ruler-ruled relations. The questions put, the data
sought and answers rendered, given this commitment,
are obviously different from those which arise from
other principles.

In the biological and physical sciences, the involvement of principles of enquiry as the ground of investigation only occasionally gives rise to the existence of pluralities of answers to questions, because these sciences have long since adopted the habit of obtaining a consensus of principles within the field. Most practitioners of most such sciences use the same principle of enquiry within a given era of research, changing or replacing it when it ceases to be useful, but doing so mainly in concert. The only general exception to this rule is a subscience which has not yet developed one conception of its subject matter demonstrably more reliable or more embracing than competing conceptions (in recent times, for example, ecology).

Most of the social sciences, on the other hand, are in the condition of ecology. Numerous conceptions of community, society, culture, personality, learning, and so on, exist. None is seen by a substantial majority of the concerned scientific community to exceed other conceptions in both reliability and comprehensiveness. Hence, the community splits into "schools," each pursuing enquiry in the terms of its preferred principle. Thus, diversities of view and pluralities of knowledge arise.

The principles of an enquiry are rarely stated in reports of the enquiry. (Indeed, enquirers are often not conscious, or not fully conscious, of the principle they favor.) Hence, the diversities of knowledge they unearth will often appear to the reader as competing answers to precisely the same question. In fact, they are answers to somewhat different or radically different questions. In consequence, they are not so much competitive as complementary. They can be treated as complements, however, only if we can discern the ways in which each is related to the investigated subject matter, hence to each other.

In the absence of a clear statement of the principle, it is nevertheless possible to discover something of the way in which an enquiry is related to its subject matter and to other, closely related enquiries. The possibility exists because the principle is represented in the report even though it is not explicitly formulated there. It exists in the particular terms and distinctions used, in the questions asked or answered, in the data sought and in the interpretation made of them.

Given two or three related enquiries, students can proceed by contrast and comparison to identify differences of terms, distinctions, data, interpretation. They are often able to reconstruct the questions being asked with sufficient precision to show the similarities and differences among them. Occasionally, it is possible to follow the trail back to a formulation of the principle itself.

Depending on the clarity and coherence of the paper under study, the harvest of such an enterprise will be at least the discovery that the papers are not contradictions of one another; it will usually identify the perspective from which the enquirer has viewed the subject matter and what of it is visible from such a perspective: occasionally, it will permit the student to see when and under what circumstances of practice and application one view is preferable to another, what each can do that the other cannot.[3]

3. It is sometimes asked why one cannot simply identify inferior principles and discard the outcomes of their use. In the long course of

The curricular arts which discriminate principles and their operation use much the same raw materials and microprocesses employed by the arts of recovery. The search for principles, consequently, requires no special place or technique or budget of time in its own right. It can and should be interwoven with the recovery of meanings which pertain to the subject matter per se, for each will facilitate and add to the other.

The services rendered by this curricular resource are of the first importance in view of the corrupting or restrictive character of available alternatives. The most despicable and common alternative is the suppression of plurality. The curriculum includes only the favored dogma of the professor in charge or makes only passing and invidious reference to alternatives (often excused as in the interest of the student, to avoid "confusing" him). Unfortunately, this dogmatism itself leads to radical confusion of the intelligent student, for he does encounter alternatives (in

enquiry in a given field, this useful elimination occurs. Some principles are discovered to be merely special cases of another or parts of another. And out of the conflict of principle which characterizes the social sciences, the effort toward such elimination is pursued with considerable energy. It is unlikely, therefore, that the casual adventurer into the field, or the generalist in the social sciences will easily identify "unnecessary" principles overlooked by the specialist. Meanwhile, another factor mitigates any such good fortune. The richness and complexity of the subject matter provides such a scope for diversity of enquiry that principles brought to bear tend to subsume quite different data sources (for example, economics and psychology), or data sources with relatively small overlap (as learning theory and personality theory) or treat much the same data source but in ways which differ radically (as personality theories which hypostasize organlike parts of the personality and interpersonal theories). In consequence, elimination of principles must often await the invention of new and radically more comprehensive ones.

his private reading or in courses from other dogmatists). The encounter teaches him that professors cannot be trusted and may teach him also that academic discourse, and rational discourse in general, cannot be trusted.

The other common alternative consists of a conspectus of principal alternatives made accessible by lecture, textbook, or readings. This alternative is not despicable but it is sterile. In the absence of arts by which alternatives can be understood in their relations to one another all the student can do is dismiss them all as mere opinion or select a favored one on the basis of unexamined and probably inappropriate criteria.

There is a second service rendered by the recovery of principles. It yields, as a by-product, a sense of being "on top" of an enquiry, of knowing not only what went on and why, but what else might have been done but was not done. This by-product is illusory to some extent and involves a small risk as well. The risk consists of the student's mistaking afterthought for forethought. He may suppose that because he can, in the light of the finished enquiry, see more than may have been seen by the enquirer, that he, the student, could have seen the same before the enquiry, hence that he, in one respect at any rate, is superior to the enquirer.

Whether he consciously receives this impression or not, he may behave as though he had—engaging often in the ferreting out of principles, using them to preside critically over the enquiry and deriving such satisfaction from the process that he uses it when he ought to be concerned with the recovery and use of the outcomes of the enquiry or engaged in enquiry itself.

This risk, however, can be controlled. It can be controlled by blunt, invidious recognition of it as it occurs in the course of discussion. It can be controlled by forewarning of the risk. It can be controlled by exhibiting, through invitation to the effort to do so, that mastery of the principles of enquiry is not sufficient to comprehend its fruits, and that mastery of the principles of a past enquiry is not a sufficient basis for new enquiries which will further contribute to it.

If the risk is so controlled, the further positive value accrues. The sense of mastery of the enquiry mitigates for a refreshing interlude the otherwise continuously submissive and beholden character of the student role. We do not often take account of this factor, treating it as if it were an inevitable accompaniment of the role, easily borne and of no particular consequence. It is, however, of some importance to teaching and learning. It is easily borne for a time, is even, perhaps, desired and beneficial in certain childhood periods. After eleven or twelve years of it, however, it begins to be irksome and by the end of the first year of college may be positively erosive, making it more and more difficult for the student to marshal his energies in the service of learning, thus contributing substantially to the very common second-year goof-off and second-year dropout. We would do well, then, to use available occasions to mitigate it.

Resource 4:   Arts of Enquiry

The curriculum can put such materials, facilities, occasions, and invitations in the way of the student that he is moved and enabled to pursue enquiries in his own right: focus on an interest of his own, shape a problem concerning it, search out materials, choose his methods, apply them, formulate the products of his enquiry.

Thanks to various pressures from the scientific community, this curricular resource is no longer a novel one in the telling. Unfortunately, however, when it is used, it is usually used too rarely and at the wrong time. It takes the form of a bachelor's thesis or the climax activity of an extended program or long course, and hence it occurs only once or twice in the student's career, and late. The reasons usually given for this tardy scarcity are plausible: the student must master a great deal of information, must mature and grow responsible, must have developed capacities for organization and expression, must have mastered techniques of enquiry, if his work, his contribution, is to be a respectable one.

These would be good reasons if the quality of the product were of first importance and if, in fact, other, equally effective resources existed in the curriculum for developing the required competences. If we are to consider engagement in enquiry as a curricular resource, however, the respectability of the product is not the point, and its production should not wait on developed competences but, on the contrary, be the means for their development.

In such a service, the resource must consist of considerably more than an assignment or a mere invitation, even with adequate time allotted, to engage in an enquiry. There must be an invitation to select and register an interest. But this is only the first step, for students exhibit a profound ignorance and incapacity at this earliest point in the process of enquiry (weaknesses which constiute one of the strongest of reasons for frequent and early use of this curricular resource): they do not know how to move from a felt interest in a global area to a problem. They are able to say, for example, "I am interested in personality theory" (or social mobility, feedback amplifiers, genetic determiners of behavior, the morality of the novel, learning in children) and they are usually half-conscious of the fact that such an interest does not constitute a problem but do not know what to do next.

The second step, then, must be a situation (preferably one-to-one interview) in which the questions are put which reveal that an "interest" is not a problem. These questions will indicate that a massive subject area requires delimitation, that the first step in delimitation is some analysis of the "interest" into parts or constituents, that an appropriately modest subdivision is not, for that reason, an insignificant one, and, above all, that a problem as distinct from an interest must indicate what will solve the problem—the kinds of data required and the use to be made of them. For example, "What in personality theory interests you? The different therapeutic practices each implies? The shifts of principle which generate the diversity of theory? The data and argument which supports one or another?" For another example: "The teaching of literature to whom? And for what purpose?" "If you are interested in the effect of such readings on ability to suspend impulse, what will you need to find out?" "What about the effects of sex, age, and social-class differences?" "Can you be sure your different interview judges will be using roughly the same criteria?"

Such an interview sends the student away with some understanding of what is required of a problem formulation which will be adequate to guide his later work. When he returns with a first formulation, questions are raised which indicate its inadequacies and raise questions about the materials, equipment, or other resources required, whether they are available, how they can be procured and processed. Still another brief meeting may be necessary to thrash out questions of method and technique. Only then is the student ready to embark on his study.

Ideally, the student knows that he may make use of further consultations in the course of amassing the raw materials of his enquiry, and, in any case, consultations ensue upon completion of this first large step, for with the materials in hand, a new group of problems arise for the student to discern and solve: problems of ambiguity of his data, alternative interpretations and alternate modes of interpretation; problems of adequate formulation.

At first glance, all this may appear to be far too formidable a demand on instructorial time and energy. It would be, for any substantial group of students taken singly, but they need not be so taken after the initial meeting, and with a gain from conjoint work rather than a loss. The students embarked on such programs constitute a colloquium to which each of them submits his proposals, problems, and early drafts and receives approval and criticism from his peers as well as the instructor. The gains involved in such a procedure include, in the first place, a large component of learning by surrogate: in work examined early, many students will be able to see parallels to their own errors and omissions. Hence, the second, third, and successive proposals brought before the group will exhibit an abruptly declining incidence of ineptitude. In the second place many of the indecisive students and students at a loss for an area of interest or problem will find in the exhibited interest and areas of interest of other students sufficient guidance for their own selection and sufficient stimulation to an interest of their own. Meanwhile, a few students will discover in the interests or selected problems of others such relations to their own that bases for collaboration and mutual support are established—and these are encouraged by the instructor, up to and including partnerships and collaborative production of the finished product.

Finally, the colloquium becomes the nucleus of the informed and rewarding audience before which each student presents an abstract of his finished work.

The services rendered by this curricular resource include, in the first place, the manifest one: a contribution to understanding of the character of problems, some initiating mastery of the arts of enquiry. An unpublished study of graduate student dropouts in the social sciences indicates how poorly this service may be performed—and how badly needed it may be. It was found that one of the largest dropout groups consisted of students with excellent course grades and satisfactory completion of their preliminary examinations who faced as their next responsibility the selection and formulation of a research problem. Doubtless, financial and domestic problems, and restiveness over the further postponement of professional status played some part here. But there is also little doubt that lack of preparation for enquiry was a major factor.

A second contribution arises from the extent to which any mode of study or experience of finished products—whether scientific researches or lyric poems —falls short of providing a full grasp of the product in the absence of an attempt to make one like it. The essay at making, in short, completes and illuminates much of what is half-known before the making is undertaken. A third contribution is toward mitigation of the wearing passivity and submissiveness of the student role.

Its fourth and perhaps most needed contribution is best discussed in the section to follow. This context will also indicate why the experience of enquiry should come early and often.[4]

Resource 5: Diagnostics

If other curricular resources are to be well exploited and pointedly used, the diagnosis of "where the student is" as basis for the conduct and tempo of a course must involve factors beyond those ordinarily examined. It must take account of certain attitudes, habits (both intellectual and other), beliefs, and biases, as well as of the information and techniques possessed by the student. A brief retrospect will indicate what is at stake here and why.

The recovery of meaning begins by confronting the

4. It need hardly be added that the colloquium is a contributing instance of "community," entirely apart from the particular curricular service it renders here.

student with a kind of material and a problem concerning it. Students will respond variously to such an
initial challenge. It will constitute a stimulus to one
student, a source of anxiety to another, invoke retreat
in a third. Those from whom anxiety or retreat is evoked
by an initial challenge will respond favorably to different later efforts. Some will respond to the invitation to
be critical of first efforts. Others will be drawn into the
educative experience by invitations to fill out the
topics and subheads sketched by an initial respondent.
Still others will require even more gentle handling—
asked only to supply a summary of preceding contributions, for example—before they are ready to risk
more complete involvement. Clearly, means must be
used that will permit a student to withdraw grace-
fully from an unacceptable challenge and, thereby, tell
the instructor who is ready for what.

The recovery of meaning constitutes a discipline.
This means that students must tentatively accept for
test, feel out, and examine a definite pattern of questions to be addressed to the text under scrutiny and
postpone for the moment the questions which past
habit, immediate impulse or whim may have dictated.
Students will differ in their readiness to postpone their
own questions and accept those proffered. Clearly, it
is desirable to know what student is likely to respond
in what way, for in some situations a first response
from a disciplined student will maximize the effectiveness of the ensuing discussion; in other cases, the
impulsive or whimsical may be needed.

Involved here, too, are certain intellectual competences: sensitivity to the precise terms in which a
question is put; ability to speak to these terms pre-

cisely and to avoid the confusions which arise from taking the terms analogically instead of literally and from shifting their denotation into the cloudy regions of connotation which surround them.

These competences, too, will vary from student to student (and from one group of students to the next), and the effectiveness of the enterprise will depend in some degree on invoking the participation of the right student at the right time. When the elements of a discipline are being tried and exemplified for the first time, precision is desirable. When alternative interpretations are to be treated, it is the exploration of analogies and connotations which can disclose the ambiguity of a subject matter as an object of enquiry and show how men of good will can arrive at alternative views of it. Further, the extent to which each of these competences exists in the group as a whole determines what one's teaching problems are, how one is to proceed in the course of discussion and at what rate.

Another and different distribution of talents is of importance to the adequate institution of articulations. Some students are very good at the task of hitting on the concrete instance, the telling example. Others are good at the work of perceiving the idea, the generality, lurking in a collection of instances but poor at hitting on an instance. Still others excel at the work of developing the clear and distinct formulation of what is involved. A reasonably good idea of which students excel at which of these is of importance in two ways, as before noted: for the sake of steering the course of discussion, but also in order to reward students of differing talent by invoking the help they are best able to give and in order to work toward ameliorating their particular deficiencies.

Certain interpersonal competences also play parts among our resources—both as competences to be developed and as competences required for exploitation of the resources: ability to respond well to criticism and to give it constructively; ability to compete, to play a subordinate assisting role, to collaborate, and to assume a directing role, in an enterprise. The effective pairing and grouping of students for such conjoint work again profits from reasonably reliable anticipation of the behaviors to be expected from different students. (There are also, of course, interpersonal competences pertaining to the ability to work well with the instructor in his various roles.)

Finally, a quite different class of variables exists in the relations of disciplines to the students' previous education or miseducation. He will have assimilated certain platitudes: "All values are relative." "All behavior is socially determined." "Novels are either realistic or romantic." He will have been instilled with certain habitual behaviors with respect to different kinds of materials. He may, for example, habitually read novels for their moral or "philosophical" "lesson," attend only to certain auctorial devices (narrative mode, treatment of time, way in which "character" is communicated, use of "nature"), or treat novels as a kind of history or memorial, that is, as expositions or expressions of times, places, classes, and cultures. He will possess many oversimplifications which it would be unfair to call mere platitudes, for example, a classification of psychological types or governmental constitutions, a model of atomic structure, operant conditioning as the model of all animal behavior.

These platitudes, habits, and oversimplifications often function in two ways as barriers to further education. For each student, they are among the cognitive structures to which he tends to assimilate recognizably related new materials. The power of such structures to select and transform the new—whether read, heard, or seen at first hand, can hardly be overestimated. Statements are revised (unconsciously, of course) to fit the structure. Where they resist revision, they are overlooked. If they are imposed by insistent repetition, they are soon forgotten. A similar fate awaits things perceived. They are not noticed, are twisted in the act of perception, forgotten promptly or altered in memory. In the second place, these habits, platitudes, and oversimplifications often represent to the student the gift and symbol of a well-remembered teacher or are valued by him as his own warranted truths. Hence they are often consciously defended by the student with every available device of refutation.

Such cognitive structures can be dealt with effectively and defensibly only by being treated in their own right: first identified, then carefully formulated, their incoherence with other possessed structures sought out and spelled out with the student, the evidences and arguments for them scrutinized and judged by criteria already affirmed by the student or by additional criteria which he will not reject because of other of his structures. (Of course, they can also be removed or revised by favorable affective loading of their replacements. This may be effective but its defensibility is questionable.) Hence, again, there is a diagnostic task: the structures possessed by students which may affect the new work of a course must be discovered.

There are conventional diagnostic devices which serve some of these needs. The pencil-and-paper test can do all that is needed with respect to information and technique, and do so not only for the group as a whole but—if the test is well constructed—for individuals as well. With some measure of expertise in tests and measurements, pencil-and-paper tests can be devised to measure sensitivity to precision of terms. With somewhat more expertise, they could probably be designed to discriminate differences of competence with respect to instances, ideas, and formulations, and perhaps to explore ability to apprehend analogical and connotative meanings. With the addition of a large amount of information about students and their various preparations, they could, conceivably, identify students' handicapping cognitive structures.

The latter services, however, would require greater and greater ingenuity on the part of test constructers, great increase in the time given over to testing, and the validity of the tests, the extent to which they are measuring what we wish to measure, would be increasingly questionable. Meanwhile, such factors as the student's response to public challenge, his readiness for discipline, and his interpersonal competences are extremely unlikely to be measurable well, if at all, by pencil-and-paper means.

Accumulated experience also serves some diagnostic purposes. We acquire over a few years a good idea of the information and technique possessed by students. We begin to anticipate with considerable success the handicapping cognitive structures which students acquire, and learn to react with considerable accuracy to signs of response to challenge proffered in the ordinary course of discussion, and to indicators of interpersonal competences. Accumulated experience, however, is subject to attrition, as well as to certain sources of error. It is much affected by the vividness of an incident, whether the incident is genuinely representative or not. As it grows, it tends to become less flexible, less responsive to indications of change in the student group. And changes do occur: admissions standards rise and fall; high school programs are reformed; the social and political climates alter and by their change generate unanticipated new states of readiness and unreadiness, new attitudes and new resistances and difficulties to be overcome.

These traditional diagnostic devices need a supplement, then, especially since much diagnosis wants doing in the moment, in the course of discussion, and without noticeably interrupting it. The available supplement consists of a permissive and unstructured pattern of discussion which stands in marked contrast to that suggested for management of arts of recovery, articulations, and discrimination of principles. Where the latter are demanding and the instructor's role dominant, the pattern appropriate to diagnosis operates by providing deliberately vague ("unstructured") occasions for student expression, and requires the instructor not only to receive all offerings with equal interest and attention but to be visibly doing just that. His permissiveness may extend to any or all of these: who responds, to what question he responds, what he says. "Jones, do you or Smith or Alpert have any feeling about this?" accompanied by a glance at each,

opens the door to multiple responses, while the unstructured question and the equal welcoming of early,
incoming responses expand the other two factors.

Wayne Booth suggests one example:

One never asks, first, "What kind of work is this?" or "How does
it illustrate this or that concept or fit this or that scheme" or
"Does it fit Aristotle's definition of tragedy or Frye's definition
of a Mennipean satire?" Instead, one begins, at every academic
level, with statements from the students about what they have
found in the work, what there is in it that interests or repels
them.[5]

The least unstructured question for such a service
might be the obvious one, "What did you like best
about it?" The classic unstructured question is, "Tell
me about it." (This form is especially important for
diagnosis of cognitive structures, since the indefinite
reference of "it," permits the student to reveal his own
choice of sub-subject as well as the terms in which he
treats it.)

In many cases, the question is not patently unstructured and its diagnostic function is carried out by attention to the form of the answer rather than to its
manifest content. One may ask of a number of students, for example, "What do you think causes such
behavior?", the reference being, let us say, to a hostile act portrayed in a novel or reported by a social
scientist. One then notes that one student seeks a psychological stereotype as "the" cause ("Such people
overreact"); another seeks the cause in social organization ("He belongs to a minority group"); another
in the immediate past history of the actor ("Maybe
he'd just been put down by his instructor").

A third class of permissive question openly invites

5. In *College English*, October 1965.

self-election, postponement of, or withdrawal from a task: "Now we need a series of formulations and revisions. Would you be willing to do the first one, Bart, or would you rather wait?" "Who will undertake to be Bart's critic?" "Are there further criticisms?" "Now how about a reformulation, a second round, which takes account of these criticisms?" (One notes, of course, not only whether Bart accepts or not, but if he declines, who volunteers in his stead, who responds to the lesser challenge, at what point Bart reenters the discussion, and who remains silent.)

A fourth evocative device is silence, or near-silence. It is made to be so by establishing expectations to which the silence is an exception. Three such silence patterns are available, one which is addressed to an entire group, one which is addressed to a particular student, one which is addressed to other students with reference to one student's statement. For the first of these services, one will have established a pattern, let us say, of beginning each meeting with a highly structured query whose content sets the subject for the meeting. On the nth occasion (concerned with an unusually difficult work or one deviant in other respects) one enters, takes his chair, hesitates, and looks around with raised eyebrow until someone breaks the silence. Similarly, one may have established a pattern of commenting on each student response or immediately conveying it to another student. In the diagnostic moment addressed to a particular student, completion of his response is met by a silence in which one continues to address that student by direction of gaze and facial expression. In the third service, completion of a student response is met by a gaze which moves on to other students, one by one, as silence is maintained.

Among the many functions which these patterns of silence can serve, there is one of special importance which goes beyond the diagnostic: it mitigates the inherent vice of the led discussion. The character of this vice is obvious enough: the led discussion has its origin in the instructor's question and maintains its momentum through his further questions; the student may learn how to answer them but does not learn to ask his own.

In effect, then, the device of silence, the withholding of guiding questions, appropriately and frequently used, is the means by which arts of recovery, articulations, and search for principles are related to and merge into enquiry. The silence addressed to the whole group gives students occasion to find their own questions to be addressed to the text or problem. To the extent that this text or problem has some relation to those previously dealt with but is set apart by special deviance or difficulty, the student has some guidance in the task but is not taken by the hand. The silence addressed to a student on the occasion of his own remarks urges him to be his own critic, to reflect on his statement: its connection with the text or problem in hand, with the question previously put, with the pool of material on which he is drawing for evidence or argument. The silence addressed to others on the occasion of a student's response applies the same urgencies to these others.

Finally, it should be noted that enquiry, reciprocally, has an indispensable contribution to make to diagnosis. It performs a service as inaccessible to permissive devices as it is to accumulated experience or pencil-and-paper tests; it reveals a matter, indeed, which is largely inaccessible to the instructor by any device. It permits the student to discover what effort is required of him by various tasks, what it feels like to perform them, what satisfactions derive from increasing competence at the tasks and from the niceness with which they are accomplished. These diagnoses, which must be made by the student because they address what is accessible only to him, bear, of course, on the quality of the decisions which he makes with respect to his own career—his choice of major field, of the academic life as such, of what to do with his time and energy (see Diagnosis 1).

Resource 6: Students and Professors

The curriculum can cast both professor and student in many more roles than are ordinarily envisaged. We have spoken of the professor in his seminarial role and as model of a style of life, as witness to the satisfactions of scholarship, sensibility, and expertise. He can also function as model of a learner. Consider, for example, the existence of a "course" or program in which the "students" consist of students in the conventional sense and members of the faculty, both sitting as peers over an extended period to master a subject matter or a discipline as unfamiliar to the faculty members of the group as to the student members. (An example might be scientist professors mastering a discipline related to the arts.) Both kinds of members submit alike to the guidance of an expert, master the materials he proposes, respond to his example, guidance, and criticism in discussion. In the process, the professorial member functions as a model of the humility, pride, assiduity, and openness to learning and correction appropriate to the role of student. Consider as another pattern, the existence of a mixed group (students and faculty) who meet without guidance or official leadership, to master a discipline equally novel to both kinds of members. The group deliberates about its purpose, selects its materials, appoints its members to serve in rotation as chairman, undertakes the work it has settled on. In this situation, each faculty member serves as model of a man who knows his station. He functions as peer of students in the situations in which they are peers in fact; he functions as a master in those moments and relative to those matters in which he is a master in fact, and does both with the dignity appropriate to each role.

The curriculum can also make the professor visible to students as a peer among fellow faculty members. Students can be enabled, for example, to witness the reception of a scholarly paper by the author's colleagues. The student sees the effectiveness with which the scholar's peer critics balance concern for the truth and respect for the scholar's person in the way they question him, examine flaws, challenge conclusions, debate issues. The student sees the reporting scholar's reception of criticism, question, and challenge.

The curriculum can make visible the scholar's transfer of the generalizable virtues of his craft to other spheres: the responsibility, the patience, the charity, the willingness to endure the inevitable arid stretches, the intellectual competences, which he brings to bear as member, say, of an administrative committee. (Obviously, the professors chosen for such a role will have to be selected with great care.)

In similar ways, students can be cast in extremely fruitful teaching roles, functioning with faculty members and acting as a link between faculty and younger student. We will postpone further consideration of these possibilities, however, until later.[6]

Students can also be made visible as students and professors as teachers to an extent and in a perspective not afforded in the ordinary teaching situation. In the ordinary situation, the teacher is properly far too preoccupied with the specific task in hand to see himself as teacher or even to see students as learners in all their aspects. This limitation can be overcome by customs and institutions which bring other students and other professors as observers of the teaching and learning undertaken and undergone in classes other than their own.

Resource 7: Affective Transactions

The transactions between student and instructor can be made to convey a useful affective content as well as a cognitive one. The instructor's propounding of question or problem can be put to such service— by the person he noticeably chooses to direct it toward, the name he addresses him by, and the voice and manner in which it is directed. Given the context of past exchanges in the group, the instructor can thereby convey recognition of a particular student's particular competence, or a challenge to try again what has been ill done in the past, or an offer of support and help, or even an appeal for help on a kind of problem at which the student is better than the teacher.

The instructor's reception of students' proffered so-

6. See "The 'Community' Prescriptions," pp. 257–303.

lutions to problems and other formulations can be put to the same service with even greater ease by devices ranging from conventional approval and equally conventional identification of formal inadequacies, through conveyance of irritations, surprise, boredom, interest, appreciation, excitement, to the direct confrontation of the student with an unevadable statement of a cogent, habitual difficulty ("I had hoped that, for once, you would have qualified your statement with a hint that you might be wrong." "Once again, you have ignored the problem." "Hasn't it occurred to you that some people might undertake actions from motives quite different from your own?" "You weren't born liking rare beef or martinis, either.")

Such affective or affect-rousing transactions have three functions. They convey what should, by now, be valued responses of a valued judge—to some students, at least. They also lay a necessary and sometimes sufficient ground for two other responses by students. The student witness or recipient of such freedoms on the part of the instructor is himself freed to some extent to respond in similar ways to the instructor. Instead of retiring in the face of boredom, confusion, or incomprehension into protective politeness and remoteness, he feels and uses some scope for expressing his state, thus supplying a kind of feedback which enormously enhances the effectiveness of teaching. The student witness or recipient of such freedoms on the part of the instructor is also moved to respond and invite response with respect to fellow students. The praises and dispraises, reluctances or appreciative receptions thus generated among peers who are beginning to share a discipline can often find points of entry and effect where the instructor's cannot. Often, too, they pave the way for a later effectiveness of the instructor's responses.

Resource 8: Briefly Noted

Curriculum can also include control of the times, places, and situations in which students are invited to conduct their own discussion, be their own critics, subject the instructor to questioning and challenge, dissolve the group in favor of solitary and small-team work, give over a problem to the instructor for solution, meet the instructor alone to deal with a major effort or persisting difficulty.

Finally, curriculum can include the effecting of transactions between students (singly or in subgroups) and materials in their raw state, unsystematized and unformulated—events and situations, problems and dilemmas posed in "field" and laboratory—and return of the experiences undergone to the discussing group for commentary, formulation, and criticism.

CURRICULAR COHERENCE

This discussion of curricular resources grew from one of two glaring problems posed by the budget of needs implied in our diagnoses: whether curricular resources could possibly meet these needs. The resources cited speak for themselves, I think; they are rich enough to serve our purposes.

The second glaring problem arises from the number of needs in the budget. How can we do all these things and teach calculus too? If each item in our budget of needs required its own course or substantial segment of a course, we could not teach calculus too. Indeed, in a mere four years we could not encompass the budget. Fortunately, each need does not require its specific instrument; many are related needs and the nutrients which will satisfy them bear analogous relations to one another.

This can be seen immediately in many of our resources. The recovery of meaning and the discrimination of principles not only make use of the same materials and the same modes of instruction but enrich one another. The institution of articulations contributes to and extends meanings recovered and becomes possible only in the context of meanings sought and principles discriminated. All of these go on in the same classrooms at the same times and, indeed, some of them would require more time alone than they require when aided by the others.

The same kind of connection can be seen or established among many of the needs. Ignorance of what is involved in decision and choice (Need 1.2) and incompetence in the arts of decision and choice (1.4) can be dealt with, in part, through the same materials and at the same time. Less obviously, cleansing of susceptibility to impulse and rejection of diversity of habit and value (1.7) together with incompetence in collaboration (1.5) are not only related to one another but closely tied to the need for resources of durable satisfaction (3), for the same processes which lead to occasions for collaboration (enquiry, recovery of meaning, reflexive scrutiny of debate) are also processes by which competences are developed which yield enduring satisfactions, evoke suspense of impulse and require and reward diversities of habit. Moreover, all of these are either occasions for, prerequisites to, or instances of community (6).

The same sort of economy of means can be established among most of the prescriptions to be suggested. A few of them can be assimilated to one another. Many of them can be assimilated to conventional courses in conventional areas of the curriculum: philosophy, literature, graphic and plastic arts, language, mathematics and the social sciences, and to some extent, the natural sciences.

I am tempted to suggest, indeed, that the cardinal principle of practical curriculum making (if there is such a principle) is that we can rarely afford a curricular device which serves a single curricular purpose. And we shall, in general, adhere to this principle. Most of the curricular needs I am able to serve are assimilated to three groupings of prescriptions and most of each of these can be assimilated, in turn, to conventionally recognizable parts of most collegiate curriculums.

One aspect of this coherence deserves special attention. The first and second prescription groups ("practical" and "curricular") are both curricular in a restricted sense of the word—concerned with teaching aims, behaviors and content which take place mainly in classroom and laboratory in close connection with spoken and written materials. In this restricted sense of curriculum, the prescriptions of the third group ("community") are extracurricular. They concern the lives of students outside the classroom—their housing, how and where and with whom they eat, their friendships and alliances, their loyalties, their memberships. Nevertheless, these prescriptions are of a piece with those which go before. The kind of community which they commend is one required by the commended curriculum and the curriculum commended in turn contributes to the formation of this community. The community is a collegiate community.

THE PRACTICAL PRESCRIPTIONS 3

INTRODUCTION

There is "method" in the prescriptions here suggested. They take account of most of the needs indicated by our diagnosis and bring to bear on them the curricular resources described in chapter 2. They do not, however, constitute a whole curriculum, nor must all of them be taken together as a package. Institutions will differ in their willingness and in their ability to make use of them and such differences are taken into account to the extent that some of the prescriptions stand alone and others require only an additional one or two to constitute effective instruction.

Let them be taken individually in the first instance, then, only as suggestions and examples. Where one or more is given further serious consideration, it will be reasonably plain what it requires from others by way of support.

Let it be admitted at once that the aims of this first group of prescriptions are modest ones. They will not, for example, constitute an instant psychoanalysis. We shall not undertake to transform deep hostilities to impulses of love. We will not replace callousness with compassion or change malevolence to well-wishing. Students who are deeply hostile, callous, and malevolent will probably stay that way.

These prescriptions will not make moral men even of those students whose impulses are appropriate, for moral maturity, as remarked earlier, involves richness of experience leading to good judgment. For this, four years is not enough time, nor is the range of collegiate experience sufficient.

These modest disclaimers do not mean, however, that a well-devised and well-executed curriculum coherent with the prescriptions will not make a contribution, and in many cases, perhaps, a substantial one, toward morality in one of its defensible formulations. I have in mind a formulation suggested and partly implied in student notions of active selfhood and service. In this view, morality does not, of course, refer to the conventional notion which comprises mainly chastity, truth-telling, and paying debts. It does not, in fact, refer primarily to any specific set of values but rather to how and by whom specific "values" (choices among means and proximate goals) are selected and acted on. In commonsense terms, it is more nearly a conception of good character than of goods in general, and of good character expressed in action.

More specifically, "moral," in this view, qualifies actions rather than things sought or feelings or unenacted impulses. The moral action as against the nonmoral action is one which is justified by its conformity to choices grounded in good deliberation. Deliberation in turn is good when it conforms to the criteria suggested earlier: that it be corporate (that consensus is sought by reasonable means); that the parties to it constitute a variety of habits, attitudes, outlooks; that it devise and consider a very wide variety of alternatives; that "rehearsal" be involved; that the facts of the case be treated as real particulars and not as instances of general classes.[1]

This justification entails, however, more than is superficially apparent, for deliberation can meet its criteria only if the individuals who engage in it possess certain characteristics. In the first place, they must be competent at carrying on deliberation. This requires ability on the part of each participant to suspend his own impulses and reflect upon them and ability to receive and reflect upon the proposals of others. The latter competence in turn requires tolerance of, and participation in, diversities of habit and outlook. Further, since deliberation is an onerous process, it can be sustained only if the participants find satisfaction in their participation with others in the process and in the precision and thoroughness, the quality, of their contributions.

These characteristics in turn imply, at one pole, possession of the sort of self-discipline which can act to modify the force and tendency of felt impulses and, at the other pole, the courage, assiduity, and energy which permit one to carry out the actions required by a deliberate choice. Between these poles, still other characteristics are entrained: good temper, informed confidence in one's abilities and equally informed awareness of weaknesses, ability to confess error, generosity toward others, especially with repect to gifts of time and energy, a considerable knowledge, and intellectual competences over and above the deliberative competence itself.[2]

1. See especially Diagnosis 3, p. 22; Summary Diagnoses 1.2 and 1.6, pp. 37–38; and Needs 1.2, 1.4, and 1.6, pp. 44–47.
2. It is of some importance that the *im*moral act, in this view, is an

It is in view of these entailed characteristics that a conception of morality which begins in commitment to intelligent consideration of alternatives and intelligent communications toward consensus ends by being a morality of good character. It is clear too that most of the entailed characteristics are in substantial part intelligent habits, ways of behaving capable of being instigated, internalized, and even, eventually, passed on to self-control by means of education. It is for these reasons, then, that we can hope that a well-designed and well-executed curriculum can make a contribution to the morality of its students.

The practical prescriptions concern those needs (Needs 1.1–1.7) which represent privations of certain of these characteristics. There is, first, the problem posed by the platitudes of "sincerity," "selfhood," and "service" which students use in ignorance of what is involved in a well-grounded idea of the self and its integrity (namely, the characteristics cited above and their use in action) and in the conditions for defensible determination of what is serviceable to others and what is not.

The second curricular challenge (need) concerns a related ignorance: of what is involved in practical decision, that is, that principles are brought to bear on cases only approximately and with great difficulty. This is essentially the problem of facing the student with "reality," that is, of discovering to him the sense and extent to which real cases are not mere instances of general rules or mere members of classes. He will need to see that classes and rules are neat abstractions

act undertaken to corrupt one or more of these characteristics or knowing inaction with respect to their development in oneself or others. In this sense, a few activists and a number of "educators" are immoral.

(selections) from the real and that real cases seen in terms of rules and classes are confused and complex. He will need to see that the application of principles to problems of choice and decision, given this disparity between rule and case, takes on a special character and requires its own art, the art of deliberation, involving the envisaging of alternatives, the weighing of alternatives, and the rehearsal of probable consequences.

The third challenge is to supply some experience of deliberation, either as a process actually engaged in or as a process seen in detailed retrospect, preferably both. Ideally, such deliberations actually engaged in should be real ones, and they will be so to the extent that the choice problems dealt with are the student's—and responsibly so. That is, action by the student will ensue on the decision made by the student, and he will have to live with the consequences which flow from the action. Our prescriptions will provide only approximately for this ideal and even then only for some students, not all. For the most part, something less than the ideal will have to suffice.

The fourth challenge is closely related to the third: to provide experience and practice in collaboration. This experience should emphasize the shared work of corporate decision and corporate execution of decision, work which requires diversity of mind, value, and habit among participants and which leads to discovery of the usefulness of diversity and the satisfaction accruing from participation in it.

The fifth challenge is to contribute to the habitual suspension of impulses and reflection on them.

With respect to all but the first two of these challenges, the closing point of chapter 2 applies with special force: that the curriculum should be conceived, so far as possible, not as a machine with a separate part for each function but as a fabric of experiences in which each area involves many functions. This point was formulated in chapter 2 as a counsel of economy. It is also a counsel of effectiveness. One does not master a competence as an intelligent habit if it is practiced only in one of the places or areas in which it is relevant. One does not learn to write lucidly in a writing course if it is only there that lucid writing is required, if everywhere else one may be half-coherent, equivocal, and imprecise. This applies with particular force to three of the practical needs dealt with here. Experience of deliberation, collaboration, and suspension of impulse will be rewarding only if they are done and undergone in many places and in different contexts throughout the curriculum.

For this reason, needs 1.1 and 1.2 (concerning the moral platitudes and the character of practical decision and choice) will be treated only by the practical prescriptions. Need 1.3, which concerns student ignorance of curriculum, educational possibilities, and his own educational needs, will be treated almost entirely in the second and third group of prescriptions; so also the problems of the corrupting character of opaque electives and early choice of major field. The need for competence in deliberation, collaboration, and responsibility will be treated in all three groups of prescriptions.

Three anecdotes to introduce the practical prescriptions.

First anecdote. After one of their more pointless and merely defiant sit-ins some students asked what punishment might be meted out. I said that I did not know but thought it should be a real one and would, myself, make it suspension for an academic period (which would carry with it the risk of military draft and loss of fellowships and scholarships). Their eyes and mouths rounded and they wailed, almost in chorus, "But we were sincere!"

A part of this cry was only a translation of the six-year-old's "I didn't mean to." A large part of it, however, was cognitive. They meant that "sincere" was to be equated immediately and unquestionably with "good." This group knew no other basis for the making or defense of moral choice than an inner feeling of self-righteousness. It did not occur to them that some Polish Catholics in Chicago sincerely hate Negroes and consider them animals; and that some Negroes in Chicago sincerely hate Polish Catholics and consider them animals. When I flung this point at them they looked at me in indignation, then muttered a few words about my putting them and *those* people in the same class. They had had an immediate experience of their own sincerity, and from their gut believed that such a feeling could attach only to their own estimates of situations. In short, they believed, unknowingly and uncritically, in a moral faculty or intuition, an automatic conscience which rings infallible bells of warning or approval when bad thoughts or good thoughts are thought. They had no knowledge of the civilization-long struggle to find reliable bases for moral judgment, no notion of the diverse, incomplete but defensible solutions to this problem or, in consequence, of the diversities of ways in which moral judgments can be made and defended.

Second anecdote. Another student, one of the mildly paranoid, had just finished referring to the mysterious "they," who, somewhere, inaccessible to pleas and argument, were making the decisions which would rule students' lives. I tried to tell him about the way the university's decisions were in fact made: the deliberations engaged in, the varieties of interests consulted, the tangle of considerations which are taken into account, the web of checks and balances through which deans and provosts are as frequently constrained by their constituencies as the constituencies are by them. As I spoke, outrage mounted higher and higher in the student's face until he blurted out, "That can't be true!"

"Why?" I asked.

He answered, "If it were true, there would be no power for us to take over."

There is an element of nastiness here, but let us ignore it. The important point is the ignorance portrayed of ways in which decisions are made and the innocence which reduces a university faculty and administration from real persons with real interests and options to abstract lay figures from an immorality play called "The Power Structure."

Third anecdote. For more than a decade I have used a simple projective technique for annual assessment of students' awareness of the variety of factors involved in the determination of punishment under the law. Each year from 1956 through 1967 student groups of eighteen to thirty identified, among others, the following six: (*a*) effect of punishment on the prisoner, (*b*) its deterrent effect on others, (*c*) protection of others, (*d*) the circumstances of the criminal act, (*e*) the background and condition of the criminal, (f) maintenance of the dignity of the law.[3]

In the last three years, no one in the sample groups has named the dignity of the law, and in the spring of 1967 half the group perseverated on the extenuating background of the criminal. Moreover, it has become increasingly difficult over these three years to convey the idea of the dignity of the law and obtain responses indicating students' grasp of its importance, namely, that it ceases to have the force of law if it can be abrogated at whim, and that without its force, civil peace collapses. On the contrary, students have increasingly voiced the unexamined view that law consists merely of arbitrary regulations, or regulations in the interest of a ruling clique, in either case rigid and incapable of change except by violence. Their proposed substitute is an anarchy which they think would function benevolently if law and authority were completely removed.

These three anecdotes commend practical components corresponding to each of the anecdotes: (a) an examination of morals and moral choice; (b) an examination of the character and role of law; and (c) an apprenticeship in public affairs concerned with the ways practical problems arise and decisions concerning them are made and carried out. Additional practical components are commended by the need for experience of deliberation and suspense of impulse.

Practical Prescription 1: Morals and Moral Choice

"I was sincere," then, constitutes one student note to be organized into a defensible ground for moral choice. The sillier, more childish part of this platitude

3. See the illustration of reflexive scrutiny, p. 62.

can be dealt with out of hand, after the fashion of our remarks concerning the sincerity of Negroes and Polish Catholics in Chicago: by seeking articulations out of student experience and within the diversities of student prejudices which indicate very obviously the contrariety and diversity of "sincere" valuations and actions and point unmistakably to their parochial character, their obvious connection with particular fears, insecurities, ambitions, propinquities, and social origins. Such search for and use of "facts of life" from and within students might well constitute the materials, methods, and purposes of the opening sessions of any course on morals and moral choice.

When mere "sincerity" is dealt with in this fashion, there still remains the factor of "*We* were sincere," the idea that some people, a moral elite, have such states of mind and character that *their* "instinct" for the good and bad, *their* sincere reaction to events, persons, policies, and actions can be trusted. Inherent here are two further factors which constitute the ground in student privations for this prescription. There is, first, the notion of a moral intuition or faculty (whether possessed by all or some, whether arising by nature or requiring cultivation). There is, second, the very fruitful notion of a state of competence and character from which defensible moral decisions can flow.

To these two, a third must be added from our diagnostic data, the platitude of "service." This platitude takes three forms, often at the same time. The first and simplest is the notion that an act performed for the sake of others is ipso facto good. The second is the notion that a sacrifice of self or disregard of self-interest is ipso facto good. The third is a union of the first two: that offerings to others involving sacrifice of self are the best of all.

These three diagnostic factors point to three central foci for this prescription: (1) an examination of the possibility and scope of a moral intuition; (2) an examination of the states of character and competence required for warranty of moral choice; (3) a scrutiny of the notion that self and other, selfish and unselfish, are contraries which distinguish the immoral and the moral. (The second and third together take care of the question of what would constitute desirable service to others.)

For this work, portions of three texts are well-nigh indispensable as the foundation materials of the course: David Hume's *An Enquiry Concerning the Principles of Morals,* Aristotle's *Nichomachean Ethics,* and John Dewey's *Human Nature and Conduct.*

Hume's is not only the classic exposition of the grounds for supposing a moral intuition but a tough minded one, expounding with great clarity and simplicity the evidence that such an intuition may exist and indicating its limited scope and strength and the possibility of its corruption. Further, he directly joins the issue of self-other (with emphasis on other), directs attention to the need for determining the specific and concrete utility of "service," links both "service" and moral sentiment to state of character, and raises, when the document is examined critically, the question whether the moral can be limited to approvals and disapprovals or ought to qualify action primarily.

The *Nichomachean Ethics* possesses four complementary advantages. First, it is above all an ethics of action rather than of approval-disapproval, feeling or impulse. Second, it is a "natural" ethic, grounded in a "psychology" (hypotheses concerning the potential competences of members of the species and of the relations of happiness and pleasure to the development and use of these competences). Third, rather than holding up ideals of human character, it takes full account of individual differences among men and is concerned with achievable goods rather than remote ones. Fourth, in its special conception of "friendship" and its account of the role of education in ethics, it, too, takes notice of the question of "service" and joins the issue of self-other (with emphasis on self).

It has one disadvantage, however: though it fits almost perfectly the commitments of students, it runs counter to one commitment likely to be found among philosophers of recent vintage, and instructor's prejudices, as well as those of students, require some attention. The difficulty arises from the extent to which Aristotle's treatment of the program rests on the notion of an array of characteristics, of potentialities, typical of the human species. Although this would appear normal enough to biologists and many psychologists, some philosophers find it repugnant, calling it "ontological" or "metaphysical," despite the obvious empirical content to which the work appeals.

By utilizing an additional text, this disadvantage may be turned to an advantage so far as students are concerned. A number of recent philosophers have "rediscovered" the Aristotelian program and have been sufficiently moved by its cogency to attempt a redevelopment of it which avoids the repugnant ontological feature. One accessible example is *Ethics and Education* by R. S. Peters (Chicago: Scott, Foresman & Co., 1967). To use this work or a similar one in juxtaposition with the Aristotle would afford a first-rate occasion for the search for differences of principle and location of the differences of meaning which arise therefrom.

The advantages of the Dewey book for our purposes are manifold. First, in juxtaposition with Aristotle it provides a remarkable instance of the transformations which can be wrought, the greater light which can be thrown, upon a common subject matter by bringing to bear on it different principles. Dewey and Aristotle are alike in their conception of the problem and subject matter of morality. They are equally concerned that it be a morality of choice and action. Each sees choice and action becoming moral as they arise from good character brought to bear on the facts of existence and the desires of men. Each conceives character as constituted of flexible, intelligent habits. Each recognizes a dual function of character-in-process—used on the one hand to reshape the facts of the environment which can alter the course of external events; used on the other hand to reshape the conditions of the environment and the behaviors which further modify and develop character itself. Yet, one of these men is, to put it briefly, Aristotelian; the other is pragmatic. Each, therefore, makes emphases which the other does not; each clarifies relations which the other remarks only in passing; each makes distinctions which the other prefers to merge. The result is two perspectives on a nearly common object which, when taken together, are vastly more educative and informative than either taken alone.[4]

In addition to serving with the Aristotle, the Dewey

4. If time is a major consideration, the Dewey work can be used in lieu of, rather than in addition to, the Peters with relatively little loss, except for the glimpse afforded by Peters of more recent philosophic methods.

book makes valuable contributions of its own. First, its contemporary syntax and rhetoric makes it accessible to students who find the denseness and the archaic English of many translations of Aristotle difficult to penetrate, and the contemporaneity of Dewey's cited examples and vocabulary facilitate articulation. He takes a hard look at notions of freedom generated in mere opposition to social control and an equally hard look at notions of righteousness generated out of unexamined passion for conformity and for existing social structures. He faces immediately the question of moral intuition, of pretending to know the good by "insight" and out of connection with actions and their consequences, thus challenging the appropriateness of Hume's conception of the problem. He indicates precisely the indispensability and mutual dependencies of emotion, impulse, and reason in the initiation of choice and action. Each of these issues is perennial; each is also part of contemporary student efforts toward a defensible morality.

As to desirable special emphasis on materials in these texts, I shall make no recommendations with respect to Hume. The *Enquiry* is recent enough and stylish enough among current philosophers to ensure that they will have their own ideas. With respect to Aristotle, I shall (diffidently) make two suggestions. There is a single sentence in book 1, chapter 3, the sense of which, in context, is crucial to a practical grasp by students of the relevance and meaning of the doctrine to their own lives and views. The sentence reads, "A young man is not a proper hearer of lectures on political science; for he is inexperienced in the actions that occur in life, but its discussions start from these and are about

these." It is important that the apparently simple sense
of the remark be probed with respect to what constitutes "experience." To most students, the word refers
only to the objective side of experience, a mere wit-
nessing of events. In the Aristotelian pattern, however,
(as in Dewey) it is also experience on the subjective
side, experiences of the impulses, reasonings, and emotions which initiate actions and those which arise as
the actions and their consequences are undergone.

A related statement occurs in chapter 4, "anyone
who is to listen intelligently to lectures about what
is good and noble . . . must have been brought up in
good habits." Students should first be faced with the
apparent question begging in the statement, the fact
that an author trying to determine what the good is
refers to "good" habits in the very course of the investigation. They should then be challenged to find
and formulate the sense in which the question is not
begged: that if an argument is to appeal to experience
of the inward effects and satisfactions of certain kinds
of actions and undergoings, those inward effects and
satisfactions must have been experienced by those the
argument addresses.

The second suggestion concerns Aristotle's list of
developable competences (the so-called moral and intellectual virtues). The list as it stands has its own
cogency to the argument as developed. Nevertheless,
the list is "dialectical," that is, finer or coarser dis-
criminations of competences can be made and they
can be developed along lines other than Aristotle's.
I recommend that instructor and students develop
(or examine) alternative lists or alternatives to members of the list, a list, let us say, developed from the

Dewey material. Such a procedure has two advantages. It invokes a measure of enquiry; it helps to clarify the soundness of the Aristotelian emphasis on developable competences by divorcing the point itself from the particular list of competences in which it is embodied.[5]

I shall make one recommendation concerning special emphases in treatment of Dewey. He is especially concerned with the positive values of impulsion, emotion, and emotional sensitivity in the making and execution of moral decisions. Hume and Aristotle are also concerned with these matters, but give neither as explicit nor as vivid treatment as does Dewey. They deserve special attention in Dewey, therefore. Indeed, one may wish to supplement *Human Nature and Conduct* by chapter 3 of Dewey's *Art as Experience,* with its especially poignant treatment of these matters.

A further word about materials. The foundation texts will profit from a group of auxiliaries drawn from recent psychology. A number of modern personality theorists have developed views involving the self and its development which deviate sufficiently from Aristotle's and Dewey's to permit fruitful comparisons. Works of Erich Fromm, Gordon Allport, and A. H. Maslow offer examples. These works, like Aristotle's, center on notions of "self-realization" or "self-actualization" but subject the materials of human nature and behavior to differing analyses. Hence they serve both to demonstrate the durability of this approach to the problem of morals and to suggest some of the issues in psy-

5. I hope that this second suggestion, together with the suggestion that Peters' formulation may be useful, sets at rest the notion that Hume and Aristotle are recommended here because they are "great." I have not been moved by the age of the works or by the reverence sometimes accorded them. They are suggested because I can think of no better materials for serving the purposes of this prescription.

chology which give rise to different solutions of the problem.

In addition to these treatments of personality, I suggest an examination of a few representatives of the current laboratory researches which bear on the tendency of many animals to "seek problems" and "act to enrich their environment" rather than, as the earlier behavioristic biases have it, merely to respond to stimuli or "drives" and in their absence to curl up and go to sleep. References can be found in a paper by Harry Harlow in *Current Theory and Research in Motivation* (Lincoln: University of Nebraska Press, 1953). See too the paper by J. McV. Hunt in *The Nebraska Symposium on Motivation, No. 13* (Lincoln: University of Nebraska Press, 1965).

So much then for materials. As to method, all possible resources for the recovery of meaning and the search for principles are to be brought to bear. The first is indispensable since our aim is to supply an ordered content with which to fill relatively empty platitudes possessed by students unaware of their platitudinous character. The second is important if we are not merely to impose a moral doctrine which will be vulnerable just to the extent that we have not suggested alternatives and variations to which it is subject. Above all, however, this prescription calls for all possible articulations of word and idea with the language, ideas, and facts of the student, for we are concerned here, in the question of morals, with what is probably the most fundamental cognitive privation as far as student conduct is concerned. Hence, we are concerned that he know not merely the facts of the case but begin to know them as some of the facts of life.

Discussion of the texts would only begin, then, with

their explication. It would move from there to a thorough probing of the plausibility of each. Students would be invited to cite instances and counterinstances relative to its points, to voice beliefs and disbeliefs, to explore reasons and grounds of prejudice for or against. Students would be called upon to criticize one another, to support one another in their arguments, to comment on the terms, the distinctions, and the identifications with which each student takes hold of problems posed to him. Above all, each student would be called upon to play devil's advocate to himself. That is, each student who voiced a strong position on an important matter would be asked to turn immediately to the contrary view and to marshal and formulate the evidences and arguments in its favor. This is a device to emphasize again and again that intelligent discussion is not a competition in which one marshals only the evidence on one side (eristic) but a process by which to probe jointly with others into the meanings and defensibilities of conceptions of important matters (irenic).

After disciplines begin to be mastered, assignments would cease to be the same to all. Instead, two or three students as a team would be asked to undertake an intensive investigation of one problem while other teams investigated others, each team to formulate the fruits of its study and deliver them for the benefit of the whole group. This device is intended, not only to shorten the extent of materials to be treated by any one student and thus permit exploration in greater depth, but also to establish relations of duty and being indebted, to set to the members of each team the problem of developing ways of fruitful collaboration, and to create a situation, when teams reconvene and report, in which students are impelled to ask as well as answer questions and begin to discover the difficult art of asking good questions.

These procedures are recommended here for a special reason as well as for the reasons which commend them as curricular resources in general. We are concerned in this prescription to afford students a telling view of the notion of developed competence, of intelligent habit, as a foundation for soundness of moral judgment, and to provide a moving glimpse of ways in which moral judgments may be tested and justified by rational means. Such a program cannot afford not to be transparent to its own principles. If it is to talk about developed competences, it must develop competences. If it is to praise the reasonable it must be reasonable. If it is to urge practical morals, concerned not only with moral choice but with actions pertinent to the choices, it too must be practical: it must affect and modify the students whom it treats, not merely instruct them. If it is to talk about responsible service and responsible collaboration, it must exemplify these activities.

Practical Prescription 2: Prudence

At bottom, Prescription 1 is a conventional affair, except, perhaps, for its practical transparency to its own principles. Hence, it can achieve only limited objectives. If all goes well, students will emerge from it with a reasoned grasp of the issues it treats—the possibility of a moral intuition, the possibility of a morality grounded in developed character, the relations of self-service to the good of others. If articulations have been pursued as they should, this grasp will have its affective component as well as the necessary cortical one. The ideas will be "felt" as well as understood—that is, known in connection with actions and undergoings (real and possible) involving the inward side of experience as well as the outward, approaching, if not quite achieving, that merger of the two which constitutes the conscious experience of having had an experience. Third, these undergoings and actions will have included experience of actions which develop competences and of undergoings which consist of awareness of growing competences, increments of selfhood.

In two closely related respects, however, the prescription is deficient. The competences it has contributed to do not include the one competence which marks the practical—competence in deliberation. In virtue of this omission, the second arises: its students' grasp of the idea of practical wisdom or prudence and of the deliberative activities which flow from it is deficient; it is cortical but not affective, not even vivid. This second brief prescription aims to begin the repair of this deficiency.

Twenty years ago, Colonel Ross dared say, it would have been his first thought; and (not without a certain rigid pleasure in seeing duty clearly; and, every other consideration put aside, doing it quickly) he would act—hew to the line, and let the chips fall where they may!

Colonel Ross was not sure whether today's different attitude came from being twenty years wiser or just twenty years older. He had, of course, more knowledge of what happens in the long run, of complicated effects from simple causes, of one thing stubbornly leading to another. Experience had been busy that much longer rooting out the vestiges of youth's dear and heady hope that thistles can somehow be made to bear figs and that the end will at last justify any means that might have seemed dubious when the decision to resort to them was so widely made. Unfortunately, when you got to your end, you found all the means to it inherent there. In short, the first exhilaration of hewing to the line waned when you had to clean up that mess of chips.

Thus, on page 51 of a longish novel, *Guard of Honor* (New York, 1948), James Couzzens tells us what he is up to. What follows is, in its simplicity, virtually a morality play. Colonel Ross is Prudence. Colonel Carricker is Impulse; Mowbray, Stupidity; Botwinick, Corrupted Prudence. And Lieutenant Edsell is Inexperience, the man of principle without prudence. They act out their respective virtues and vices against the background of a World War II Air Corps establishment in Florida, in situations which include almost every component we might wish: the world, the flesh, a racial integration problem, the issue of war and peace, rule books and needs to violate the rule book, loves, loyalties, and friendships.

I suggest, in short, that where actual experience may be hard to come by, recourse be had to literature, that traditional source of "vicarious experience."

Let it be admitted at once that, badly done, this can be a highly dangerous procedure. It can corrupt the book, the student, and the "lesson." It corrupts the book (and literature generally) if it conveys the notion that this is what literature is and what it should be read for: the "lesson," the slice of life, the philosophic truth. It corrupts the "lesson" and the student, if it suggests that the "lesson" (which *is* one aspect of the work) is necessarily the true lesson, the poetic insight.

These dangers are minimized by the procedure outlined in Articulations (p. 72): to give as much attention to the parts of the work itself and their organization (who is involved, what they are like, what they are involved in, how they relate to one another and to the circumstances) as to the articulation of the work with the knowledge and experience of the student. The work of recovery of the parts and organization of the work constitutes a vivid statement of what the work comprises (more than its lesson). And what is discovered thereby in the present instance is almost sufficient to guarantee that its "lesson" will not be swallowed whole, for the work in question is not a very good work. Its characters are bas-reliefs, its organization loose; and weaknesses in these respects are enough to suggest that the author is not likely to be infallible with respect to his "lesson" either.[6]

Attention to the articulations of the work is suggested, however, for much more concretely curricular purposes than the preservation of the chastity of literature. As indicated in the general discussion of this procedure, the work will not serve its curricular purpose if it does not impinge upon the experience of the student and collide with his prejudices. But if it does so, the first impulse of the dogmatic or undisciplined student is to assimilate the work to his own experience and belief, misreading or rejecting it where it runs counter to his own experience and his own interpretation of that experience. It is to counter this impulse, to

6. I am, in fact, suggesting that second-rate works are probably to be preferred for such purposes. The better a work, the more persuasive it is, even if it is wrong; and the better a work, the more demanding is the search for its parts and their manifold relations, leaving too little time and energy, perhaps, for articulation with the experience of the reader. In a nearly perfect work, I suppose, this would not be the case: recovery of the work would simultaneously articulate it with the reader, assuming that the reader possessed the necessary, corresponding richness of stucture.

suspend it for time enough to reflect upon its origins, that attention to the work's articulations is commended. Attention to the work is itself a suspense of the impulse to assimilate it forthwith. What is discovered in the process—the complexity, the coherence, the plausibility of the work—becomes a challenge to the impulse by constituting the work as a further experience *of the student*, existing in him side by side with earlier experience and demanding, therefore, that adjustment of the two to one another be done reflectively, with critical attention to both and the possibility of modification of the earlier as well as of the later, instead of by peremptory dismissal of the later.

Of course this end will not be achieved if attention to the work is too intense or sustained too long at a time. In that case, the work's interpretation of the experience it affords is likely to be divorced from any possible engagement with the student's, relegated to the limbo of so much formal instruction. The appropriate treatment is, then, a rhythm which swings from engagement, in which parallels between work and student are evoked, voiced, debated; then to disengagement, in which the student's past is momentarily set aside to make room for the present; and back to engagement again. In each successive engagement (if instruction has been effective) the present and forming experience will grow more and more toward peerage with the student's earlier assimilated experience and belief.[7]

This method poses two problems which call for

7. I am indebted to Thomas Robey for much of this formulation. He is currently engaged in the construction and test of an extensive curricular experiment of this kind aimed at suspense and repair of a highly specific impulse of a highly specific student goup: Negro junior college students and their experience and interpretation of the minority, scapegoat role in which they have been cast.

comment. First, the duration of each phase of the rhythm must be nicely timed, and the effective timing will change as the cycles proceed. The problem must be met by close attention to the purport and the emotional tone of student contributions. Suppose, for example, that in the cool phase of the cycle (concerned with treatment of articulations within the work), the instructor asks, "What do you think the author is trying to tell us by having the murder take place on the highway?" A student answers (with affirming nods from other students), "It doesn't matter. Nobody would kill a girl that way." Such urgent movements by students toward their own experience and convictions about such matters, if frequent, are signs that the cool phase must be sustained and vigorously kept to its business. If such movements become rare or entirely disappear, however, one has gone too far and too long. The optimum turning point will be signaled by the still-frequent appearance of such movements checked in midcourse by the students themselves. The warm phase of the cycle will tend to run indefinitely, becoming harder and harder to divert, especially in the earliest cycles. The problem is to note and grasp the moment in which it has served its present purpose and threatens to get out of hand. The sign is a noticeable increase in the vehemence with which opinions are voiced or challenged. As cycles follow one another, this signal should come later and later. It should never wholly disappear.

The second problem concerns the phase with which to begin. In one sense, there is no choice: the book or some part of it must be read. The discussion which follows, does, however, afford a choice. It is riskier and requires greater courage to begin with the warm phrase

("What do you think of Lieutenant Edsell?" "What is your opinion of Colonel Ross's treatment of the Negro reporter?"), since it may loose a torrent. It will be the more rewarding start with students who expect and are resigned to the unarticulated, academic treatment of most matters. It will be the poorer start with students in real or posed rebellion.

Practical Prescription 3: Public Policy

Experience with *Guard of Honor* or a similar work should serve to clothe the idea of prudence with some vividness and detail. But even with this added vividness, it remains only an idea, and an idea only of the exterior surface of prudence—the man of prudence identifiable by certain marks: judiciousness, calm, focus on the proximate goal, concern for the inelegant fact. This is the barest (though useful) beginning. Prudence is the name for a propensity and a competence; propensities and competences become real, become visible, become genuinely knowable, only in the activeness they imply. What is wanting, then, is a visibility of the acts of deliberation—the discrimination of proximate goals, the weighing of alternatives, the scrutiny of possible means and the rehearsal of consequences.

To supply this need (though only for a limited number of students) I propose a program, a "course," concerned with public policy. The program consists of two components: apprenticeships, and a forum in which what is seen in the apprenticeships can be discussed with others.

The apprenticeships, or, more accurately, watching briefs, are to be served in those locations in each community where practical problems of public import are noted and dealt with. I have in mind executive, legislative, and administrative offices in city and state, business corporations, unions, organizations involved in the raising and dispensing of money, even, on occasion, the administrative and policy-making bodies of schools and universities. Since the locations available for such watching briefs will depend on the resources available in each community, I shall say little more about them. Note, however, that they need not be large or pretentious. The community council which passes on urban renewal plans and zoning waivers or the grievance committee of a union local or factory may be as useful as the police commissioner's office or the office of the superintendent of schools.

I envisage the student as serving his apprenticeship in either of two relations. He might serve his term, a semester or a year, in attachment to a specific person—the executive, administrator, or chairman of the enterprise—occupying an inconspicuous desk in his office, permitted to be present at phone calls, interviews and parleys at the discretion of the executive, and accompanying him to such meetings as the executive sees fit. He might also serve a roving mission, attending meetings and parleys but also observing at first hand the situations with which parleys deal and watching the reception and execution of decisions made in conference and parley.

It is obvious enough that the success of such a program, whether measured by the profit accruing to the individual student participant or by the ability of the college to maintain the cooperation of the necessary agencies, requires careful selection and preliminary briefing of the student participant. He must be able to keep his mouth shut; he must be prepared to conform to the exterior signs of acceptibility required by the cooperating agency. He must realize that the more he guards his manner, his replies to questions, and his speech generally (in itself a kind of silent deliberation), the more he will be permitted to see.

It is the need for selection of this kind, rather than the supply of available resources, which sets a limit on the number of students who could participate in such a program. It is also this selection, however, which may operate to extend the educational fruits of the enterprise relatively widely in a student body. Persons so selected are likely to be among the persons who will be heard by their student peers, whether in student offices or in informal groups. Hence, the changes of attitude and the accruals of competence which result from the enterprise may have distinct effects on the ways in which students generally begin to see and deal with prudential problems.

I envisage the second component of this program, the forum, as requiring a distinct format. Ideally, perhaps, it should serve as the place where the detailed content of deliberative processes seen are related, scrutinized, recognized, and evaluated—but this is out of the question. The important parts of deliberative activity are its details and its details seen in their sequence. This would require recording, which would rarely be permitted, or a prodigious memory. Since these are out of the question, other means must be found to evoke deliberative detail and identify them as such.

For this purpose the reports of student observers might be juxtaposed in the forum meetings with relevant bodies of social scientific theory. The deliberations of policy bodies and the ensuing executive events by which decisions are carried downward and outward would thus be examined against theories of administration and decision-making. Behaviors of political bodies would be contrasted to formulations of political theory; economic decisions compared with economic theory; community decisions seen against the backdrop of formulated views of the ways in which communities organize and act; and individual and small-group behaviors viewed against the dicta of social psychology and theories of individual behavior.

In all such forum confrontations between reported fact and formulated theory, the whole purpose of the program requires that the relation of the fact to the theory be maintained strictly as the relation of criterion to thing criticized. For the aim of the forum is not to "explain" the facts or to use them as evidences or buttresses of social scientific theory but to make the facts visible and especially to make visible the intelligent and the deliberative character of the facts. The more clearly the facts appear as "buts," contests, contrasts, and exceptions to the neatnesses of formulation, the better this will be done.

By use of such a format, an additional service will be performed and an additional function will be served by the program. It will, as the additional service, provide experience to indicate the weaknesses and enrich the meanings of such stereotypes of social scientific theory as "power structure," "élites," "political bosses," "organization men," "big business," and "free enterprise." The additional function lies in the possibility of the use of such a program as a major component of the social science curriculum. I envisage two such usages.

It could be constituted as a degree program, a "major," making appropriate use of conventional courses in economics, political science, and sociology, but culminating in apprenticeship and forum, in turn leading to a bachelor's thesis. It could also serve as an "integrating" focus of all or most programs in the social sciences, serving not only to establish connections among the various fields of knowledge but also serving in the students' senior year to establish an additional focus of community among them.

In addition to contrasting fact and theory, the forum should contain a second component arising from a second responsibility of the student observer. He is to be concerned not only with the deliberations and actions of the body to which he is attached but with the "silent" deliberation by which he himself earns, or fails to earn, increasing access to the privacies of communication on which he depends. His second responsibility to the forum, then, is to report his successes and failures with their attendant circumstances and submit them to the forum for discussion, analysis, and criticism as essays in deliberation.

Such occasions must be anticipated in the construction of the forum. A formal means should be devised by which each participant can notify the forum chairman of a notable success or failure and arrange for its presentation. A further means should be devised by which to make clear to student participants that accounts of such failures and successes are among the most valuable resources of the forum and constitute one of the major obligations of participants. Finally, means should be devised by which to distinguish such forum occasions as especially serious and valuable moments.

This program will not be easy to maintain. It exists only as long as its emphasis is on the practical, on the concrete and ultimate particulars in their messy incoherence and resistance to neat formulation. As we have indicated earlier, the academic, on the other hand, loves neatness and order and tends to impose neatness and order where they do not exist. The tendency will be, then, to enlarge the scope of theory at the expense of fact, to assimilate the fruits of the watching briefs to political and social theory rather than to use the facts in enrichment and criticism of theory and as objects of attention in their own right.

I suggest one safeguard against such a reversal. A lawyer, an able administrator, or a professor deeply involved in the channeling of his special knowledge to the formation or execution of public policy should be an active cochairman of the program and a presence in its forum.

Such a presence may also render an additional service. The forum exists as a place where students learn to ask appropriate questions and where students are the major sources of materials for questioning. Its management, therefore, calls for a chairman who is discreet, sensitive, and an austerely sparing speaker. The last, at least, most professors are not.

Practical Prescription 4: Law and Legal Reasoning

There is a special form of deliberation and a special arena for it which are crucial to western social order and of which our students (and our graduates) are profoundly ignorant. The special form is the form employed to adapt our laws to changing times, differing situations, and changing needs. The arena includes the courts as briefs are presented, facts alleged, precedents urged, and decisions rendered. It includes the administrative agencies and police executives charged with execution of legal judgments and enforcement of the law. It includes as a third component the pressures and urgings which initiate consideration of a possible new statute, the maneuverings and debates through which legislation is drafted and modified with an eye to its possible passage as well as to the need it is intended to serve.

The deliberations carried on in these places are, of course, neither simple exchanges of statement (except in the case of the courts) nor readily accessible. Further, they take place on a historic time scale and not in a sequence of afternoons. They are not matters of easily accessible record (again, except in the case of the courts), being neither within the scope of textbooks nor available, as in the case of scientific research and humane criticism, in monographs or learned journals. They constitute, in fact, a neglected area of sociolegal historical research.

The process whose existence is recorded in these materials—the progressive modification of law and its application to case and circumstances—is a peculiarly vulnerable one: it can continue to function only as long as its beneficiaries are convinced that it exists. That is, the law, its institutions and agents can function only as long as law as such is respected and its agents trusted. The apparatus cannot function if it must function entirely or largely by force. (Consider, for example, the dependence of the income tax law on voluntary compliance: the cost and consequences of extensively applied forced compliance would make it and the whole apparatus of democratic civil order impotent.) This respect and trust in turn require belief in the beneficence of law. This belief is undermined if there is widespread ignorance of the fact that law earns its power and respect by its capability for responsive change and adaptation to case and circumstance.

This ignorance is widespread, and belief in the beneficence of law is currently under challenge. Hence I strongly urge that immediate as well as middle-term steps be taken to make accessible to students some view of the processes by which the law refreshes its effectiveness.

The present inaccessibility of some of the desirable materials will not prevent a decent first approximation. It can be constructed, indeed, wholly or largely from materials of record: statutes themselves, court cases, briefs submitted to the courts, decisions rendered, and studies of the consequences of decisions in changing the meanings and application of the statutes and conforming them to changing circumstances. Let it be emphasized, however, that what is needed is cases, decisions and consequences in all their particularity, not banalities and generalities of manifestos, declarations, constitutional preambles, and pious commentary. The aim is not to praise the law but to exhibit it, for we are proposing a program for intelligent students, not sheep, and praises which exceed the patent present facts will exacerbate rather than mitigate the distrust of law with which we are concerned. The array of cases, decisions and consequences should, then, exhibit the ways in which the law is often insensitive as well as sensitive to changing times, show that it is almost always slow and ponderous in its change, indicate something of the vice as well as the virtue of its ponderousness, and above all, exhibit the detailed, deliberate process by which change is guided and effected.

Concern for the intelligent student and for the facts of the case dictate a second component of such a program: a component concerned with the challenge to law when it is somnolent or corrupted: civil disobedience and the issues it involves. Some of the traditional materials for such a segment, Thoreau, for example, or Gandhi, are not wholly suitable, precisely because they are less concerned with the issues involved than with the praise and proper conduct of civil disobedience and the occasions for it—or else they assume the need for it. The traditional Platonic materials, on the other hand, *Apology, Crito, Phaedo,* are eminently suitable. Instead of a simplistic opposition of law and justice, they are concerned with justification of the law. The indispensability of law is recognized. Distinction between civil disobedience and mere defiance of the law is made with dramatic clarity. The dialogues are concerned with the importance of embarking on a course of civil disobedience only at the right time, the right place, and before the appropriate witnesses, and they emphasize that it is to be undertaken not for the dubious satisfactions of martyrdom but for the effect it is likely to have. They are clear about the uncertainty of the right effective action in the world of actuality (the deliberative factor), yet equally clear about the necessity and possibility of decision and action despite uncertainty. Finally, in the persons of Socrates and his students, these matters are imbued with the elements of heroism, pathos, and love which are inherent in the issues themselves.

I assume, of course, that the full forces of articulation and recovery of meaning are to be brought to bear on the material of such a program. Each issue and distinction is to be discovered, clarified, related to current problems and actions, and debated. It is especially important that full use be made of the affective elements involved, the tendency of our students to identify with the students of Socrates and to be deeply moved by the figure of Socrates. Students would be first engaged in these emotional tugs, then disengaged from them, in much the way Socrates handles the problem of his own students in *Phaedo*. Without the first phase of this rhythmic treatment,[8] our treatment of the material is likely to be no more than an intellectual exercise. Without disengagement, it will deteriorate into an affirmation of emotion as the proper apparatus for the making of decisions.

It is important, too, that such material be dealt with in the context of the first segment of the proposed course. Without an adequate account of the processes of law's revision, a dramatic treatment of civil disobedience becomes entirely one-sided: law remains an abstraction while disobedience is figured in vivid detail.

Preparation of the syllabus and readings for such a program will require interdisciplinary collaboration. Choice of the statutes, cases, and decisions to be examined must be made with an informed eye to the kinds of issues and "causes" which will engage students' attention. They ought also to be issues and "causes" of more than passing importance. At the same time, they must be well represented in the legal literature

8. See Practical Prescription 2, pp. 134–35.

by materials effectively representative of legal reasoning and the legal process. The minimum need, then, is for a legal scholar, a political scientist, and a historian. At least one of them, and preferably, all of them, ought, in addition, be in close touch with undergraduates.

But why, indeed, leave the important matter of selection for effectiveness with students to the chanciness of "close touch with undergraduates"? Here, surely, is a proper place for student participation in the construction of curriculum. I suggest, therefore, that a useful purpose would be served and a useful precedent set if a foundation were to sponsor the development of such a syllabus by a team consisting of the three necessary specialists together with, say, a first-year law student and an upperclassman in one of the other two involved fields.

I make this suggestion with an additional end in view. The program suggested is only a first approximation, restricted in content to what is readily available. Its materials are cut from the middle course of the process which ought to be displayed. For prior to a statute and ensuing court action interpreting it, there is the matter of the pressures, needs, and circumstances which give rise to the statute and the maneuverings which lead to its formation and passage. Posterior to court action there are the problems of enforcement—not only the resistance or responsiveness of those bound by the statute in question but also the resistance or responsiveness of those charged with its enforcement.

These materials, too, would be represented in a wholly effective program of the kind envisaged. To effect this representation, a substantial, though not intimidating, body of fundamental research would have to be undertaken, involving sociologists and social psychologists as well as representatives of history, political science, and law, the aim being to discover and formulate the beginnings and ends of the processes whose middles constitute our first-approximation program.[9]

Why not, then, our first-approximation team as pilot of the larger project? Such a two-part program would, ironically, set an even more spectacular precedent: to the best of my knowledge it would be the first time in modern academic history in which fundamental research was undertaken for the sake of education.

Practical Prescription 5:   The Possibility of Simulated Deliberation

Prescription 1 treats primarily the *ideas* of morality. Secondarily, it articulates most but not all these ideas by way of experiences which begin to make them "real." It fails to do so, however, for the idea of prudence and for the deliberative competence prudence represents. Prescription 2 begins to repair this deficiency by embodiment of the idea of prudence in a fictional person. Prescription 3 affords students an extended experience of deliberative situations and actions, but only as observed, as carried on by others. Prescription 4 affords a similarly distant view of a form of deliberation of special magnitude and importance. It

9. A few studies of roughly this sort have been done by such people. Unfortunately, most of them aim for generality and theory and desert the particulars which resist this academic tendency. Stephen Bailey's *Congress Makes a Law,* and Robert Dendiner's *Obstacle Course on Capitol Hill* on the other hand, have courageously included some of the messiness of the practical. Their work suggests that a special breed of political scientist is needed for the work we suggest, together with a competent Washington newspaperman.

remains, therefore, to bring the experience of deliberation to the student as an activity of his own.

Ideally, of course, this would be done by way of real cases. The student would participate in deliberation on problems affecting his own welfare, and the deliberation would be undertaken in the company and circumstances which would render the experience educative. Real experience of this kind can be arranged for a small percentage of students, perhaps 10 percent.[10] For the majority of students, however, we are probably limited to some kind of classroom simulation of the process.

This circumstance has blocked most efforts to conceive of a practically oriented education as even remotely feasible; it has led, instead, to the dictum that "practical wisdom cannot be taught." It appears to be virtually impossible to reproduce the essential characteristics of deliberative problems in situations to which artifice contributes. Furthermore, it is held with some justice that the development of deliberative competence occurs only as character in its entirety develops, and that this development occurs only through experience of choice and consequences of choice so penetrating that they modify even the firmest of prior habits of thought and feeling.

These two arguments are on the whole sound. Plan, pattern, artifice are, in certain respects, contraries of the qualities of a deliberative situation. And the exercise of practical wisdom at its ripest involves attitudes and sentiments (as well as competences) which are normally the product only of extended and poignant experience.

10. See Practical Prescription 6, p. 282.

There is a loophole in each of these arguments, however, through which the possibility of educationally effective simulation of deliberative situations can be glimpsed. In the first place, although sheer randomness in the presentation of a deliberative problem is probably impossible, it should be possible to eliminate many of the visible effects of planning and to disguise others. With respect to the second argument, although complete exercise of practical wisdom may require mature experience, mastery of parts of it by way of simulation is clearly possible. The important question is whether the parts so mastered are mastered and retained in such a state that the remaining parts of the whole process which accrue later, slowly and by way of the vicissitudes of real experience, will couple onto the elements mastered through simulation and thus constitute them as educational advantages. In the last analysis, this remaining question can be answered only by devising and testing promising simulations.

Meanwhile, however, we can be sure that if the simulations used with students omit crucial aspects of the real thing, or worse, possess the contraries of some of them, the possibility of future coupling on will be seriously impaired. Just such omissions and contrarieties characterize many of the proposed simulations of the practical which I have encountered. In some of these cases, the flaws and omissions seem to have arisen because the authors were so enthralled by the notion of simulation as such that little or no attention was paid to the characteristics of the real thing.[11] In most cases, however, these flaws and omis-

11. This preoccupation with the novelty of simulation is often marked by use of fancy names, such as "the role-playing approach," "psychodrama in the classroom," "the problem-solving approach."

sions are due to the fact that a summary analysis of
the practical is unavailable in the educational and
psychological literature.

An immediate need, then, is for a summary analysis
of the defining characteristics of the deliberative problem and some suggestion of possible counterfeits and
approximations suitable to a simulation. Such an analysis follows.

Condition 1. For deliberation to be real, the deliberator must feel the pinch of the problem in one of
two ways. In one class of real cases, the problem arises
in a felt need, and urgency, of the deliberator. In the
second class it arises in an urgency felt by others, but
the deliberator stands either as the responsible and
sympathetic decision-maker to those who feel the need
—for example, as father to children, as excutive or
legislator to a constituency—or as sharer of the problem
by virtue of affective ties—for example, as friend, neighbor, comrade.

This condition is imposed by two factors in the deliberative situation. One is the peculiar character of
the deliberative process: that it is not only lengthy
but has no discernible steps or stages and no clear
indicator of its conclusion. Plateaus in the process occur
when one class of facts has been scrutinized or one
group of alternative solutions rehearsed, but up to some
indefinite point the quality of the outcome of deliberation is largely proportional to the extent that such
plateaus are felt as only temporary resting places from
which to discriminate the relevancy of facts not previously envisaged and to conceive possible solutions
not so far considered. This is especially vivid in cases
where a possible solution to the problem is seen to en-

compass all the facts under consideration, including facts concerning feasibility. Such cases have all the appearance of a conclusive solution to the problem. In fact, the totality of facts encompassed by it are only the facts so far recognized as relevant to the problem, and "the" problem is only the problem as so far conceived.

There is need, then, for a constant and importunate reminder that the deliberative problem is one of satisfying a real, existent need and not merely of fulfilling logical and evidential conditions appropriate to scientific problems. Nothing serves this purpose better than the need itself. There is also need for some external pressure toward termination of deliberation and its transition to action since the process can be indefinitely prolonged. The importunate need obviously serves this function, too.

The second factor requiring a felt pinch of the problem is simple enough but obscured by prevailing beliefs and language habits involving the word *need* and the ideas expressed by it. As a noun, as in *a need*, the word has polar ambiguity. It can refer to a state of deprivation, a state of requiring, lacking, needing, or it can refer to a material thing or set of conditions which fills a lack, fulfills a requirement, rectifies a state of deprivation. "I am hungry," "I am thirsty," "I am tired" express needs in the first sense. "My need is a weekend of rest," "Water, water!" "My kingdom for a horse" express needs in the second sense.

The unfortunate result of this ambiguity (abetted by the fact that *need* is a verb as well as a noun, and can be either transitive or intransitive) is the habit of speaking and thinking as if every experience which we identify as a lack, deprivation, demand, requirement, is always and necessarily accompanied by awareness or knowledge of the material object or altered condition which will fill the emptiness, rectify the felt imbalance. Some of the very phrases used as examples of *need* in the first sense illustrate the point. "I am hungry" is almost universally taken to mean, "My need is bread and meat." "I am thirsty" is similarly taken to mean "My need is for drink." Only if we encounter the archaic (or poetic) "I hunger" or "I thirst," are we encouraged to ask rather than assume what it is that is thirsted or hungered for—and thus begin to entertain the possibility that a felt sense of need may not always be accompanied by clear and certain grasp of what it is we need.

This diremption of felt need and fulfilling object frequently characterizes problems of deliberation. More often than not, the problem has its origin in a need so novel or so complex (in itself or in connection with other needs) that we do *not* know what it is we need, what material object or condition will satisfy our want. In such cases, discovery of the appropriate object or condition, discovery in the sense of discerning the characteristics it should have and identifying the possible objects or conditions which may possess these characteristics, is itself part of the deliberative process.

At first glance, one would suppose that this condition of deliberation—that the subject feel the pinch of the problem—is the one most difficult to simulate since in effect we are asking that the simulated situation evoke at least a counterfeit feeling of a need which the subject does not have. In fact, evocation of feelings is a commonplace of drama, the novel, and some of the other art forms, and some of these concern characters and situations which constitute deliberative problems appropriate to our time and place and to our students. Moreover, similar evocations take place in a number of areas where ingenuity and money has made it possible to design elaborate simulations. I am informed, for example, that in the training of air pilots, visual simulation of an approaching landing strip and kinesthetic simulation of plane movements and instruments is so effectively done and is so thoroughly responsive (by computer, of course) to each move of the student pilot that every physiologic measure of his reactions and almost every piece of subjective testimony bear witness to anxieties, anticipations, urgencies, and needs which seem to be very close to the real thing. In the same fashion, we can imagine well-planned video projections of, say, classroom situations (grounded in appropriate materials of other kinds) which would evoke in a teacher trainee something approximating the felt needs of a real teacher confronted with a real problem in a real classroom. Why, then, could not similar evocations be designed for deliberative problems appropriate to the college student? Considerable and intimate knowledge of student life and thought or a series of pilot trials and studies may be necessary to effective choice of scene and situation, but neither of these should be beyond our resources. A warning, however: just as literature can descend toward bathos by making us feel *for* rather than *with* a character, so may we if we become enamored of the merely generic evocation of feeling and fail to take the toughest of critical views of our plans and products.

Condition 2. The deliberator must believe that, short of a miracle or his own further deliberation and action, he must live with the consequences of his decision. (In cases of the second class, where the need is a need of others, the deliberator must know that he must continue to live with those who live with the consequences.) This condition is imposed by one of the factors which impose the first condition: the need to insure against premature termination of the process. The importunateness of the need provides necessary energy. Felt responsibility, however, the realization that we are concerned in deliberation with solutions which are solutions in fact, not merely in formulation, is required to resist seduction by the neatness, coherence, and "logic" of an early, envisaged solution.

Here, it seems to me, simulation will inevitably be weak. At least I have been unable to construct a possible and reasonable facsimile of responsibility, though two relatively remote substitutes appear to be feasible.

The first derives from extension of the two-step series mentioned above. Although students will not live with the consequences of their choices or even with those other persons who must live with the consequences, they will in fact continue to live with the fellow students (and instructor) who bore witness to their deliberations and choices. This factor can be intensified as a simulacrum of responsibility to the extent that (*a*) the student group becomes a community: that is, each member interacts with others, gives and receives approbations and criticisms, learns to know others; (*b*) individual contributions to deliberation and choice are memorialized: given individual attention and characterization by the instructor, appealed to in the course of subsequent discussion, made a matter of record by written formulation by the student and by preserved tape recording; (c) the sequence of problems dealt with by the group have connections with one another; (d) the successive contributions of each sudent are themselves made objects of discussion and critical attention (reflexive scrutiny of debate).

The second substitute is more exciting, though possibly more difficult. Suppose that some of the problems posed in simulation are problems which the student can immediately identify as members of a class of problems with which he will in fact, in the palpable near future, be involved. Suppose that additional problems can be related to characters in plays or novels in whom the student can identify points of similarity with himself, similarities significant to the problem posed (*not* merely "identify with," in some mildly stirring but vague way). Suppose, finally, that at least one of the range of possible solutions to each problem so related to a fictional work is developed by the drama or novel to the point where disastrous consequences (overlooked because of inadequate deliberation or impoverished character) are acted out.

A wide range of appropriate literary works are available. There is Hamlet, of course, young enough and confused enough to serve extremely well. There is poor Edward Ashburnham in Ford Madox Ford's *The Good Soldier,* who sees everything through the pink fog of his notions about what he ought to do and ought to feel. Leonora Ashburnham, with her own unexamined notion of her duty, would serve almost as well for women students. There is Nabokov's Humbert

Humbert mistaking Lolita for the girl of his dreams despite all the patent evidence to the contrary. There is Anna in Elizabeth Bowen's *Death of the Heart* who can recognize her fault but not that it is a fault: "Though she and I may wish to make a new start, we hardly shall, I'm afraid. I shall always insult her; she will always persecute me." And thereupon she makes the fatal decision: "Well, then, it's decided, Thomas— we are to send Matchett?" (I do not mean to suggest, of course, that these are the "right" interpretations of these books. The books are being put in our service.) With such an organization of devices, one could, I think, hope for a simulacrum of responsibility approximating that achieved by controlled display of aircraft-landing problems.

Condition 3. The facts of the case must be discriminated by the agent. That is, just what facts constitute the facts of the case is itself a question to be settled only by deliberation. This condition arises from the fact that deliberation is concerned with possibilities as well as actualities, with what might be brought about but does not yet exist. Hence neither existent conditions nor established rules or principles are competent by themselves to determine what data are relevant. The determination rests in the ability of the agent to envisage possibilities and then to scrutinize them for the connections they may have with actualities.

This condition imposes on any simulation the requirement that the facts it may make available to the student *not* be characterized by a visible orderly relation to one another or to the problem situation. On the contrary, the potentially available facts must be disordered and of considerable variety. The plan and pattern which governs construction of the simulation must not become visible in the simulation itself, else scope for student discrimination of what facts are relevant will not exist. At the very least, the plan and pattern must be minimized or well disguised.

Dramatic and novelistic materials again afford a convenient way to indicate how such minimization and disguise can be effected, for a first-rate novel or drama (and we need good ones) will be tightly planned. The deliberative problem for whose presence the work has been chosen will emerge from character and circumstance as revealed in the work; the materials dealt with by the fictional deliberator will be just the material which will enable the author to work out the fates he has in mind. Further, they will appear in the work in an order appropriate to its plan. The decision made and the events ensuing on it will be similarly planned. Obviously, then, a mere reading of such a work will afford no scope for deliberation, nor will it even exhibit a realistic one, because of the element of plan.

But consider the following possibilities. First, we isolate and present to students only that portion of the work which establishes character and sets forth circumstance, time, place. Then let us suppose that the number and variety of facts entertained in the fictional deliberation are large enough to approximate the real thing, the only flaw being the neat ordering with which they are presented. We can then do away with this order by entering each such item on a separate card or sheet, shuffling them and presenting them to the student in now random order.

Suppose, on the other hand, that the facts are neither numerous nor varied enough. Then as part of the simulation materials, we generate additional facts with possible bearing on the case and possessing an appropriate coherence with those from the original source (not *too* coherent, however: mainly, not flatly contradictory).

Whether we add to the fictional facts or not, we can now introduce an additional step toward verisimilitude. We can suppose that the mere possession of fact cards will mislead students into acting as if all of them had to be taken into account, or suggest to students, by way of recognition, the notions of relevance he ought to be generating himself. To repair this fault, the mass of information items can be treated as a bank on which each student can draw only as he identifies and demands the kinds of facts he holds to be relevant. Moreover, such drawing on the fund of information can take place not once but again and again, as the deliberator deals with his first-wanted facts, envisages and tests decisions, and perceives new needs.

The advantages of such a procedure can then be multiplied by holding each of several series of withdrawals (by single students or small teams) in confidence, maintaining a record of materials drawn and uses made of them. For with such a record of the course of the practical enquiry, *different* patterns of deliberation (whether eventuating in the same or different decisions) can then be subjected to reflexive scrutiny by all parties to the several efforts.

Anticipating a fourth condition of deliberation (see below) we can take another and giant step toward verisimilitude with respect to the facts of the case: we can render them ambiguous. The obvious and highly desirable device is to afford in the bank not one but several versions of a number of the facts, each version being a report of the fact as seen, understood, distorted or adapted by different characters in the novel whose self-interest, bias, and so on, are revealed in that portion of the work excised and earlier presented to the students. This device will reach its maximal verisimilitude if the work has been so chosen that the reporting characters themselves are also ambiguous—revealed to the reader not by fiats of the author but by actions and reactions requiring interpretation by the reader, or by reactions, descriptions, and ascriptions voiced by the characters themselves about one another.

Finally, two minor caveats and a further comment. The disordering and itemizing of the facts of the case should not be done merely by recording sentences as composed by the author, since a sound work will reflect many aspects of its plan and pattern even in the structure and word choice of isolated sentences. Second, this sort of denaturing is especially wanted should there be authorial sentences flatly formulating the problem faced by the central character, for the terms in which a problem is formulated to a considerable degree plan and direct the enquiry which solves it. The situation which gives rise to a practical problem must be known in all specific detail of time, place, and circumstance, but the problem itself properly has form and direction only as constructed by the deliberator.[12]

Comment: It may be that video rather than bookish presentation of some parts of such a simulation here is preferable. Nevertheless, let us caution ourselves once again about the flatulence which so easily attaches to

12. See Conditions 6 and 7, pp. 163–67.

exploitation of a medium as such, and the tendency to use relatively new media merely because the promise of profits from novelty moves an entrepreneur to make extra funds available. (The same warning applies to the notion of simulation itself, as I have previously remarked.)

Condition 4. Many of the facts of the case, perhaps most of them, must (*a*) be sought out by the agent and (*b*) their reliability as facts estimated by him.

They must be sought out rather than merely "found" for the same reason that they must be discriminated by the agent—the fact that the possible (as well as the actual) is central to the process. This means that the relevant facts will not often have been the object of scientific researches, will not be codified at all, or if they are, will likely be coded in connection with subjects remote from the central focus of a deliberation. (For example, facts wanted by a corporation executive for testing the feasibility of a new idea may be recorded in his comptroller's or accountant's files as raw data, but it is extremely unlikely that they will be accessible as an entry on a balance sheet or retrievable by any of the programs normally used in the corporation's computing machines.)

The reliability of the facts must be estimated by the deliberator for the same reasons. Since they bear in part on a novelty, it is extremely unlikely that they will have been subjected to the validation process characteristically applied to scientific data—collection and scrutiny by different, independent observers. Furthermore, if they have been collected at all, they will have been collected, in all probability, for other and different purposes. Hence, the defining marks which determined their inclusion in the record are unlikely to coincide with the marks which would define the data wanted for the deliberative problem in hand.

It is also characteristic of the deliberative process that many of the facts wanted for its purposes can be obtained only by hearsay. In this situation, judging the reliability of the facts becomes the problem of judging the credibility of witnesses—their intelligence, their responsibility and, above all, the degree and direction in which the bias and interest of the reporter distorts his view and memory of the facts.

Condition 5. Since deliberation is concerned with determining *feasible* means toward some proximate end in a definite, particular time and place and under equally definite and particular circumstances, the raw materials of deliberation must be facts of equal definiteness and particularity. Theoretical considerations and generalities have a small place in the process, but they are neither sufficient nor characteristic. The problem of selecting a man for a managerial post is not a problem of selecting one who belongs to an appropriate personality type and exhibits the levels of competence required by the job. The man we hire is a man, not only a personality type and a bundle of competences. He is a multitude of probable behaviors which escape the net of personality theories and cognitive scales. His past experience has endowed him with particular prejudices, tendencies, tics, and mannerisms. He is married to some particular woman with her own endowment of prejudices, habits, tics, and mannerisms. And all of these manifold particulars will affect his work and the work of those who interact with him. Moreover, the theory which yields the classificatory scheme by which he is typed and the further theory which determines the tests by which his capabilities are measured are inevitably theories with their own special emphases and limitations. Hence even these limited generalized data are unlikely to be wholly appropriate to the decision in hand and will require interpretation in the light of additional facts about the man and about the job situation he is to fill.

Condition 6. The limited role of theoretical knowledge and the special treatment it requires should be represented. Generalizations and theoretical formulations are not the sufficient or the typical materials of practical problems but they have their place. The personality type and the measured levels of competence of a man we propose to employ are as relevant in their way as the details of his personality and the specific complications of behavior through which his formally measured competences do their work. Their role, however, is not merely additive; rather, they constitute the generalized ground which must be *modified* in the light of the concrete particulars of the case. Calculation of the changing rate of fall of a body which takes account of the medium of fall and the vagaries of temperatures and winds as well as the force equation; treatment and prognosis of John Smith's particular way of having typhoid fever, in view of his age, his history, and his present state, as well as the classic description of the syndrome, are cases in point. The equation for force or the classical description of typhoid fever enter the problem, but its solution involves much more than solving the force equation for a particular set of values or inferring treatment from the typical prognosis and typical effect of therapeutic agents. Instead, effort must be made to identify factors in the particular situation which do not enter the force equation or the typical case of disease but which are *likely to* affect the course of falling object or disease, and then to estimate the *probable* effect of each such factor. In short, the same sort of envisaging of possibility and rehearsal of its consequences are involved in the deliberative treatment of theoretical formulations that are required in the treatment of concrete particulars themselves.

With respect to simulation of this factor, two procedures are possible, one easy, one more difficult but more important. The easier possibility is implied in the examples cited. They are instances of the art or quasi science of engineering which normally brings theory to bear on stubborn materials only partially encompassed by the applicable theory. For undergraduate students in the physical and some social sciences (economics, for example), one can then develop or retrieve from existing teaching materials any number of cases involving the *modifying* application of theory to particular circumstances.

Such cases will introduce students to the kind of problem involved in assimilating theoretical contributions to the practical and will afford limited practice in the art but they fall short by virtue of their relative simplicity. The simplicities which require correction are of two sorts. In the first place, the number of factors modifying those encompassed in the theory is relatively small and their modes of interaction are also few. Second, and more important to the matter of verisimilitude, most of the factors involved, whether theoretically encompassed or not, are prefocused from the outset on only one or two targets: to carry a given burden of traffic over a river at a given rate; to effect a given volume and clarity of sound in a given auditorium; to increase the efficiency of repair of radar equipment for the navy via effective selection of trainees. Contrast to these the problem of a chief of state cogitating a change of policy re the conduct of a war. The ostensible focus of the problem may be to maximize the possibility of bringing the antagonists to the conference table, but *any* action the chief may take (indeed, any statement or simply silence) will simultaneously affect not only the chief of the opposing state but a host of other targets as well: the morale of his own fighting force, the attitudes of allied chiefs, their military forces, their civilian constituencies, his own constituency, the behavior of neutrals, his ability to maintain executive control, the behavior of competitors for his office, his own moral and mental health, the moral and mental health of his advisors and subordinates. Each of these targets is of great importance in its own right. In addition, each effect on each of these targets will constitute a further source of effect on other targets, including that of a possible peace.

To involve the multiple target factor, simulation must add to the conventional problem of physical or economic engineering problems drawn from biological and social "engineering" in which a modicum of theory is involved; for example, the problem of tracing the multipath consequences of possible actions involving, say, control of an insect pest; transforming the biological character of some region (a nitrated lake, a bog, an arid dune); the route and design of a highway which passes through residential and recreational areas as well as industrial zones; altering the social-psychological-economic character of a community by urban clearance and zoning plans.

Such simulations as these will be more difficult to acquire than those of conventional engineering problems for two reasons: the body of "engineering" lore is itself sparse; and little of it has been incorporated into materials suitable for students. Nevertheless, some lore exists and so does the talent which could transpose it to simulation form.

Condition 7. The notion of multiple foci of political problems suggests the seventh criterion of a valid program of deliberative simulation. The simulation must present a problem situation and not "the" problem; and the problem situation must be characterized by the same particularity and definiteness which mark the facts of the practical case.

The need for differentiation of problem situation from problem arises from the fact that *any* formulation of the problem forecloses or shadows some possible solutions or emphasizes others. The question "Should I take on additional consulting commitments?" diminishes the visibility of asking a raise in salary as a possible resoluton of my financial problem situation. "How can I increase my income?" obscures the possibility that reduction in spending might be the preferred resolution. Even the general question "What shall I do about my financial situation?" obscures the possibility that the better formulation of the problem is one of reducing anxiety level rather than modifying finances. In short, formulation of the problem, like determination of what facts constitute the facts of the case, is itself a problem to be solved by deliberation.

That the problem situation must be specified with respect to time, place, and circumstance is obvious enough. "What shall we do about water pollution?" can lead only to platitudes and generalities (a common enough consequence of a number of badly inspired proposals for mock senate committees and aldermanic chambers), for a plan of action can be stated only in terms of what is at hand to act with, act upon, at what time, and under what circumstances. The appropriate formulation of the problem-situation must, then, specify (or hold ready for specification on demand) who pollutes what lake, with what materials, with what effects, both present and probable; in the context of what possible legislative and enforcement mechanisms and counterlegislative powers, etc.

Condition 8. Rehearsal of consequences must be involved, and rehearsals must in turn involve predilections of the deliberator which require scrutiny, as well as judgment concerning the need to control them.

I have earlier indicated what is involved in rehearsal. With respect to each possible choice which meets other criteria, one constructs in imagination what it would be like *in detail* to live with the consequences of one's choice. Is the possibility a new position in a good, New England, village-located college? And is the deliberator south-central urban? Then one considers as a matter of course the salary, the duties, the colleagues, the facilities for research, size of class, and quality of student. But one also rehearses what it would be like to join the maze of social obligations of a small, closed community (or deliberately live outside it); to live amid such consciousness of the community that desire for consensus and approval may override other considerations about one's behavior; what a New England winter and its confinements will be like; the muddy March thaw; the outdoor freedom for one's child; one's wife's needs, and the effects of the community on her; the risk of seduction by gardening or house construction; the summer-only vacation.

Needless to say, this conjuring up must be affective as well as cognitive, for one is asking not merely what would be entailed in the change but how one will feel if involved in the new condition. It is this affective requirement which calls for the second half of this requirement—that predilections be evoked and scrutinized. For granting an effectively imaginative rehearsal, and identification of a strong like or dislike for what is evoked, there still remains the question whether this propensity is alterable or not (a question, often, of its age and yours) and, if alterable, whether it should be; that is, whether, if it is a dislike, it stands in the way of other advantages that far outweigh it, for example, or marks an underdeveloped competence which could become a source of great satisfaction. Of course, it may also be a strong liking, in which case the question is whether the satisfactions afforded may seduce one from efforts of other kinds which would be, in the longer run, more rewarding. Finally, it is equally important that one may suspect that the predilection in question is so firmly a part of one's limitations and powers as to admit of no change. In such a case, one makes the indicated decision or, to the contrary, one plumps for a crucial test of the suspicion of firmness by subjecting one's self to the strongest pressures toward change.

In brief, this requirement touches on a crucial identifying feature of most practical problems—that among the relevant possibilities open to deliberative choice, as well as among its actualities, are the states of the deliberator himself. If we do not evoke this kind of scrutiny and judgment in our simulations, we are capitulating to the student fantasy that likes and dislikes are unalterable bastions of "ego identity."

With respect to simulation of this requirement, consider the following possibility. Let us suppose that the course of deliberation on a given situation has eventuated in two quite different choices by two students or student teams. The two teams have met, reported their decisions, given each other an account of the deliberations (up to but short of rehearsal) which have led to their respective decisions. They have scrutinized them and debated them but have not necessarily resolved the differences of consideration or weighting which have led to the difference of choice. The moment of rehearsal of consequences is at hand. The teams separate with two obligations accepted: on the one hand, to write, dramatize, or photograph a rehearsal of the crucial moments, periods, circumstances, involved in the situation of their choice; on the other hand, to write, dramatize, or photograph a rehearsal of the choice of the other team as this choice appears to those who have rejected it.

This work completed, the teams reconvene. Team A presents its rehearsal of its choice. Team B then presents its rehearsal of team A's choice. The two constructions thus confront one another immediately. At its most dramatic (and most educative, perhaps), team

A recognizes and recoils from consequences it has not envisaged; or it denies the validity of what it recoils from. In the latter case, a matter of probable fact, the question is debated and resolution sought, either from the two teams involved or from an additional (and knowledgable) arbiter. In this way, rehearsal is not only invoked under the lash of an audience which can be anticipated to be a searching one, but the kind of error by omission which can so easily arise in the enthusiasm of deliberation terminated too soon, is seen and felt in considerable depth. (Of course, the two rehearsals may be substantially the same. Of course, too, we are assuming that, in any case, the pattern of presentation is then reversed, the choice of team B being the focus of attention. We are also assuming that the relations of the two teams to one another and to the umpire of the simulations have been such as to maximize the responsibility of the participants: the teams are not competitive, eristic, but concerned, as friends, that the other's final choice be a good one.)

Obviously enough, if this facet of simulation is added to the suggested others, this adventure in deliberation will be a major one. It will require the equivalent in time and energy of at least a semester course, perhaps two. (Let us suppose that, in fact, it is the senior student's sole responsibility for the last half of his last semester.) As such, I would still deem it a desirable addition to the curriculum, taking, for some students, if not all of them, the place occupied by a bachelor's thesis in some collegiate programs. It might well deserve its place as the valedictory of collegiate education, a modern and practical equivalent of Hermann Hesse's Bead Game.

Emphasis on rehearsal in simulation of the practical performs a special service over and beyond its normal function. It reminds the potentially complacent that something lies beyond the status quo. Deliberation, like all modes of thought, has its corruption. Science is devoted to warranted knowledge; humane criticism to the clarification of the meaning and order of works of art. But science is corrupted to trivial counting by many of its practitioners because the trivial poses few barriers to the achievement of warranty. Humane criticism often deteriorates into the sly cleverness of detection of "devices," of betraying the armature inside the sculpture—because the exposure of devices calls for little test of the judgment and sensibility by which we discover and make accessible what the devices are for. Deliberation can deteriorate too, most especially in those who are good at it and, because of their competence, gain administrative or executive office. It can deteriorate into mere calculation, devoted to conservation of means instead of to their deployment. It can deteriorate into a sterile game of frustrating one means by another for the sake of retaining the executive power to play the sly game. Only the rehearsal of goals beyond the present condition and firm discipline of the habit of rehearsal can complete the character which can guard against these corruptions and keep alive the sense of new possibilities.

A postscript. The simulations suggested under conditions 2, 3, and 4, involving a dismembered-novel-cum-prosthetic-devices,[13] were adopted for illustration because they permitted a particularly helpful emphasis on

13. Pp. 156–60.

the possibility of introducing randomness. There is no reason why the dismembered novel cannot be replaced by materials developed (and videotaped, for vividness and the facility of instant replay) for the purpose of the simulations. It would be well, however, if *non*-collaborating authors were used, one for the original presentation of problem situation and character, another for the variety of possible facts of the problem situation. A similar replacement of the two-team presentation of rehearsal of consequences is also possible—a bank of video tapes, one or two pertaining to each possible decision in the situation, the appropriate one or two utilized as the foils for a team's own rehearsal of the consequences of its choice. This has the advantage of putting a trained talent to work on the problem. It has the disadvantage of depriving students of a pattern of collaboration and challenge which may have great educational value.

The notion of dismembered and pied materials is, nevertheless, an attractive one because of its wide applicability. It could be applied to court cases (with special reference to the credibility of witnesses and to the problem of deliberation on proper punishment where judicial latitude obtains); it could be applied to sets of formal arguments on national issues (again with emphasis on the ambiguity of practical fact but also with emphasis on the role and treatment of theoretical materials in their practical use). It also could be applied to such special pleadings as those of geneticists and ecologists on issues of population and pollution controls. I hesitate to suggest this use, however, because of the amount of high-handed arrogance which invests so many documents of this kind, arrogance which misuses theoretical knowledge and passes off obiter dicta for the fruits of deliberation.

In summary, then, the criteria which define valid deliberative problems and practices are these:

1. The deliberator must feel the pinch of the problem.
2. The deliberator must know responsibility with respect to the consequences of his decision.
3. The facts of the case must be discriminated (identified as relevant) by the agent.
4. Many of the facts of the case must be sought out by the agent and their reliability estimated via estimate of the credibility of witnesses.
5. The raw materials for deliberation must be mainly facts definite and particular, not generalities, not theoretical subsumptions of facts.
6. The special treatment of theoretical knowledge required by deliberation (*modifying* application) must be represented.
7. The initiation of deliberation must be by cognizance of a concrete problem situation and not a formulated version of the problem.
8. Rehearsal must be involved, and through rehearsal, a scrutiny and judgment by the agent of himself as part of the matter deliberated upon.

Practical Prescription 6: Real Deliberations

In larger institutions, a hundred practical problems arise during the course of a year which immediately concern the welfare, the convenience, and the comfort of students. I have in mind the manifold problems concerned with their housing, their feeding, their recreation, their facilities for study; and problems of decision which lie closer to the academic—problems of scheduling and housing of classes, registration, library hours and procedures, bookstore facilities and services, recording and dissemination of grades and other records, the operation of the academic advisory system, payment of fees.

In too many cases in too many institutions, such matters are settled as well as acted on by a petty bureaucracy: campus police officials, building engineers, "Buildings and Grounds," cafeteria manageresses, registrar's clerks, deans' secretaries, assistant deans, and administrative aides. Occasionally, no doubt, decisions made by such officials are made in the interest of the clientele. Inherent in the roles and relations of such petty officials, however, is a continuous pressure toward treatment of the clientele as sources of problems and irritation, not as clients. Decisions are made in the interest of "efficiency," of relieving pressures from officials one notch higher in the administrative structure, of maintaining petty power and petty empire involving members of the structure one notch lower. The result, in the vast majority of cases, is the institutionalization of a steady and chronic source of resentment and friction for faculty and students alike. The resentment, moreover, has two sources. In addition to the frustrations and impositions of the rules and acts themselves, there is the further frustration of the petty tyranny usually practiced—the absence of channels of appeal to bodies other than the next tier of petty officials.

A mechanism which would ameliorate such frustrations and tyrannies, even if it had nothing more to commend it, would constitute a marked contribution to whatever of community the institution enjoys. Much more important, these hundreds of problems constitute a wasted educational resource, for most of them conform to most of the conditions which define an educationally useful practical problem. They touch felt needs of students. The outcomes of their treatment are outcomes with which the students must live. Allocation of scarce resources, the choice of alternative means and ends, the discrimination and estimate of the relevant facts—all are usually involved. In addition to meeting most of the conditions of practical problems in their general form, they exemplify the practical problem in its political aspect: the existence of legitimate differences of interest among those affected and the existence of persons, prejudices, and habits which are parts of the means and obstacles which must be used and dealt with.

Why not, then, use these resources? I suggest the following procedure, designed on the one hand to release the educational potential inherent in these problem situations and on the other hand to insure that decisions made will be at least as good as those made by petty officials. The heart of the plan is simple enough: the appointment of numerous committees of a certain constitution and with *seriously* delegated powers, one such committee for each problem.

The plan has three simple parts: a means for identifying the relevant problem situations and coordinating their treatment; the constituency of each committee; a procedure for review which does *not* withdraw at whim the delegated powers of the committees.

I suggest a special assistant to the president as the identifying and coordinating agent. He has two responsibilities, of which one will be delicate and difficult (at first): to extract from petty officialdom the arrays of problem situations to be used. A presidential letter will inform officialdom of the new procedure and empower the special assistant to perform his function. He will then meet the officials (one at a time), determine with them the impending, relevant decisions each faces, and choose with him those which most affect student life, are most amenable to client-centered treatment, and especially, those whose urgency does not require extremely rapid decision.

I have no doubt that officialdom will resist and evade. It will postpone selection, seek problems of least importance or one or two designed to bring disaster on the mixed committee which sits upon it. But this is an ordinary risk of any shift in administrative procedure. In a very few cases the shift will doubtless require surgery: removal and replacement of an occasional official. There are good reasons to expect that, in most cases, however, officials, too, will adapt. Indeed, some of them will even be educated, for they, too, will serve a role on the committees established.

With appropriate advice from president and deans, the special assistant will then enter upon his second responsibility: appointment, convening, and attendance at all the committees called. Appointment will be patterned as indicated below. Meetings will be scheduled at convenient times and in a special place: a room (later, rooms) marked by its location and its furnishings as part of the apparatus of administration (especially *not* classrooms, student common rooms, professors' offices). The special assistant will join each committee at each of its meetings—as a member but not as a chairman. His role will be largely a silent one at first since his station as presidential surrogate is likely to invest him in the eyes of students and faculty with status he will have to live down. He is not wholly silent, however, since deliberations of any one committee are likely to impinge on others—if only by way of limited facilities and resources which must be shared. These overlaps indicate his coordinating function: to inform committees at appropriate moments of the parallel, competing, or otherwise related work of other committees.

The constituency of each such committee is the heart of the matter. I envisage each to consist of two or three students, two or three faculty, the special assistant and the official (or his agent) in whose domain the problem falls. (The chairman is drawn from the student-professorial membership.) Each will have his own role to play and learning it will be painful. The official is present as informant and, usually, as executor of the decision made, but he is likely to begin by telling the committee what its decision ought to be, telling it that its decision is impossible of execution, conjuring up every rule, by-law, city statute, health ordinance, or contract term which might stand in the way of solutions envisaged. It will be the task of the special assistant to resist these tactics insofar as they are exaggerations and displays of force. It will be the responsibility of student and faculty members of the committee to conceive pathways around or over real obstacles of a kind which officialdom does not normally consider. Eventually, it will also be their responsibility to convince officialdom that they are serious and can learn to be practical.

Selection of student members must be made with

wisdom, not with mere caution. Most student bodies are well-supplied with anxious young conformists, itching and able to detect what their "betters" want and to agree with them. If the student contingent on a committee consists wholly of these, there will be no education in the practical and, in all likelihood, no good decisions either. As far as possible, then, let there be one activist or independent soul and one who, though "proper," is self-possessed. In that event, each will contribute to the education of the others. The activist will learn why off-with-their-heads solutions won't work. The conformist will discover that an eye to the problem (as well as an ear to the ground) can be a route to approval. The proper student, like the official, may learn to expand the boundaries within which he seeks the possible.

Selection of appropriate faculty members will be difficult, since a number of criteria must be met. One of them at least must know the campus through and through. No more than one should be a student-lover. One must have practical competence. (Unfortunately, faculties are almost as innocent of practical wisdom as students. Hence this need rather than the number of appropriate problems will be the limiting factor in the operation of the program.)

The roles of student and faculty members alike is to deliberate—to take account, not of their special interest alone, but the interests of all those affected, to inform each other of the special interests and needs of those they know best, to invent, envisage, and judge possible means and ends. Like the official, however, they will need to learn their role. Students are likely to begin in conformity or overcompensation for conformity. Faculty are likely to begin with pontification, suspicion of students, or the assumption that the professors are there to lead and teach and the students to listen and follow. Only as time, chance, and wise choice of the problem operate, will the professor discover himself in error on occasion and witness the resourcefulness of students sufficiently to begin to accept them as peers in an enterprise at which neither is expert.

In brief, it is the situation which will teach. Hence the review procedure is of first importance, not only as a safeguard against poor decisions, but as a catalyst of the education. I envisage a simple one. Each committee decision will be reviewed by the special assistant alone, by him and the official, by him and the president, or, in very important cases, by the three together. In every case, however, the review will be made in the name of the president and its result transmitted to the committee by him. If the review finds the committee action effective, well and good. The committee is complimented, thanked, and discharged. If the decision is found wanting, the want is specified (conflict with other decisions, lack of the needed resource, other claims on the resource, undesirable consequence identified) and the problem returned to the committee for reconsideration.

Obviously, all this hinges on the quality of the special assistant, on the competence of the president, and on the extent that his office permits the added burden. I have no solution for the problem of a pompous or tyrannical president, but for the other two prime needs alternatives suggest themselves. A poorly chosen special assistant can be replaced by another. The president's burden can be shared with or given over to provost, academic vice-president, or dean.

As the novelty of this operation diminishes and practical experience accumulates (among professors as well as students) at least three channels of expansion of the program can be entertained. First, as capable students are identified, they can take over some of the chairmanships of new committees and share the burden of the special assistant. Second, the program can be proliferated at an appropriately smaller scale within each academic department and division. Third, and especially at the level of departments and divisions, the program can begin to assimilate some of the problems central to the institution: curricular problems. I have in mind matters of examination procedures, degree requirements, and the when and what of course offerings. Fourth, and by no means to be dismissed as impossible or impractical, student participation can begin to pass over from participation in deliberation to participation in execution and management of decisions made. On the non-academic side, they can participate in the management and operation of their snack bars, coffeehouses, other places of entertainment, reading rooms, bookstore, dormitories. (Have we forgotten in this egalitarian era that the fraternity house was traditionally a student-run affair?) With respect to the academic side, I shall have more to say in the sections to follow.

For all the space given it here, the practical is only an addendum to the curriculum. It is invoked in the service of sore needs. It is commended to college and university as their responsibility because it draws on the commonly recognized academic disciplines, is itself an intellectual discipline in part, and because it most conspicuously attaches itself to the intellectual, moral, and characteral disciplines, which are also indispensable to the commonly recognized intellectual disciplines: suspense of impulse in the interest of reflection, respect for diversities of interest and competence, capacity for sustained effort. It is, nevertheless, only an addendum, and its use in the absence of a sweeping reform of the commonly recognized curriculum fields will not only constitute merely a cheap placating of student pressures, it will not work. It will not work because the disciplines it requires in students will arise only as these disciplines support and are supported by development of their sister disciplines.

THE CURRICULAR
PRESCRIPTIONS 4

The general character of the sweeping curricular change commended by our diagnoses is clear enough. Its purpose is to return to the curriculum an intellectual challenge to students and the fullest possible opportunity to develop the arts of recovery, enquiry, and criticism appropriate to each discipline. In view of the section on curricular resources, a brief description should suffice.

The foundation of the whole effort is extensive grounding of all programs and all courses (early as well as late courses, specialized or "general") in materials which contain structured meaning and reward the search for it. For such fields as the sciences, the social sciences, history, and philosophy, this means, in general, no "truth" without the evidence and argument which supports it or from which it grows. It means—especially for history, philosophy, sociology, and psychology—no "truth" with its evidence and argument without some sampling of the alternative choices of principals, evidence, and interpretation which confer on these fields their characteristic pluralism: in psychology, for example, no B. F. Skinner without some Harlow; no Freud without a Harry Sullivan or equivalent *and* a stab at a "cognitive" theory of personality. For literature and the arts, it means works of some quality addressed at first hand rather than second—neither treated as instances of some class of generalities nor mediated by a professorial authority.

Curricular Prescription 1:   Materials and the use of them

If challenging materials are to serve their full complement of purposes, they cannot be merely challenging. They must also be representative of the problems and the methods of the disciplines they represent, and the meanings discovered from them should be meanings of consequence in the field. The reason for the latter condition goes without saying: we are not proposing that search for meaning and arts of recovery be *substituted* for knowledge and knowing but that discovered structures of meaning shall illuminate and complete the knowledge gained.

The reasons for the former condition are almost as obvious. We are committed to correction of the situation in which students must almost blindly commit themselves to a field of concentration. This choice will cease to be blind only if the early curriculum affords opportunity to the student to discover the disciplines of recovery and enquiry characteristic of a field and discover them, not merely in the sense of learning their names and being told about them, but in the sense of discovering what they feel like, what demands they make, what rewards they afford him. This kind of firsthand representativeness, I must add, is not afforded by the mere hasty addition to courses and programs of passages on the "logic," "methods," or "philosophy" of this field or that. Such passages— a lecture or series of them or a full course—are much more likely to be an addition to the burden of unsupported generalities we are trying to replace than to occasions for discovery and trial of relevant competences. If a "philosophy" of science or of history is to be found, let it be sought first in histories and reports of scientific enquiries under the guidance of instructors in these fields who can, themselves, exercise the requisite arts of recovery. If a faculty member's training is deficient in this regard (and this is true of many) and hence requires the help of a logician or philosopher, let it be clear from the start and throughout that the consultant's aid is sought in the interest of science or history, as the case may be, and not in the interest of a philosophic dogma. (The emphasis here is on "dogma," and more important, dogma insinuated; it is not intended to denigrate philosophy.)

There is a second and related reason why challenging material should be representative of the state of the disciplines they represent: they constitute the materials and afford the occasions through which the lives of the faculty become accessible as instances (models) of styles of life of which, otherwise, the student will probably remain forever ignorant. It is the evident competence displayed as the instructor exemplifies the appropriate disciplines of recovery and criticism, his visible satisfaction in the work, and the clear usefulness of its fruit which ground his role as accessible model. It is his effective guidance, support, and criticism when the student, in his turn, embarks on tasks of recovery or enquiry, which further make him accessible. Hence, again, the materials must represent what the instructor should represent: the state of a discipline.

Appropriate materials are, of course, only a foundation for the commended curricular reform. They can serve only as texts for sermons and as reading supplements to the sermons unless there are also adequate curricular occasions for the exemplification, trial, and exercise of the competences of analysis and enquiry which the papers invite and suggest. This means, in general, that a substantial proportion (one-half? two-thirds?) of the meetings of most courses (and especially those in the first year and the last) must be of a size which permits face-to-face community of work. The group must be small enough to permit most students to discover and know one another as collaborators and competitors. This means, on the one hand, to discover the diversities of talent present and the usefulness of each; it means, on the other hand, to discover the deficiencies, foibles, and mannerisms which accompany talents and to learn how to tolerate them or help to ameliorate them as occasion affords. The group must be small enough to permit the instructor to discover and know the diversities of his students and afford most of them (in person or by recognizable proxy) the different sorts of guidance toward mastery of disciplines which they severally require. The group, on the other hand, must be large enough to contain the diversities of talent, and of developed and undeveloped competences which permit the work of recovery and enquiry to go on and make possible a range of helping and being helped, tolerating and being tolerated, which will constitute an experience of collaboration.

The number which will constitute the desired community will vary with several factors. The greater duration of semester or trimester permits a larger group than does an academic quarter. An instructor with energy and an excellent memory can support a larger group than one who tires and forgets more quickly. A tendency toward social-class and aptitude uniformity in a student body may dictate a larger group for achievement of adequate diversity than will a varied student population. In general, I consider twenty to twenty-five as modal, thirty and fifteen as frequent; thirty-five as approaching the dangerous, and ten, the precious.

The kind of material suggested and the kind and size of group are joined and made viable by the kind of work they permit. They are the conditions which permit the student to become more and more an agent instead of a passive recipient of his education. They permit the work of recovery, enquiry, articulation, diagnosis, and criticism. Under these conditions the students can essay their first "readings" of a body of materials, voice beliefs and disbeliefs, explore the grounds of their prejudices and preferences, give and submit to criticism, discover the possibility and use of reflexive scrutiny of their debates. The group alone, without the material, will permit debate, liveliness, excitement, and confusion. The materials alone, without the group, will permit developing awe of great men and great books, submission to them, to "the" rules, and, in most cases, either the habit of submission or mindless revolt. The materials and the group together, and the capable instructor, permit the assay of debate, its reflexive scrutiny, which can lead not only to rules but the reasons for them, hence, not only to discipline but to the measured breaking of the rules,

knowing what and why they are, on which the en-
largement of enquiry depends.

All such "right" combinations have their inherent
vice. This one is no exception. Its endemic threat is
that of discipleship, coterie-ism. Some number of students of each effective instructor are infected by the
model of competence he affords, discover (or think
they discover) the requisite competences in themselves,
mistake the satisfaction of good work and the pleasure
of developing competence as gifts peculiarly of this
man and this discipline. They then scramble to take
as many more courses from the same man or his allies
as schedules permit, cultivate his discipline to the
neglect of others, hotly attack alternatives cultivated
by other students and hotly defend their own choice.
They end by being identifiable in three minutes at
thirty paces as a McIver man, a Parsonite, a Buhlian.

This is not an unmitigatedly bad thing. It even has
its uses. It is not wise, however, to give it the keys
of the city. The general solution is, of course, gentle
pressure toward variety of models by way of distributed requirements of one kind or another. There are,
however, smaller-scaled guards which can be woven
into the day-to-day texture of discussion.

One consists of carefully cultivated, early reward of
"good stubbornness." In the early days of discussion
the pattern of enquiry or recovery aimed at by the
instructor is still unclear to students. His questions,
therefore, are ambiguous, and different interpretations
are made by different students. The instructor listens
carefully to identify two quite different resources—
interpretations which move toward the question meanings intended; interpretations which move elsewhere

but are sound. Both are given full hearing. The first is identified and rewarded frontally: "That is exactly what I meant. Thank you." The second is recognized and rewarded with similar directness: "That is not what I had in mind, but it is an interesting line of questioning. Go on with it." (Or, "What suggested that line?" "Are you especially interested in that sort of analysis?" "That leads in a direction we shall probably need.") One identifies students who respond with pleasure to recognition of their "unwanted" interpretation and, again and again in the course of the semester, one diverts the arguments to them, with an invitation to pursue a counter line.

This pattern puts students on notice that the "official" line is not the only line honored by the instructor and that adventure into other lines is, itself, honored. It also serves an additional purpose. It makes possible a clearer identification of the character and purpose of the official line by affording contrasts, and by the same means, exhibits some of the limitations of the official line.

After disciplines begin to be mastered in the early weeks, a second pattern can be invoked, a pattern suggested in Practical Prescription 1.[1] Assignments cease to be the same to all members of the group. Instead, three students are asked, as a team, to undertake investigation of one problem; a second and third team are asked to investigate others. Each team formulates the fruits of its analysis and names a spokesman to deliver its contribution to the group. Before general group discussion of a report ensues, one asks the team members who did not report for whatever of doubts,

1. P. 130.

disagreements, or alternative interpretations they may have had, and again one honors a "deviant" line of investigation which is sound by indicating the kind of contribution it makes. This pattern can be extended by appointment of two teams to the same problem, urging on them the desirability of different attacks on the problem and suggesting that they confer on the alternative lines they will take. Again they report, and again reflexive scrutiny by the whole group identifies the character of each line and the contribution it makes.

A third pattern removes the instructor's hand entirely and patently. A vexed problem which has had some discussion, a new problem or a fresh document is handed on to students for analysis and discussion—without the presence of the instructor. Depending on circumstance and personalities, his absence can be arranged in various ways. The students can be informed simply and matter-of-factly at the time of an assignment that they are to handle its discussion under their own direction. They can be told at time of assignment that the instructor has another duty at the time of the next group meeting, and asks as a favor that they conduct the meeting without him and report its outcome at a subsequent meeting. They may receive the assignment in the ordinary way and be informed at the next meeting that the instructor cannot meet with them and requests that they proceed without him.

Each of these patterns has much the same effect as far as our purpose here is concerned; it lightens the heavy hand of authority and personality; it inserts some space between person and doctrine. Both effects are to be sought as conditions in which students can explore more freely and therefore more fruitfully what competences they possess and what satisfactions ensue on their use.

The device of the absentee instructor deserves attention in its own right, as a curricular prescription in general, because of other desirable effects. Note, first, that the absent instructor leaves no instruction as to chairmanship or other apparatus of organization. That remains as a problem to be recognized and solved by the student group itself. Hence the device makes another small contribution to occasions for collaboration (community) in direct relation to the primary work and character of the collegiate community. In the second place, the device constitutes an important, almost irreplaceable, addition to diagnostic resources. Nothing is more persuasively illusory than the increasingly well-*conducted* discussion. As we learn the idiosyncracies of each student, his special competence, his limitations, his idiom, our questioning grows more and more adroit and, in consequence, discussion proceeds more and more smoothly, finds its mark more quickly and with less misdirection. We can easily mistake our own progress for progress by the student group. It is only what they can do without our help which will serve to distinguish our increasing competence from theirs. Finally, non-governor-controlled discussion permits expression of interests, concerns, emphases which will not be brought to bear in controlled discussion, concerns which often yield substantive results of surprising kind and value.[2]

These three patterns for mitigation of personality have two additional properties in common which con-

2. This statement is implausible; I can only suggest that it be tested.

stitute a caveat: (*a*) their use depends on the individual instructor, not on bureaucratic machinery; (*b*) they rouse instructorial anxiety (especially the third), since they begin to indicate that the instructor is not indispensable. They will be widely used, then, only as the climate of the institution encourages them. If they are not widely used, they may constitute a mild risk, for they may be read by students or other instructors as marks of an indulgent man or a theatrical one.

Curricular Prescription 2:   Subject matter

So much, then, for the general character of the curricular reform envisaged. It is primarily a matter of the quality of materials, what is done to them, and the circumstances of the doing. Except for the commendation of a practical component, the traditional curricular problem of *what* shall be taught does not arise primarily. This shift from traditional emphasis is dictated mainly by our starting points. We are concerned with deficiencies of competence among students and not with deficiencies of information—at least as far as the traditional academic fields are concerned. It is also dictated by concern for responsible judgment on the question of subject matter; concern that judgment shall be rendered in each field by persons who know the alternatives—in brief, by the specialists. The fact that many of them are irresponsible in their judgment by virtue of disdain for the student as a factor to be considered is not rectified by an equal and opposite irresponsibility on my part.

Nevertheless, the problem of subject matter arises secondarily at two points. One of these is relatively trivial. It concerns the cloud—considerably larger than

a man's hand—of "experimental" colleges now arising
in response to student protest. Many of these colleges
are looking desperately for a way of being experimental, or at least of appearing so, and some are finding it in ill-conceived and ad hoc "new" fields of
concentration generated by rearrangements of traditional filiations. One proposes a Division of Semiotic
coordinate with divisions representing traditional fields.
Another proposes seven "newly structured provinces
of knowledge." Among them are such defensibles as
Mathematics and Logic; Physical Science; and Biological Science. But also present is a Province of Behavioral Science *separated off* from a Province of Social
Science, and a Province of Mind and Spirit.

I have no quarrel with fresh filiations and segregations as such nor have I a doctrine which pretends to
legitimize traditional field divisions as right or true or
natural from the beginning. It is the case, however,
that when subject matters have been successfully discriminated for enquiry, principles are brought to bear
upon them which define their boundaries, their significant constituents, and their modes of organization.
Such principles determine what data are sought concerning that subject matter and the way in which the
data are interpreted. Hence knowledge of that subject
matter is embodied in the terms of the same principles—not merely expressed in a language borrowed
from them but taking its meaning from the terms of
the principles and relating to the subject matter as true
and false by way of the same terms.

It is also the case that different discriminated subjects are pursued in enquiry by means of different principles. Hence there arise bodies of knowledge about

each such discriminated subject matter which can be
made coherent with one another only insofar as there
are terms common to their principles, or as bridging
terms relating some terms of one principle to terms of
the other can be devised. In many fields (philosophy,
history, social sciences) the contrary holds. Knowledge of a subject matter is pursued concurrently by
different scholars with different principles and in different terms. Hence two or more bodies of knowledge
arise of roughly the same subject matter. These bodies
of knowledge stand in an important relation to one
another: they are each other's critics; the very existence of each announces the incompleteness of the
other and begins to indicate how it is incomplete.

New filiations and segregations are not, then, to be
undertaken lightly, that is, filiations and segregations
of bodies of *existing* knowledge. (The formation of research groups, temporary or indefinite, to pursue enquiry, that is, to try to construct new knowledge on
subject matters which bridge traditional fields, is another kind of enterprise. So is the initiation of a new
curriculum unit to represent a recently developed
body of knowledge.) If new filiations are not to be
spurious or illusory, we must be sure that common or
bridging terms exist; we must know what they are;
we must be prepared to trace out the connections they
make possible. This is not only a work of expertise but
of rare talent. Further, if new segregations are made,
some appropriately complex way must be found to
replace the critical function of the materials excluded
by the segregation. This, too, is work which requires
rare talent and the alternative to it is the covert import into the curriculum of dogma which misrepresents

not only the enquiries on the subject matter but the subject matter itself.

Consider the second case cited above. The province of mind and spirit is said to be "evolved" from philosophy and religion. Consider first what dangers of irresponsible segregation might be involved. Are we to suppose that only philosophy has something important to say about mind? That psychology has nothing to contribute? Are students to be barred from discovering what can be known of mind from seeing its operation in the intellectual disciplines generally? Have sociology and cultural anthropology nothing to teach us about the genesis, the variety, and the operation of mind?

In the same way, consider the segregation of social science and behavioral science. The former is said to be evolved from history, political science, economics, and geography; the latter embraces psychology, sociology, and cultural anthropology. The latter, then, would treat in one way or another the composition, relation and tensions of social classes, the mechanisms for dissemination of a culture's values, the degree of community which cultures foster, the degree of alienation they condone, the ways in which they respond to communications from other cultures. Have these matters little or nothing to do with history, economics, geography, political science?

Consider, too, some of the filiations involved. A province is said to require similar skills, knowledge, and modes of thought. Are the modes of thought of philosophy the modes of theology or even similar to them? A hundred philosophers would deny it. Do history and geography use similar modes of thought? A hundred of each would deny it. Or are we, for example, to suppress from the curriculum on mind and thought all philosophy which does not support, bear upon, or share its mode of thought with theology?

Such problems of new filiation and segregation of existing knowledge are not impossible of solution. I have, in fact, encountered two authentic cases. It may be that the instance in question is a third. It is clear, however, that many such rearrangements of the cards are undertaken innocently, that is, irresponsibly, without grasp or solution of the problems involved. And some, surely, bear far closer connection to the recruitment possibilities they seem to afford than to the curriculums they claim to describe.

In fact, one extremely interesting *mechanical* solution to the problem suggests itself. Suppose, for example, that students are exposed in their first year to a curriculum which treats a selected political science only in the context of classical economics and appropriately selected history, without connection with another course, which considers appropriately chosen selections from psychology and sociology, and a third which teaches selected philosophy and theology in close connection with one another. Suppose that in the next year the student encounters the same philosophy juxtaposed to Freud, Marx, Durkheim and a modern philosophical analyst or two; the schemas of polis and polity in the context of sociological and psychological studies of institutional structures, authoritarian personalities, administrative structures, and decision-making; and psychology and sociology in the context of the destructively critical warfare of method and principle which goes on in each of these sciences. If he survived the shock, he might learn more vividly than in any other way what challenges of doubt, uncertainty, and ambiguity man's knowledge poses. The third and fourth years might then be devoted to mastering something of the competences by which the confusion is unraveled.

In any case, the moral of such stories is clear enough. If rearrangements of existing bodies of knowledge are installed without solution of the problems the rearrangements pose, the result must be to exacerbate the conditions we are trying to overcome: the piling up of unsupported and vulnerable dogma, the proliferation of tautologies and generalities. It then becomes vastly more difficult, rather than less so, to launch students on a voyage of recovery and enquiry. There will be much vociferous debate but little ground for reflexive scrutiny. In consequence, there will be little consensus, few solutions to problems, and little increase in the competence to solve them.

In this matter of alternative filiations and segregations, there is, however, a potential for a very fruitful contribution to the curriculum. I shall consider it under a later prescription. Meanwhile, let us turn to a more important matter of curriculum.

Curricular Prescription 3: Diversity and Unity

The more important problem of subject matter is an exacerbated version of a perennial problem (for which I have no competent solution)—the eternal tension between, on the one hand, real differences of competence and irreversible differences of interest among students and, on the other, the equally real need for a shared tradition, shared experience, shared problems, values, and idiom.

The arguments for each of these are very good ones. Almost every ground of curricular argument speaks for a commonalty. First, a complex culture cannot function without a substantial body of shared values—a sense of commitment of its members one to another in the interest of common needs requiring pooled effort. Even the store of practical means on which we draw to solve our problems, especially deliberation itself as a means for choosing means and obtaining collaboration, arise from a shared lore. Community, in its aspect as a desired good in itself, rests on a shared tradition and a shared idiom. (By "idiom" I mean more than vocabulary: I have in mind also the wealth of allusion, sentence rhythms, dated slang, shared sources of simile and metaphor, and other forms of shared remembrance by which we communicate layer on layer of meaning by way of apparently simple statements, and especially the meanings which remind each other of shared membership.) Friendship itself grows in the soil of shared experience. And "solidarity" in the face of an external threat arises almost as much from a shared tradition as from the shared danger.

It is equally true, however, that a complex culture requires the diverse cultivation of diverse talents. The adroit use of chosen means requires the varied competences which develop from diverse talents. Community (and friendship) fall apart from boredom if everyone is the mirror image of everyone else; it is the exchange of *different* experiences ("What did *you* do to-day?") and the differing characters and points of view which arise from differing experiences which nourish both friendship and community and enable them to be something more than bread-and-butter loves.

There are additional reasons which commend attention to individual differences. First, there is the waste of life, time, and talent involved in requiring of all that they strain ineptitudes to meet official demands. Second, there is the boredom which can appear even to the normally immature nineteen-year-old as a price he cannot pay. Third, there is our commitment to a curriculum which enables students to discover and cultivate the competences most likely, in each case, to become a resource of enduring satisfaction as well as of productivity.

This curricular problem, then, is a classic example of the practical, with its perennial feature of requiring that we find a way of obtaining the most possible of mutually excluding goods, not simply choose one against the other.

On the whole, the academic world has not been practical in its treatment of this problem. It has preferred the pendulum swing (from the free elective system to the earliest commitment to a major and devices which prescribe much the same program for all) or decision by default. As I write, the tendency is toward decision by default. The young talk about "my thing" and "his thing," and the dean of arts and letters hastens to heed and comply. Our patent failure to teach a great many Negro children effectively has evoked a rash of studies which "prove" how different people are: they "prove" that some learn only with emotions; others learn with their muscles; large numbers cannot learn via language. These frail straws, too, (shades of the "ear-minded" and the "eye-minded" of the 1920's) are being grasped as principles which dictate radical differences of curriculum for different students. In general, it is now chic to opt for election—either self-election by the student, assignment on the basis of social class or ethnic origin, or, I think we can anticipate, on the basis of hastily constructed psychological tests.

Another unacceptable solution operates by way of the admissions machinery. The highly specialized small institution admits only those students whose aptitudes fit them for its specialization. This conception, enormously multiplied, would establish, say, twenty kinds of institutions representing as many specializations, each kind attracting and admitting only those students with evidenced competence in the specialty. By this means we would satisfy one of our goods. We would also create another modern equivalent of a Tower of Babel, populated by groupings of citizens as effectively alienated from one another as, say, a native speaker of Swahili from a Tyneside dock worker.

Our diagnoses do not permit such sweeping solutions. We are committed not only to a commonalty which will suffice for community and collaboration; we are also committed to the development of individual competences. In addition, we are committed to curricular occasions adequate for differentiating in students between irremediable differences of competence and interest and those which are fantasies or reversibles grounded in the accidents of experience and nonexperience. We need, in short, devices which will maximize each of these mutually excluding goods.

The very common year or two years of required "general education courses" (or the equivalent in "core" requirements), followed by two or three years of mixed concentration and election, is one effort to accommodate these mutually excluding goods. Presumably, the student of wide interests can discover his lesser and greater strengths in the common years; mistaken interests and dislikes will be disclosed and new interests generated, thus laying a firm base for choice of special field. And so, to a considerable extent, it might be, if the courses were of the appropriate kind—challenges to competences, trial runs of disciplines. By conviction or default, however, the majority of these required general courses and core-requirement fulfillments are of another kind: surveys of knowledge, instillation of "principles" abstracted from their meaning-conferring structure, or intensive drills in "fundamental" facts without the framework which confers their significance on them.

Of greater importance to our present point are certain inadequacies which exist even when the constituent courses are good ones. The weaknesses are simple ones. First, the student with incorrigible distastes must spend from a quarter to a half of his first college years in acute boredom or distress, and the student who lacks the competences required for some of the courses —whatever his high competence in the others—may suffer even greater stress. This is especially true where the required general courses enjoy a local high esteem among students, and ineffective functioning in them pushes the student to merely peripheral membership in the student community. Even where this degree of esteem does not exist, the student's self-discovered inadequacy can be, as already indicated, a heavy burden for his only partially developed ego. Add substantive consequences: early dropouts and dilution of the grade-point average on which, unfortunately, the student's future may hinge.

It will not solve our problem merely to do away with the required courses which create these hazards, for then, to repeat our dilemma, we will have no machinery by which to rectify mistaken notions of likes and dislikes and evoke unrecognized competences. What is wanted is a full array of challenges to the test of interest and the exploration of competences, challenges which will not dissolve until the tests have been faced but which will be mitigated or removed in the event that test and challenge evoke reaction instead of response.

One merely mechanical means toward this end suggests itself. Suppose for the sake of simplicity that our challenges are embodied in four, year-long general courses, one each in the social, physical, and biological sciences and one in the humanities. Suppose, further, that all are required of all in the student's first or second year. But suppose, further, that at the end of the first quarter or trimester, students have the privilege of electing a special grading scheme for two of the four. The special grade, whatever its symbol, (e.g., "P"), is assigned three properties. First, it can be earned by the minimum attendance, assiduity, and quality of performance which would ordinarily constitute a barely passing grade. But, second, it will either not figure in grade-point averages at all or be treated as a "B" (as in the common A-B-C-D-E grading scheme). Third, the option may be rescinded by the student at the end of the course in favor of a standard grade. Suppose, finally, that this option is firmly established in the local mores and clearly explained on record transcripts simply as a form of elective.

There is a distinct possibility that such a plan might have surprisingly far-reaching results. Its firm establishment in the mores should remove almost entirely the stigma which might otherwise attach to poor work in the courses for which "P" is opted. A very large part of the stress involved in trying to meet standards which competence cannot reach is removed. The disproportionate amount of time and energy which would otherwise be devoted to stretching minimum competence to meet the standard demand is released for use in other courses. Even the occasions for boredom are substantially reduced. Meanwhile, two separate tests of apparent distaste and untested incompetence have been maintained: the intensive test in the first trimester, before the option becomes available; the much milder one, permitting what may be a salutary degree of relaxation and remoteness, in the remainder of the course. (It is the possibility of such a salutary consequence of relaxation and relative distance which suggests the desirability of a reversible option.)

Now consider an extension of this device which sacrifices a portion of one of our goods in the interest of increasing the other. The student is privileged to elect the "P" for half of one course and to replace the second portion of a second course with an equivalent added program in one of the remaining fields. The additional loss and additional gain involved here are obvious.

A third possibility deserves a prescriptive number in its own right.

Curricular Prescription 4:   Additional Diversity

Consider for a moment the curious phenomena known to the nineteenth century as idiot savants. They were lightning calculators, vast storehouses of immediately available and accurate memory, instant learners of musical instruments, demonic chess players, minutely accurate draftsmen, faultless retracers of blindfolded journeys, who were otherwise incompetent, dull, stupid. In the romantic versions known to the nineteenth century, such persons do not constitute a curricular problem. They stand as a caricature, however, of a segment of college students of great potential value for whom our usual ways of imparting a common idiom and a shared tradition constitute a sometimes insuperable barrier to discovery, enjoyment, and use of their talents. They are the persons who display, in the midst of a merely adequate or average intelligence, a peak of specialized competence or interest.

Such persons may be vastly more numerous than we suspect, since the competence tests most widely used for collegiate admission do little or nothing to identify them. (The widely used scholastic aptitude tests try to predict college performance as colleges currently require performance—based largely on verbal competence. The scores which refer to "quantitative" aptitude are still heavily verbal—insofar as teaching and learning of mathematical competences takes place in a context of the received and spoken word.) Certainly every college professor either is or knows a professor who is a witness to the existence of such people: able critics of art and literature who cannot start a car; the able biologist who has trouble with long division; even mathematicians who have trouble following a verbal argument. And what is suggested by such anecdotal evidence is borne out by more formal studies. B. Bloom reports one such, involving tests of seven (unnamed) special abilities. He found that more than 60 percent of a college population fell in the upper decile of one *or more* of these tests![3]

If it is likely that 50 to 75 percent of students are of this sort, some efforts should be made to develop tests which will identify them and to do so in terms relevant to existing fields of knowledge, competence, and expertise. There are a few such, for example, in law and medicine, but the bulk of efforts in this direction have been narrowly psychological—attempts to identify "independent mental abilities" such as space visualization, rather than the complexes which would identify the musician, the plastic artist, the theoretical physicist.

Meanwhile, identifying signs of some usefulness already exist: on the one hand, strong interests expressed by students; on the other, records of disparate precollegiate achievement—high grades in some few fields, lower grades in others. What is wanted is some stretching of curricular flexibility to accommodate at least a little of what these signs suggest.

I have two sorts of increased flexibility in mind: on the one hand, to permit the earliest possible student exploration of supposed special competences and interests even at the price of some loss of commonalty; on the other hand, flexibilities designed to exploit specialized interests and possible special competences in

3. *Handbook of Research on Teaching,* ed. N. L. Gage (Chicago: Rand, McNally, 1963) chap. 8.

the service of *broadened* interest and *broadened* mastery.

Consider humane subject matters and disciplines in the context of general courses as a case in point. (This choice is dictated by the frequency with which art, music, and dance are mentioned as foci of special interest and competence.) Consider, too, that the prevailing pattern of such courses places its emphasis entirely or mainly on literature and overwhelmingly on the finished literary work.

There are good arguments for these emphases. Literature is not only an art but a conveyor of cognitive content in a sense and to a degree to which music and the plastic arts do not aspire. Hence, it can be argued, the study of literature, as against music or painting, conveys an important burden of ideas and attitudes as well as critical competence and a durable source of satisfaction. The argument for study of finished works follows easily: they are the works which convey the burden of meanings which constitute the continuity of our culture.

These are good arguments. I do not propose to deny them. (Indeed, I have used them.) It is also the case, however, that there are causes as well as reasons for the prevailing academic emphasis on the wordy arts and on the finished product of such arts. With respect to the latter, the humane academic faculty is overwhelmingly a critical and not a constructing faculty. With respect to the former, the humane faculty has its dim origins in the written and spoken word and not in the graven image and tends to perpetuate itself as it was constituted. Why not, then, in the interest of the refreshment of faculties, as well as in the interest of student needs, some mild alteration of existing emphases?

Consider, first, an extension of the last device suggested in Prescription 3, the privilege of replacing a part of one general course by an added program in another field (for instance, replacing the second half of a general course in the humanities with an appropriate additional half-course in the social sciences). Suppose that in addition (or instead) the humanities course itself were constituted in a branching design: a first quarter or trimester common to all students; a second portion embodied in alternative but parallel programs among which each student chooses. A conservative start could be made with the traditional trio: literature, music, the plastic arts. But Terpsichore was also a muse, and dance—"primitive" as well as western-sophisticated—is now the object of much critical attention. It should not be outrageously difficult to develop a "literature" of the dance (via motion picture and videotape) which would permit the same sort of curricular attention to it which I assume here for the other arts: a concern for the art objects as such and the developing competences of sense and intellect which render them accessible and constitute of them an enduring source of satisfaction. (For reasons which will be indicated presently, architecture—including the planning of large areas—industrial design, and history could also be treated as compositions, works of art.)

The branching pattern described above is designed to concede a measure of commonalty in the interest of earliest possible student exploration of supposed special competences and interests. Consider now the possibility of exploiting special interests in the service of broadening that interest to embrace the literary arts with their special burden of cognitive content. For this purpose, the branching pattern would be inverted. Each student, if he so chose, would begin with his choice of an art form or medium other than the literary. The bulk of instruction in the art form of his choice would put its main emphasis, as before, on the art object. But as perception and sensibility developed, emphasis would shift toward issues of critical theory concerning parallels and connections among art forms. This shift of emphasis would in turn lead to examination of literary works in connection with questions problems, and analogues encountered first in the form or medium of the student's original choice.

The principle involved in this suggestion is obvious enough: to enlist an existing interest in the service of related matters. The grave risk involved is equally obvious: that the course and the student will be lost in the mazes of critical theory or will choke on a collection of ill-conceived parallels. I suggest the device, nevertheless, in the hope that experienced experts will devise a better one.

Meanwhile, it is reasonably clear that few dangers and much profit are promised by invoking the same principle as a guide to construction of the first sort of branching pattern. A humanities alternate which dealt with architecture and community planning as its art objects would enlist certain interests in the social sciences in the service of the humanities. Industrial design would invoke another and history, a third. A literature variant which dealt with rhetoric, argument, exposition (whose subjects were politics, ethics, etc.) instead of novel, drama, and short story, would harness some part of still other interests in the service of literary art.

In making these suggestions, I am guided by a special version of the principle of enlistment: we are enlisting interest in the *matter* of literary works in the service of concern for its *form and matter.* There is quite another area to which this principle might profitably be applied—to the matter of fiction, of drama, novel, and short story, as evidenced in student choices. This device is as old as the hills at the high school level and leads there, more often than not, to nothing more than the same interest in the matter with which it started— usually because the untutored choices of high school students are of books which afford scope for little else. In the present case, we are, presumably, not dealing with untutored students (nor with choices from "teenage" title lists). We are dealing with students who have completed half of a year's course devoted to the humane disciplines and to adult books. If the course has had effect, it should be evident in the quality of student choices. Further, the necessary quality can be guarded by numerous additional devices. Choice can be made from lists prepared by faculty. A student group which begins with a genre, a subject, or other matter, may seek the help of an instructor in finding titles. A student group which has chosen a list of titles must find the staff member willing to teach that list or one willing to bargain some of its titles for titles of his choice.

Curricular Prescription 5: More "Enquiry"

Whatever the arguments in favor of finished works (both in the sense of completed works and in the sense of very good ones), it is still the case that pre-occupation with them to the exclusion of work in progress—student work: enquiries, essays, sculpture, choreography, short stories, drama, and drama production—marks one of the signal failures of the academic community to use its resources and take account of the condition of the learner. I have already indicated some reasons for heavier emphasis on *enquiry* in this sense.[4] It is one of the most powerful ways—perhaps the only way—to afford experience of the ground of all enquiry: the originating problem, the first idea, the nascent plan, the seminal purpose, from which flow research and scholarship worth the doing, as well as works of art. Second, involvement in what flows from the originating notions—the wrestling with a stubborn matter, recognition of the detailed and subordinate problems which stand between plan and plan realized, search and discovery of ways of overcoming these problems, efforts at judging the efficacy of conceived solutions, experience of the evolution of plans as they meet and are modified by their matter—is indispensable to a grasp of the full character of the finished product and a proper complement of the grasp afforded by even the best of critical studies of the finished product. Third, involvement in work in progress affords the diagnostic by which the student can discover in the immediate fact whether his interest in a kind of making or doing is genuine or not, whether his competence is sufficient to make the labor of creation a fit price for the satisfactions which he discovers from it.

A fourth reason—only suggested in earlier pages: if the itch to make, to do, to shape, to alter some piece

4. Pp. 93–94.

of the world is not nurtured and channeled in the curriculum it will fade away or find its outlet elsewhere. In many students, a vast quantity of this energy takes sick and dies from what is done to it in homes and high schools. What remains requires early collegiate nurture if it is to grow again. And grow it must if the academic career of these students is to be more than a detention of bodies until the labor market can use them and yield more than a slavish storage of a small stock of mental goods for later peddling on a still smaller market. For most of the others, students who have resisted the erosion of their curiosity and their itch to mark the world, the college curriculum is a place of last resort. It is here they will find a channel for their energies and learn to discipline them or turn them loose in waves of aggression and hostility.

For the latter group of students at least, we can surely afford branching variants of first courses which afford scope for this itch and energy. The humanities program can offer scope for theater—acting, directing, staging—as well as for writing; it can offer scope for dancing as well as choreography, for sculpture, painting, and other plastic arts; for music. It can and should, I think, go further—break the monopoly of the fine arts in the interest of the useful arts—design of furniture, clothing, playgrounds, pots, and pans. (Shades of "shop" in the progressive schools of forty years ago! They had a good idea.)

Let us keep in mind, too, that not all the itches to make and do are for the shaping of physical stuff (words, paint, clay, wood, space). There are also itches to shape ideas (philosophy, mathematics, criticism, history), to discover (the sciences), to operate and modify institutions (the practical), to contribute to persons (teaching). There are curricular services of this sort, then, to be served by all the faculties of a university, in all its early courses, including the faculty of administration.

Obviously, most colleges and universities lack the men to do the nontraditional species of this work. (If they have an "artist in residence," more often than not he is preoccupied with his own making and shaping, serves mainly as an odd kind of animal on occasional display, or unwillingly and badly plays much the same teaching role as other and regular professors.) I suggest we try to find them—not writers in search of a convenient place to finish their current book but men who reserve some of their itch as an itch for contributing to persons who resemble themselves. These are men who would welcome most, then, neither the one-shot, temporary resting place nor the full obligation of regular professorship but something in between (for example, a rhythm of a half-year on, a whole year away). I suggest such persons for two reasons. They are the persons who could perform the intended function. Of equal importance, their special status and the special rhythm of their presence would minimize the strain they might otherwise create in the academic community; for good artists, in usual fact, if not by definition, make bad citizens of an academic community.

Curricular Prescription 6:   Late Diversity

Consider the student for whom three years have passed. He has discovered unsuspected talents and successfully bared some fantasies of dislike. He has

pressed some interests and found them hollow; he has
found too great disparity between some other interests
and his competences. He has mastered some disciplines
of recovery and essayed a few enquiries. From these
evocations, discoveries, and developments of himself,
he has made a reasonably good choice of a field of
specialization. He has spent more than a year in it,
enjoyed it, profited from it. His last year of under-
graduatehood is upon him. Whether by convocation or
translation into graduate work, this means the last
visible chance at further exploration, and he knows it.
He knows, too, of some special interests and half-
tested competences he has renounced in the interest
of his specialization. And this knowledge is now
mature enough to warrant its honoring.

Here, par excellence, is a crucial place for a special
kind of student election, a point in time when he can
choose more wisely and indulge his choice more profitably than in either the immediate past or the immediate
future.

I envisage, then, a blank place in our curriculum
which permits this special election and an apparatus
through which it can operate. The blank space is the
obvious kind: curricular space in the last year protected from encroachments of the special field.

The apparatus is equally obvious—and expensive.
Each student, alone or with some minimum few others
(three, five) considers and projects the course he would
like to the degree of detail of which he is capable. It
may be a special selection of works in his special field
which he does not otherwise have a chance to consider
in connection with one another. It may be a special
treatment of works already known by him in other con-

texts. It may be a treatment of works otherwise un-treated anywhere in the curriculum. It may be an adventure into a genre he has not tasted since his first year of general work. It may be a narrow subject or problem. The student also has a list in hand of faculty named for that year as available for "tutorials." The list indicates the interests and the special competences of each member on it. The small student group consults with the two or three faculty members of their choice, indicates to them their plan and interest. The instructor indicates his interest and competence—or lack of it. To-gether, they accommodate to each other's conditions and emerge, or not, with a plan agreeable to all. Then, depending on supply and demand, tutor and tutorial group strike a bargain with one another, or, each poten-tial tutor indicates his preferences among tutorial groups and each potential tutorial group files its plans and preferences with some central clearinghouse which matches, as far as possible, tutor and tutorial group.

This is, as indicated, an expensive device. It is not, however, as expensive as it may appear at first sight. The students are mature ones. They can read and they can administer their own time and they require neither interim tests nor examinations. There may be, in fact, no papers to be read by the tutor. The group meets then, infrequently, relaxedly but at some length, per-haps one late afternoon or long evening per week. This does not constitute a heavy tutorial burden.

Curricular Prescription 7: The Heart of the Matter

Whatever the scope for enquiry, for autonomous student work, for diversities of interest and talent we may choose to afford, it is still the case that the heart of the matter is scope for recovery of meaning and relation, for education of perception and sensibility, in materials traditional to the traditional fields of learning.

The science curriculum would be primarily concerned with science as problems sought and pursued. Its constituent elements would consist, not of facts so-called or of principles so-called, but of evidence and its interpretation. Lecture and textbook would speak of problems perceived or conceived, of the diversities of possible data which might lead to their solution, of those data actually sought and found, and of the interpretation of these data, with as much respect for the questionable aspects of the interpretations as for their more certain ones. Embedded in the necessarily large expanse of such exposition will be areas of depth in which the materials are not expositions and analyses duly expounded but matters requiring analysis and exposition by the student—primary reports of scientific enquiry on which students can practice and develop the arts of recovery concerned with discriminating problems, with identification and weighing of evidence, and with the critical noting of the principles and premises which give rise to problems and are involved in the interpretation of their data.

Much the same curricular pattern would characterize instruction in the social sciences. It too would be concerned with problems and their attempted solution, and with evidence and its interpretation. But because the subject matters of the social sciences are so much more complex than those of other sciences and so much less amenable to consensus on kinds of principles, problems and methods proper to the fields, the intellectually responsible curriculum in the social sciences will put much greater emphasis on "schools of thought" —diversities of ways of conceiving and solving problems—and expose to view the existence of competing resolutions of problems, alternative emphases, and the inevitable operation of bias.[5]

Similarly, education in the humanities would concern itself with its primary objects: novels, drama, music, and works of plastic art, treated in their particularity and not as instances of genera. It would be concerned to convey those competences which enable us to look at pictures instead of through them, to listen to music instead of being soothed by it, to find in works of literary art not only instruction but a high order of durable satisfaction, and to construct, with some clarity and niceness of distinction, communications of our own thought and experience.

Curricular Prescription 8: Examinations

Given the ugly start in schooling which most children suffer, it is not what a professor says which conveys what he expects of students, nor even what he himself is and does. It is what he asks for on examinations. In no useful sense, then, will our proposed curriculum exist—no matter what the planning, the staffing and teaching—unless conventional examinations are

5. It is also patently the case that the subject matters of the social sciences are loci of most of our practical problems and no amount of special pleading for their scientific purity does away with this brute fact: our practical problems are political, social, economic, psychological. Nor are students likely to be dissuaded by such special pleading from concern for these problems. Let them be raised, then, in connection with the theoretical problems which bear on them. But let them be treated with the same concern for the defensible, the same attention to the diversities of solution suggested by diverse researches, and the same attention to the incompleteness of each which we accord to the related theoretical materials.

changed in the appropriate direction and degree. The direction of change is all that can usefully be stated here. It amounts to this: they must be tests of what the student can do—not merely of what he knows.

Let us, again, use the humanities as our case in point, remembering that the sciences and the social sciences can be served analogously. Two weeks remain of the academic year (or one week of the semester, if semester examinations are envisaged). Formal class meetings have been adjourned. A work (or works) representative of the objects of the semester's search for meaning and discipline has been put into the hands of students as the basis of the examination. It is representative of the objects of the semester's search for meaning. It is accessible to the disciplines developed, identified, and exercised in that semester. The students need not be told what its purpose is because that purpose is a part of the regular function of the institution: it will be the target of problems, questions, challenges concerning its form and matter, its structure and sense, when students reassemble for examination. It will also be the focal point of problems of comparison with works examined during the formal meetings of the year—but *this* work (or works) has not been the subject of instructor-controlled scrutiny; it is new; it is fresh.

Students will obtain mastery of the set work in many different ways. Some will read solitarily. Some will join casually with one or two others to read, exchange questions and puzzlements, debate alternative readings, try to outguess the examiner. Still others will form groups of larger size—five, seven—to discuss the work in much the way similar works were discussed in the period past. Some will search out secondary

sources; others will avoid them. All of them know that
the faculty remains in its offices, available as consultants, ready to speak to well-put questions, supply ancillary information, even referee debates.

This runs counter, of course, to the tradition of examinations. Students are collaborating; they are cheating,
in fact; borrowing ideas from each other, criticisms,
tips, and caveats. Which is exactly the point. They are
doing on their own what we have taught them to do.
They are doing exactly what we do—unless we are poets
or egomaniacs—when we undertake a similar work,
for we, too, borrow ideas from colleagues and prede-
cessors (and it matters very little whether we seek their
help face-to-face or by way of their publications), and
seek from colleagues charitable enough to give it,
criticism of our thoughts and formulations. The examination, in short, is a continuation of the curriculum as
well as a certifying device.

(Rest assured, however, that as far as certification is
concerned, there will be ample scope for differentiating
the poor from the better from the best. The slavish
imitation of a secondary source will be patent—if the
faculty is as decently informed as it ought to be. The
naive construction in simple opposition to a secondary
source will be equally identifiable. The ingenious twist
which comes off and the one which does not come off
will be distinguishable from one another. The received
idea which has been digested and assimilated can be
told from the one which is parroted. In the brief and
technical language appropriate, there will be ample
range and variance.)

For the examination proper, students need not be
assembled in merely the traditional policed and lower-

ing way; if facilities exist, indeed, each student may have his own cubicle in which to work. In any case, students will not be crowded cheek by jowl but there will be ample room for each student's typewriter (if he uses one), for his marked and annotated copy of the set work, for his notes which he is free to bring with him. He will also be free to roam: to leave for a breath of air, a cup of coffee. What if he does exchange a few ironic or informing words with colleagues: whatever help they afford must be ingested and used by the recipient.

All this will function only if the questions are good ones. I can do little more than repeat the general rule: they must be tests of what the student can do. They will concern authorial devices in the set work and their effects. They will, if the work is of fiction, concern themselves with its characters and action, its plot, its scene, its "theme"; with any or all the elements of the work which the various disciplines imparted in the course have centered on. They will proffer critical treatments of the work and invite the student to respond to these as critic of them, say, or opponent. They may offer two such critical works and invite the students' attention to their systematic differences of principle and method and to what, in the set work, these differences of principle and method address themselves. They may invite juxtaposition of the set work with other works read in the course, require in the student the reaped grain of what transpired in the course of the year or semester. (They will not, however, hinge on remembrance of an incident, a character's name, his age at a moment in the work. In fact, procedures will ensure against such trivial handicaps to effective work by supplying them or by making copies of the books themselves available in the examination rooms.)

To end, these fruits of the students' education must, of course, be read well. Let us assume both the good will and the good mind of the reader: he does not know the one right approach, the one right answer to the examination problem posed. He is prepared to be edified, even entertained; he is prepared for a wide range of attacks on the problem and prepared to judge each one, not "on the curve," relative to other papers, but in its own right: how defensibly each problem question has been interpreted, how appropriate the student's attack on the question as interpreted, how well the attack is mounted and carried out, and with what clarity and distinction of statement. What remains to be said is a matter of technique best stated in the light of the following.

There is a second way in which traditional examination procedure is a barrier to effective education. It makes of the teacher a taskmaster and inquisitor, a giver and withholder of official marks of progress and success. It requires him to play propitiable god, policeman, and judge. We have proposed, on the other hand, a curriculum and a climate in which the faculty member is a possessor and imparter of disciplines in quite another sense: mentor, guide, and model; ally of the student against ignorance; participant with the student in high adventures into the worlds of intellect and sensibility. These two sets of roles—judge and advocate, enemy and friend—are poor companions. Judge and enemy almost inevitably consume the advocate and friend as far as students of college age are concerned. We would do well to minimize the predatory roles.

A number of devices suggest themselves, all center-
ing in two matters: who sets the examinations; who
"grades" them. With respect to the first problem, what
is wanted is separation within *particular* persons, as
they present themselves to students, of the roles of
teacher and inquisitor. The teacher of John Smith should
not be sole giver of the tasks on which John Smith is
judged.

One way to this outcome is obvious: let each question
put to the students be posed in alternate versions for
his choice. Thus, to continue the use of literature as
our model, a problem of major analysis of the set work
can name four or five sorts of critical analysis, from
which the student chooses one. A problem which relates
the set work to a work treated in the course can leave
to the student the selection of the latter work (restricted
in some degree or not, as the individual case requires).

But why not extend the idea of choice to its limit?
Let us suppose that the device of available faculty
during the reading period is formalized to the extent
of convening one meeting of each student group at the
period's halfway point. The student brings to this
meeting questions of two sorts: those he wishes answered as guides to his continued study; those he suggests as appropriate challenges for the examination.
As many of the latter as time permits are heard and discussed by the assembled students. They react to the ease
or difficulty of each. They scrutinize it for its appropriateness to their preparation and to the work to which
it is addressed. They repair its obscurity or ambiguity or
otherwise suggest amendments. They suggest additional
questions in turn suggested by those in hand. On his
own behalf and after the meeting is adjourned, the

instructor may make additional amendments or changes in the questions in hand and select from them some part of the examination (30, 50, 85 percent). Or the student group itself, by discussion and show of hands, may choose four or five of the questions proposed by the student group, and from these choices, the instructor in turn will choose two or three.

Where a course is taught by two or more persons (whether at different times or as a staff) other devices are available: a pool of questions from all members of the staff, grouped by kind, then each kind selected from by lot. Better still, perhaps, achieving something of the advantage of an independent examiner without his prime fault of remoteness from the course: the examination for the students of each instructor is chosen from the pool by other instructors of the staff; thus no instructor sits as examiner on his own students.

There are infinite variations on these two themes. I would plead only that some variant of each be used: some formulated and chosen by students, some by other members of the faculty.

With respect to the problem of who reads (and grades), similar devices are in order: in the case of staffs, no member reads the papers of his own students or is not sole reader; some students (selected by students) function as second readers (on papers held anonymously, of course) and differences of first and second judgment are adjudicated by discussion, and so on.

Finally, a word to indicate that the model holds for areas other than the literary. The set work in the case of science or the social sciences can be a research paper or a series of them, a monograph, a summary of recent

work in a field. Questions are addressed to the nature
of the problems treated, the soundness of methods for
obtaining data, their interpretation, the collation and
reconciliation of conclusions drawn. Questions can then
reach backward to relate the content of the set work
to relevant matters dealt with in the course—and for-
ward toward formulation of problems and methods for
solving them as agendas for future research. The set
work may also be not reports of the enquiries of others
but a problem to be attacked and solved in field or
laboratory, the report and the protocols of the student's
enquiry constituting the materials to be judged.

My personal inclination is to do away entirely with
the *terminal* examination and return to the very old-
fashioned, unscientific, unobjective business of judging
a student on the basis of his day-to-day contributions
to the course—oral contributions as well as written.
On the oral side, I have in mind his displays of courage
in entering new and untried territory, the kindness,
relevance, and usefulness displayed in the comments
he makes on others' contributions, his progress toward
speaking to the question and speaking to it well, his
growing competence for reflexive scrutiny of his own
contributions. On the written side, I have in mind
numerous small contributions (daily, perhaps) which
represent first forays into problems and, read before
the group, lay the basis for discussion; longer contributions which formulate the fruits of discussion and
carry them to additional problems; longest contributions of the sort described as grounding the final examination. (The institution of such a program would have
the added advantage of making more difficult the administrative tendency to increase the size of classes.)

Given such a procedure, I can imagine inviting the students of a group toward the end of a course to name those whom each feels has noticeably contributed to his own enlightment. I would request this participation in the form of a proportional representation ballot and take account of revealed consensuses in the assignment of grades. I suggest, however, that this be tried first only on a small scale: it is my experience that students often do not permit themselves to recognize the help they get from other students. Or one might, in view of this tendency, use student consensus only so far as it points to contributors and add to their recognitions one's own.

Curricular Prescription 9:   Overarching Disciplines and the Sampler

We have so far submitted docilely to the least examined and most pervasive of academic tyrannies: the principle of subject matter. The section on curricular resources, for example, speaks of arts of recovery and arts of enquiry, but the arts in question are arts constrained by subject matters. Each art of recovery seeks meanings embedded in a structure of knowledge dictated by principles and methods characteristic of a particular science or small group of them. Each art of enquiry is, similarly, an art controlled by principles and methods for investigation of some defined subject area.

A similar rule (or tyranny) of subject matter is visible in the problem treated in Curricular Prescriptions 3–7.[6] The problem itself arises from another principle—the student; but in these prescriptions solutions to the prob-

6. Pp. 197–216.

lem of diversity of talent among students is sought in terms of subject matter. In some cases, it is subject matter per se; the written word; clay, or bodily movement as matter subjected to pattern and shape by students' or others' creativity. In other cases, it is subject matter of enquiry: living things, the human past, cultures and societies, as subjects investigated by one or another science.

Indeed, the material of this book is shot through and through with signs of control by subject matter. The differentiation of the practical from other spheres as a special problem of student protest arises in a distinction of kinds of subject matter—the complicated, rich, and wayward particular as against the abstracted, idealized, or generalized referent of scientific knowledge. And treatment of other spheres everywhere depends on a distinction of subject matters: especially the subject matters of science, social science, the humanities.

The ubiquity of subject matter here attests to its potency as a principle as much as it reflects the habits of the academic community of which I am a part. Nevertheless, even here, there are signs of what other considerations make quite clear: that subject matter is not ineluctably a first principle of curriculum, not an objective given with which we must begin. (Subject matter as such must be distinguished, however, from knowledge of a subject matter, so far as curriculum is concerned. The latter—distinguishable bodies of knowledge pertaining to distinguished subject matters—to us *are* givens even though they were not given to the enquirers to whom we owe these bodies of knowledge. When we arrive on the scene, the bodies of knowledge have boundaries and internal structural characters which differentiate them from one another in ways which are extremely difficult to reorder. See the first part of Curricular Prescription 2, for example.[7])

What these signals portend is fairly obvious, once attended to. Either there are no natural joints in nature or, if there are, they do not everywhere coincide with the joints we have established between the fields of enquiry. The subject matters studied in the sciences of sociology and psychology have obvious connections with one another. The subjects of the physical and biological sciences touch and merge at more than one point. The subject matters of biology and psychology, biology and sociology, of the novel and of theories of personality, all interpenetrate. Indeed, it is clear that in the long course of human enquiry the separations and filiations of the sciences undergo changes from time to time, changes which are by no means obviously evolutionary or tending toward one climax (for example, merger). And one source of these changed connections and separations is clear enough: they arise from changes in the principles of enquiry of one or another field—concepts, models, which define the boundaries of a subject matter and specify elements and relations within it as directives to the enquiries which are to master it.

The fact that different subject matters are not inescapably there and the further fact that many of their differences are conferred by intellectual acts and inventions immediately suggest the possibility that some other principle for the organization of courses and curriculums, a principle which cuts across subject matters,

7. Pp. 192–94.

should be sought and tested. Four or five such have been conceived. Two of them have been recurrently successful in some hands, for some purposes, and on some students. One of these is the idea of generic arts or skills. The second is the idea of generic principles and methods. (These two often merge into one another and are rarely entirely distinct.[8])

One recurrent dream must be set aside before we can formulate a prescription which uses arts or methods as organizing principles, the dream of a panacea. This is the dream of a method of enquiry or of problem-solving or of a small set of arts, which can operate universally, on all subjects indifferently, which can be taught as an art or method (that is, in a generalized or simply generalizable form) and which, once learned, opens all doors, solves all problems. No mathematics or philosophy has yet proved that such a cure-all is impossible. But very little in the whole course of our

8. Others have been used less frequently and with less success. Fundamental ideas which cut across subject areas have been sought. For example, *freedom* and *control, individual* and *society, stability* and *change,* have been used to cut across the social sciences. *Chance* and *cause, art* and *nature, process, stability,* and *change, unity* and *diversity,* are among ideas used to organize the sciences generally. The utility of ideas as organizing principles has suffered from inherent difficulties—vagueness, slippery equivocations, mixtures of literal and metaphorical meanings—and also from incidental flaws, notably the tendency to use mere pairs, as in *freedom* and *control.* "Problems" have also been used to cut across fields, especially in the social sciences, where the search has been mainly for "practical" problems—conservation and use of resources, racial integration, maintenance of peace, conformity, and reform. Difficulties arise here from unnoticed impositions of questionable organizations of subject-matter areas (for example, the subordination of psychology to sociology-anthropology, or the reverse) and from hidden premises concerning the relations of theory to practice. In the 1930's, there was a brief flurry of efforts to organize by "area of living." That is, effort was made to draw from all fields the knowledge needed by the "citizen," the "consumer," the "husband and father."

intellectual history suggests that it is probable and much in the course of that history suggests that it is impossible, or, worse, delusive.

It appears to be impossible in the face of what seems to be the ineluctable fact of difference itself as a characteristic of thought, of action, of things. Men have generated widely different principles and methods, and many of them have worked to produce their different useful outcomes on one or another subject matter. Men have sought different ends and sought similar ones with different means, and the results have been different sorts of satisfactions received and praised by different men. A dog and a rock respond to different commands and reveal themselves to different questions. (There is similarity, too, of course, and we shall take account of it.)

The dangerously delusive character of a cure-all arises from the character of an art or method, whether it lays claim to universality or not. Any usable principle and method must, in the course of achieving effectiveness, define what a problem is and what a solution is. What then of other "problems" and other "solutions"? For a method which does not claim universality, there is a ready answer: they are problems and solutions appropriate to other methods, if such methods can be found. For the method which claims universality, there is an even readier answer: they are false problems and false solutions. If, then, a dominant institution of a culture with a highly efficient educational system at its command teaches the one true and universal method, it will realize its claim to universality: there will be no one to recognize its limitations—except heretics and the insane.

He exhibited the tone of mind which alone can maintain a free society, and he expressed the reasons justifying that tone. His *Dialogues* are permeated with a sense of the variousness of the Universe, not to be fathomed by our intellects, and in his Seventh Epistle he expressly disclaims the possibility of an adequate philosophic system. The moral of his writings is that all points of view, reasonably coherent and in some sense with an application, have something to contribute to our understanding of the universe, and also involve omissions whereby they fail to include the totality of evident fact. The duty of tolerance is our finite homage to the abundance of inexhaustible novelty which is awaiting the future, and to the complexity of accomplished fact which exceeds our stretch of insight.[9]

We are not concerned, then, with universal arts, principles or methods or even with highly general ones, but with generic ones. A generic principle, like an allegedly general one, can be given one name rather than many; it can be discussed as if it were all one piece; but it cannot be applied that way. In application, it must be specified to a subject matter, and to different subject matters it is specified in different ways. The subject matter, too, is a principle, determining how and to what extent the method, the art, the principle, can be applied.

Given these two, subject matter on the one hand, art or method and principle on the other,[10] there are two ways in which they can be usefully applied as principles of curriculum. First, we may choose to use subject matter as our organizing principle and discipline as our principle of emphasis or aim. This is the more familiar usage. Courses are named for their

9. Alfred Whitehead on Plato: from *Adventures of Ideas* (New York: Macmillan, 1933).
10. Hereafter, for the sake of economy, I shall use *discipline* as the covering name for principles-methods-arts.

subject matters (science, social studies, humanities, mathematics, history, literature); the materials of each course are drawn from a recognized field of enquiry and inform us concerning its subject matter.

They are not, however, studied merely for the information about their subject which they contain. They are also studied as instances of the use of disciplines. The information they contain is seen as arising from methods used and arts applied. These arts and methods are identified, their constituents noted, and their application scrutinized. When alternative attacks on a similar subject are examined, they yield perception of different principles and different methods applicable to that subject matter together with some idea of the differing strengths and weaknesses of different principles as applied to that subject matter.

These materials, are not, furthermore, merely studied. They are also confronted as occasions which evoke disciplines. Arts are used to discern their meanings, to perceive their arguments and their use of evidence —some of the arts of recovery. Still other arts of recovery are used to discriminate differences among them of principle, method, art. Then, when differences of "reading" are debated, additional arts are invoked—arts of expression and communication. When these debates in turn are subjected to reflexive scrutiny, still further arts are invoked and practiced—arts of rigorous formulation which record what has been done, in what order, why it was done, what was achieved—detection and formulation of the rules of the game, in short. Finally, when these rules are "broken," deliberately modified in order to bring them effectively to bear on different cases and new problems, arts of enquiry are invoked and practiced.

In the second usage of subject matter and of disciplines as principles of curriculum, the latter are used as principles of organization. Subject matter is used as a principle for the selection of material and the specification of the disciplines. Two examples will indicate what is involved here. The first uses principles and methods of restricted scope, and consists of a course for seniors. A fragment of its syllabus follows.

Senior Colloquium 3
Conceptions of Organisms as Principles of Enquiry

Part 1. The conception of typical whole and functional part

Readings:
1. Aristotle, selections from *Physics, Posterior Analytics, Generation of Animals, Parts of Animals*
2. T. Parsons and N. Smelser, *Economy and Society,* pp. 16–20, 46–51
3. William Harvey, *An Anatomical Disquisition on the Motion of the Heart and Blood,* chaps. 1–6
4. Clifford Geertz, *The Rotating Credit Association: A "Middle Rung" in Development*
5. Edward Shils and Michael Young, *The Meaning of the Coronation*
6. W. M. Fletcher and F. Gowland Hopkins, *Lactic Acid in Amphibian Muscle*

Part 2. The conception of the self-regulatory system

Readings:
1. J. S. Haldane, *Materialism* (selections)
2. J. Smith, *The Inverse Feedback System*
3. Boris Ephrussi, *Synthesis of Respiratory Enzymes in Yeast*
4. Paul Bohannon, *The Impact of Money on an African Subsistence Economy*

What is characteristic of such programs is also what is startling to the unaccustomed eye: the juxtaposition of apparent irrelevancies, of materials from widely different fields. A brief analysis of the materials of part 1 will indicate where the relevance lies.

Aristotle first outlines the notion of *species*, of the possibilities of groupings into natural kinds, and outlines an inductive method which will tentatively determine the nature of each kind. He then expounds the notion of a part of an organ as a well-adapted structure which has a function in the maintenance of the species. He then outlines the kinds of evidence pertaining to a part by which to determine—only probably, of course—its function.

Parsons and Smelser do much the same sort of thing for societies and social organs. They reproduce quickly the notion of organ and function, outline the characteristic problems of maintenance of a society toward which societal organs can be expected to function. The two accounts are not the same, partly because the authors are different authors, but partly because societies and biological organisms are not the same sort of thing, even as objects of enquiry treated at this general level. An examination of the differences are, then, extremely rewarding, both as examples of the art of constructing models for enquiry and as reflections of the subject matters to which they address themselves.

The remaining papers are concrete enquiries exemplary of the methods and principles described in the first two works. The Harvey and the Shils and Young are searches for the function of an identifiable part. The Geertz work is a search for the part which serves a known function in a special societal species. The Fletcher and Hopkins study is a similar research on the biological side. Each research taken singly exhibits some of the characteristic difficulties and rewards of research of this kind, and comparison of those addressed to biological systems and those addressed to social systems begins to show some of the different difficulties and rewards which characterize such research when applied to the different subject matters. Comparison undertaken in another vein begins to exhibit some of the crucial differences and similarities of the two subject matters and raises questions of their relationship—that is, of the extent to which biological organisms which are also social are determined by the structure in which they are parts and, on the other hand, the extent to which social structures are reflections of the needs and characteristics of the organisms which constitute them. Of particular importance is the complication introduced into the study of social systems by the necessity for taking account of intelligence, and of the possibility of deliberate and voluntary action on the part of its units and organs.

A second example, designed as a course for entering students, uses arts of very broad scope. One fragment of its syllabus follows.

Liberal Arts B
The Control of Conclusions

Part 1. Accounts: Their control by coherence and plausibility

Readings:
  1. Akut Ogawa, *Rashomon*
  2. Albert Einstein, *Physics and Reality*
  3. Sigmund Freud, *The Ego and the Id*

In this example, the relevance of the apparently disparate is established by arts rather than by such a concrete conception as that of organ and·function. The Einstein paper is a description and a praise of the invention and construction of coherent system as the aim of science, or at any rate, of physics. He first indicates the extent to which even the most ordinary-seeming "fact" is the product of a conception and given significations independent of sense impressions: "The first step toward establishing a 'real, external world' consists, in my opinion, in the construction of the concept of a 'bodily object' or of bodily objects of various kinds." He affirms as a mystery that the totality of sense impressions can be ordered by thinking and proceeds then to a careful and detailed account of the kind of ordering by thinking which physics imposes on its sense impressions. In the course of this account he suggests the arts involved in imposing such an ordering and states the criteria by which the products of these arts are to be judged.

The Ego and the Id is an exhibition, step by step, of the erection of a similar structure. Freud sets forth a fact or two and considers, as if musing aloud, alternative structures to contain them, examines the plausibility of each, chooses one. He moves on to additional facts, invents new notions to embrace them, then adjusts the fit of the new notions to those earlier devised. As the work proceeds, the structure grows more and more complex, of course, thus providing increasing scope for exhibiting the arts involved.

Freud controls his construction by rules quite different from those of Einstein and takes a different view of the status of the finished product. For Ein-

stein, a central aim is greatest economy, hence he begins with all the "facts" he proposed to subsume and
seeks the fewest possible and most embracing concepts. Freud, on the other hand, proceeds from a few
facts to a few more, hence from concept to concept,
locating additional concepts to provide coherence.
Einstein recognizes his coherent system as *imposing*
order and meaning on the constituent sense impressions. Freud, by contrast, seems to say that he *finds*
his meanings and connections in the facts. The work
of examining the Freud in the light of the doctrine
espoused by Einstein would lead, then, to discovery
of two varieties of coherence, different arts by which
to construct them, different views of the status of the
finished article; students' search for the differences
and similarities and their effort to systematize them
would use still other ways of constructing coherence.

Finally, *Rashomon* displays with frightening effectiveness the extent to which "the facts" of a case can
be given radically different signification in widely different but equally plausible, equally coherent accounts.
It does so, of course, with facts about persons and
persons' lives. Seen against Freud's work, this raises
questions about the different kinds of facts which can
claim to represent human life and the different kinds
of orderings to which the facts will submit; problems,
again, about coherence and plausibility. Seen against
Einstein's work, it raises questions about the singular-
ity or plurality of truth (whether of man or of inanimate
nature) and raises in a different way questions about
the various kinds of knowing.

A word of warning is in order. Very good courses
resting on arts or on principles and methods of en-

quiry as their organizing principle are generated only if difficult conditions are fulfilled. The set of arts or the array of principles and methods employed must be well founded. First, the whole set of principles and methods must, as a set, encompass the enquiries of the fields to which they are applied. Second, the principles and methods, severally, must each be clear, distinct, and concrete. Each must be comprehensible as a conception of the matter to which it is applied and distinguishable from other conceptions. Each must be understandable in terms of the evidence it requires, how that evidence is to be elicited and how, once found, the evidence is to be interpreted. A set of arts must be equally well grounded, encompassing the whole of the process by which it effects its results and distinguishable into the acts and sequences of acts by which it achieves its ends.

An effective set of arts poses an additional requirement. Principles and methods are necessarily sought in fields of enquiry as they exist and, when mastered by students, become tools for doing what is done in the fields of enquiry. Arts, on the contrary, are not as tightly bound to what has been done; they enjoy a degree of freedom which permits to them another function—to begin to enable students, future enquirers, to do what the fields of enquiry do not now do, in short, to be relevant to unfulfilled needs of our time. Since our time is a time of specialism, of numerous walled cities which separate enquirers as well as enquiries and their fruits, the present need is for arts which will effect communication among the cities— begin to discern dependencies among fields as they now exist and repair some of the divorces which they have entailed. (Especially poignant among these divorces are, on the one hand, the divorce of the rational and the affective, and, on the other, the divorce of thought and action—the two ruptures toward whose healing this book is directed.)[11]

Unfortunately, the principles and methods of enquiry into enquiry by which arrays of principles and methods are sought and formulated are not now widely used—nor the arts by which sets of relevant arts are discriminated and described. There is, therefore, no large number of taxonomies and descriptions of principles, methods, arts, which will make it easy to design courses and programs using them as organizing principles.[12]

Since the desirable scholarly base is lacking, I do not suggest that we engage wholesale in the ad hoc and necessarily irresponsible development of whole programs organized by arts and principles. I do commend, for reasons to be given presently, one such course, placed at a particular moment in the student's career—experiment perilous though it be.

I commend, further, initiation of a substantial number of collaborative enquiries—pooling talents of philosopher, sophisticated subject-matter specialists, and curriculum theorists—aimed at the disclosure and detailed description of overarching disciplines of this sort.

11. In this paragraph *arts* has a special sense. Arts, in general, are the acts and processes by which principles and methods are applied. In some moments in intellectual history, however, some arts are arts in a special sense: acts and processes whose principles and methods are unformulated or lost to sight. They are nascent or renascent principles and methods.

12. But see, as one fine though necessarily general treatment, Richard McKeon's "Character and the Arts and Disciplines," *Ethics*, January 1968. See as a lesser instance, pertaining to principles in a restricted field, my "What Do Scientists Do?" *Behavioral Science*, January 1960.

There are, then, two sorts of courses or programs which arise from differing use of subject matter and discipline as curricular principles. One arises from use of subject matter as the organizing principle and of discipline as the principle of emphasis and aim. The other is generated by disciplines used as organizing principles, and subject matter as a principal of selection and specification. Each kind of course has its special advantages and omissions, most of them complementary.

Among the advantages of organization by subject matter are these. First, there is a resource for reasonably firm and evidenced disclosure of what relevant principles and methods exist—indeed, a criterion by which relevance is determined. Second, these well-grounded patterns of principles and methods lay a foundation for confidence in the soundness of the patterns of art we develop in their service. Third, each one of the group of arts in question can be brought to a relatively high state of development in students in the time allotted, since they are a restricted set and practiced only on the subject matters to which they are immediately applicable. Fourth, discovery by students of the principles and methods, and practice of the arts which discover them, occur in and through enquiries characteristic of the field, hence in and through substantial portions of the bodies of knowledge they have produced. Discovery of principles and methods, mastery of the arts pertaining to them, and mastery of the knowledge of a subject matter go hand in hand and illuminate and facilitate one another. (Please note that arts of recovery—one of the overarching disciplines—are involved here as well as arts pertaining to use of the principles and methods recovered. It is *not* one of the weaknesses of this mode that it excludes overarching disciplines.) Finally, there is the practical advantage involved: that the development of such programs and their application in the classroom must begin with specialists, and specialists are in good supply.

The weaknesses of this mode are as follows. It provides minimal preparation for coping with novelty, even the novelty which may arise within a recognized subject field. This weakness is inherent, since the principles and methods involved are those characteristic of the field as it now exists and the arts involved apply principles and methods to the subject matter as it currently appears in the light of present knowledge in the field. A fortiori, this mode provides little or no ground for transfer, that is, for systematic analogizing of principles and methods as seen in one field to effective operation in another. (As an amusing consequence of this failure, note the extent to which "analogy" is so often prefaced by "mere" and conceived as an epithet by persons trained only in this mode, rather than understood and practiced as a technique of systematic transapplication. The pejorative is right; most of the analogies constructed by such persons are naive comparisons and not systematic transapplications.) Another weakness consists in the fact that though overarching disciplines of recovery are involved, they are involved as applied only to one subject matter at a time. There is no time and no place in which there can be reflexive scrutiny of what is involved as the discipline is moved from one subject matter to another. Hence, there is only accidental mastery of these arts as overarching; they are practiced first in one place, then another, but what is involved in moving them is not brought to light. Finally, and of greatest importance to our purposes here, this mode precludes any systematic use of arts which aim to discover the relations which exist or which can be induced among various subject areas—the arts which make possible recognition and repair of divorces.

The strengths of the second mode are the complements of the weaknesses above. Organization by disciplines provides for continuing confrontation by novelty (the "irrelevances" which are so striking in the examples cited), and transfer is of its essence. All disciplines involved are overarching, are practiced as such, and provide occasion for mastering and understanding the ways in which they are translocated. Finally, discovery and induction of connections among subject fields are inescapably involved.

The weaknesses of the second mode are similarly presaged. The necessary sets of arts are hard to come by. Then, as soon as they are brought reasonably well to bear on one kind of subject material, they are transferred to another. Finally, they do not entail any substantial mastery of the subject fields on which they are brought to bear. Indeed, they tend away from such mastery and easily breed disdain for well-grounded knowledge.

In summary, then, the first mode is conservative of what is known and done; it tends toward expertise and reliability. The second is innovative and frontier; it tends toward variety and the untried. The pathology of the first is stodginess. The pathology of the second is cleverness.

It will long since be patent that most of the prescriptions suggested so far are in the first mode. Since
all curriculum problems are practical, the reasons for
this choice are practical: grounded in considerations
concerning students, teachers, and the times. Specialism is with us and unlikely to go away, short of de-
bacle. Our accumulated lore will come to us from
specialties; it will be increased only as we participate
in their disciplines; they can be criticized and their
obiter dicta identified only as we know their principles
and methods. Practical problems reach us embodied
in technologies which the specialties have initiated;
hence even practical problems require something of
the lore and the disciplines of the specialties. Coping
with and contributing to the specialties require many
men; a few frontiersmen go a long way, and a few
innovations at a time are all we can usefully assimilate.
(But see the quotation from Couzzens, Practical Prescription 2.)

These are also, however, precisely the reasons why
some smaller part of the curriculum should be in the
second mode. Pervasive specialism unexamined creates in students the illusion from which we all suffer
to some degree—the illusion that subject matters as
now distinguished are the inevitable products of natural divisions. There is little grasp of the vicious diremptions created by the divisions, less grasp of the
idea that the diremptions might be repaired and no
suggestion of the arts by which the separated can be
related and the ground laid for repair of diremptions.
If, then, we are involved in a collegiate program with
four "general" courses, let one of them be in the second mode. If there is an eight-course (two year) gen-

eral program, let there be a thread in the second mode
extending through both years.

It is important to note that this is not only the
commendation of a thread in the second mode but
also commendation of a special place for it—as part
of the *initial* collegiate experience of the student. This
recommendation stems from some of our earliest diagnoses. The peculiar (unexpected) juxtaposition of subject matters imposed by an organization by disciplines
exhibits each subject matter in a strange new light.
What the former experience of the student taught him
to take as the defining properties of each subject are
separated from one another, and some of them are
given new places in the whole constellation of qualities
which characterize the work. Other qualities, formerly
subordinated or entirely lost in the background, are
made conspicuous. A biological work, for example,
ceases to be merely "a lot of facts about the heart"
and becomes an adventure in the application of a
conception of the nature of things. Yet the facts remain. Indeed, they do more than "remain" for the
student who may have learned a dislike for biology.
They become facts with a special meaning—facts made
relevant by a principle of enquiry, and facts with meanings assigned by the principle. In brief, an organization by disciplines will, for a remarkably large number
of students, breach the walls of accidental or fantasied
dislikes and open the door to the trial of competences
which might otherwise never be tested.

Second, the new character assigned to subject materials by their place in a disciplinary structure entails
new demands on the student in the course of recovery
of meaning. A fictional work, for example, is not now to

be read as primarily an unfolding of character, a plot structure, a reflection of a time, place or people, but as, let us say, a massive example of the ambiguity of fact (for example, Lermontov, *A Hero of Our Time*) or of the art of conferring coherence and plausibility (*Rashomon*). Consequently, the assignment and discussion of such a work in such a context constitutes one of the best of situations to elicit and make visible (to student as well as instructor) the habits of mind, the cognitive structures, which tyrannize individual students in their intercourse with materials of one kind or another. (In this process, there is not only a diagnosis of constraining cognitive structures but a beginning of flexibility, a move toward pluralism, toward the ability to treat a polyvalent work in terms of several of its valences.)

The close juxtaposition of subject matters and the comparisons this propinquity affords constitute a third advantage. In conjunction with other first courses organized by subject matters, they provide an extensive experience of what different subject areas demand by way of competence and interest; what scope these areas afford for the exercise of competences; what arts, principles, and methods exist, through which competences can be realized and used. In short, they constitute for the student a sampler of himself, of fields, of disciplines, in relation to one another, which will go far toward removing the opacity of electives and the blind chanciness of decision about fields of concentration.

Fourth, and of considerable importance, the inclusion of such a thread as an initial experience of the student dramatically marks his passage from "school" to "college," from "learning" to "mastery," and signals to him his induction into a "different" culture and community. Such a passage, appropriately felt, is a potent means for marshaling energies and constituting membership in the service of the collegiate community. (I assume, of course, that the induction will not be a fake, that whether disciplines function as organizing principles or as principles of emphasis and aim, they will continue to function throughout the curriculum.)

A closing word on this matter. Two patterns are available for the organization of materials by disciplines, as indicated by the two examples. One can organize by principles and methods ("Senior Colloquium 3") or by arts ("Liberal Arts B"). The latter is to be preferred in the present context: it permits relations among much more widely disparate subject matters (scientific investigation, a novel) than principles and methods are likely to afford.

I suggest the use of arts, despite the attendant difficulties and despite the weaknesses which are likely to ensue. A relevant grouping of arts must be constructed by the faculty which intends to use them—since a ready-made set is not available, and, if it were, could be conveyed, as arts, only by persuading faculties to use them and master them. But since the art of constructing sets of arts is itself involved in the effective use of arts as principles of instruction, the well-discussed plan evolved by any faculty would be a useful beginning. The course which evolved from such a plan would, doubtless, have its intervals of failure. So be it: if the course is seen by students as the brave experiment it is, they will profit as much from the spectacle of professors risking their "dignity," and daring to learn again as well as teach, as they may lose because of the weak spots in the plan.

Curricular Prescription 10: Curriculum in the Curriculum

Our curriculum is intended to be a corporate intellectual adventure engaging faculty and students jointly. It is an adventure pursued in part for its fruits —the meanings found, the lore mastered—but these fruits constitute only one of its purposes. It is pursued also to discover for students the intellectual life as one of the real lives that some men live and as one of the threads which can be woven into most lives. It is pursued as a sustained discovery of each adventurer's diverse capacities for such a part of life. It is pursued as a means for developing these potentials and for savoring the satisfactions of their development and use. Finally, it is pursued *jointly*. Student and student, student and instructor, instructor and instructor—combined one to one and corporately—discover that they are necessary to the adventure and discover the satisfaction of such joint adventures. The intellectual adventure is, in short, the defining reason of the collegiate community.

The collegiate community cannot, then, without self-destruction, set irrational limits to the use of reason, and one of the remarkable paradoxes of reason consists in the fact that it is a proper subject of itself. Rational activity is itself accessible to rational scrutiny. We can not only think but think about our thinking. Such thought about thought is visible and commonplace in most scholarly areas. The scientist rethinks his argument from evidence to conclusion (and his rules of argument). He similarly examines the arguments of other scientists. The humane critic examines the premises, the emphases, and the distinctions which ground his work and the work of fellow critics. The economist retraces the selected starting points, targets and pathways by which he infers the effects of selected changes on the economic system as a whole.

Such thought about thinking is, however, notably uncommon and invisible in the one place which matters most to the collegiate community—its curriculum. As far as students are allowed to see, the curriculum is not a subject of thought; it merely is. In many cases, indeed, thought about curriculum is not merely invisible; it barely occurs. Single courses are sometimes the outcome of single happy thoughts but are rarely accorded the reflexive, critical scrutiny we give as a matter of duty and right to our "scholarly" productions. Their origins are left obscure and their outcomes only occasionally examined. Sequences and groupings of courses are sustained by tradition and inertia and only rarely examined. Least of all do we worry about our sins of omission, the courses we do not give, the outcomes we do not seek.

This grand omission requires correction. The curriculum which is a joint intellectual adventure will include itself as part of that adventure. One of its subjects will be itself, and this subject, like all other subjects which it treats, will be accessible to the critical scrutiny of its celebrants—faculty and students, separately and together—each in the fashion appropriate to its competence. I have in mind the following devices.

The "confidential guide." This suggestion is borrowed in part from Harvard and in part from the procedure of certain consumer-testing organizations.

A small group of responsible senior students, such as the senior editors of the campus newspaper, annually prepare and present to other upperclassmen a questionnaire concerning the freshman and sophomore courses they have taken. The questions concern the quality and character of lectures, readings, discussions. They ask how well the student "did" in the course, what he got out of it, what he hoped for and failed to find. Other, less structured questions leave scope for additional comments on the courses involved and evoke some signs of the character, interests, competences, and prejudices of the student answering the questionnaire.

From the responses on each course, the editors abstract an approximate estimate of the course—what it does; what it does *to* students; what kinds of students profit much, profit little; what specific strengths and weaknesses it may exhibit. The result is not a merely statistical summary of responses or mechanical grading of the courses but a description (and not a curt one) of the course as seen through student eyes, including, of course, the eyes of the editors.

This description is sent to the faculty member or staff responsible for the course with an invitation to respond. The instructor responds or not, as he sees fit. (The numbers of respondents and nonrespondents among faculty are sufficiently well balanced as to constitute no pressure in either direction.) His response may be an announcement of changes in matters noted in the review, a statement of reasons for certain aspects dwelt on in the description. In any case, the instructor is asked to limit his response to a magnitude approximately half that of the original description.

Finally, the editorial description of each course together with the comment of its instructor are collated and published as a "confidential guide" available to students and to faculty.

The effectiveness of such a device depends on the quality of the faculty as well as the competence of the student editors involved. Assuming a faculty which is neither insecurely defensive nor overanxious to curry favor, the long-term effect is likely to be a very good one and unlikely to be disastrous. If estimates prove to be badly prejudiced or mistaken, student-clients of the guide will learn to take it lightly and faculty will ignore it. If estimates are persuasive in their adducing of evidence and argument, students will take its estimates into account and faculty will be properly sensitive to the information it conveys. (They will also be sensitive to the reactions of other faculty. That is, the faculty pied piper will know that his colleagues may identify him as such; the faculty member who panders to student whim will be similarly advised.)

The valuation session. This too is a well-tried device, though not yet widely used. (It is also a painful one.)

At the last session of a seminar or small-group course, the instructor retires from the chair (but not from the room), invites the group to name a chairman and undertake a discussion, an evaluation, of their just completed educational experience. Unless the course is exceptionally bad or superlatively good, what ensues is remarkably enlightening (and traumatic) on important matters which would otherwise rarely be brought to light. The instructor discovers evidence of his behaviors and their results of which he was unaware. He discovers how small some candles were which threw bright beams and how dim was the light thrown by some he thought were large. He discovers a remarkable variety and independence of thought among students: there is rarely consensus and, often, bitter debate on some critical matters raised by them; and they rarely take the occasion to flatter the instructor. He may discover, too, how wide of the mark has been his estimate (low or high) of the preparation and readiness of students for what he has tried to do for them and to them in the course.

At the end of the session the instructor, if he is wise, makes no rejoinder to criticisms made. He may thank a student or two for especially precise and well-judged comment. In any case, he will thank the group as a whole and depart.

Self-evaluation. We rarely hear ourselves, and in the course of the complex structuring and acute attention to students involved in the effective conduct of discussion—debate and reflexive scrutiny of debate—we are rarely able to. Why not, then, the simple mechanical help of the portable tape machine?

The taping of one or a selected few sessions will not suffice. We will almost inevitably "prepare" for the taping or be acutely affected by consciousness of its operation. If, however, a whole sequence of discussions is taped—the first or last third of a course, for example—these handicaps are overcome. (Even the intimate and confidential exchanges of psychothera-peutic sessions are uninhibited by the machine after the first few sessions.) At the end of the sequence (and not before!) one settles down in privacy to discover what one has done. I shall refrain from comment on what one hears. Suffice it to say that it is often em-barassing and usually salutary.

There is a second use of such tapes. Each instructor who has taped a sequence selects from the lot the one or two whose intellectual or interpersonal structure (not style, not dramatic flavor, not tour de force) he considers to be especially good, especially appropriate to its materials, or especially effective with students. The group of collaborating instructors who have taped their sessions then meet for a series of evenings to hear and comment on each other. The instructor whose tape is to be considered introduces his effort, runs the machine, and interpolates his judgment of the reasons for and the effects of what the tape reveals. He stops and replays to emphasize a crucial or subtle point. He stops on request to hear others' comments on what has just transpired.

There are two benefits from such a device. The os-tensible benefit is to the instructor whose work is heard and commented on. The more important benefit is to the other instructors. Under the cover of the commen-tary, adverse and complimentary criticism of the tape, they are able to take note of what others do which they have not done and to profit from their example.

The working group. We are again concerned with a device which is well tried but only spottily used. Prescription 9 ended with a staff which invents a set of arts and, under each one, juxtaposes works from disparate subject areas which exemplify the art or require it as part of the process of recovery. A course so designed is not likely to be a good one, since the arts which organize will not have been well possessed by the faculty until experienced by them in the preparation and execution of the discussions of the works under examination. The course, then, will be a course of discovery for faculty as well as students.

One assumes, of course, that the end of the first offering of this course will be the beginning of a better one: reflection on what was done, on its appropriateness to student needs, on the appropriateness of the works to the arts which examined them, and of the arts to the array of books so treated.

The open existence of such curricular experiments—*open* not in the naive sense of an "open" meeting of a Senate committee, but unhidden, a matter of course, informally reported to students, even, as I shall presently indicate, conducted with the help of selected students, will be one of the surest guarantors of the existence of an intellectual community and one of the very important ways of communicating its existence to students.

The professor's professor. The devices suggested so far are largely bootstrap operations. They tend to permit a view of the curriculum only in its own light and criticism of it only against the standards it establishes. In this respect, it is much like a course organized by subject matter and aimed at the disciplines characteristic of the subject field: it suffices for mastery and en-largement of the fields as they now exist but provides no mechanism for criticism of their roots.

(It is worth noting that the same point applies to student demands for control of curriculum—they can see only the errors and omissions which their education has so far taught them to see.)

This limit on self-criticism does not hold entirely. In the case of subject fields, subject matters and principles seasonally confront one another so as to betray incoherencies between them, thus leading to the invention of new principles and the shift of boundaries among subject matters. A similar confrontation will operate for an alert faculty in the case of course organizations. An invented set of arts and a selection of works presumably illuminated by these arts confront one another and similarly bring to light inadequacies in both. And both these processes are abetted by a working group which cherishes the diversities of mind within it and heeds what the diversities reveal.

Nevertheless, the operation of this historical dialectic is slow and chancy. It can profit from a device which speeds it. The professor's professor is such a device.

His qualifications are these. He is retired or about to be and possesses no administrative power. He is, therefore, neither threat nor competitor of the remainder of the faculty. Second, he is from a tradition at variance from that in which the remainder of the faculty was trained. This is in part assured by his age. It is better assured by an origin materially variant from that of most others of the faculty—German-, French- or English-trained, let us say, if the remainder of the faculty is mostly American. Third, he will have known a wide variety of curriculums—by observation, participation, or invention—in different kinds and qualities of institutions. Fourth, he will be a learned man and an ironic one—anxious neither to please or reform. He will not be easy to come by but he is not as scarce as hen's teeth.

He will function in two ways, one private, one public.

His private function will be to advise and suggest— as asked and only when asked by individual faculty and staffs. He will hear their present plan. He will then point to lacunae otherwise unperceived, warn of weaknesses, suggest alternatives. Precisely because of his variance in age, tradition, and learning, he will be only half-understood in some cases and rejected in most. Thus he will be protected against the risk of becoming a curricular czar. This insurance will be doubly underwritten by his irony: he will not return to discover whether and how his advice was taken—again, unless he is asked. Nevertheless, what was half-understood will be seminal and what was rejected is likely to germinate later. It will reappear in "modern" form from the cogitations of the man who half understood, or take on cogency from experience with what was adopted in its stead.

His public function will be to dissect and criticize the curriculum. He will offer one course—open only to seniors. That course will do on a grand scale and with reference to the whole curriculum of the institution what reflexive scrutiny does on a smaller scale to segments of debate. It will identify what has been done, its premises and likely outcomes. It will describe alternatives which exist in other times and places; what they assume and what they achieve. In consequence, it will illuminate for students (to some degree, at any rate) what has been done to them and what has been left undone.

By opening the course only to seniors, it is restricted to those who have undergone the experience which is under examination. This restriction also ensures against subversion, since these are mainly the persons who will no longer plague the remainder of the faculty. Meanwhile, however, the faculty will know that the course is given. They will know that some of their students will hear it. They may even attend themselves. It will constitute an institutional cherishing of diversity.

There are, of course, smaller ways in which part of his function can be performed. The philosophy program will import a visitor who pursues philosophy in quite another key. The literary critics will invite a lecturer whose doctrine is opposed to theirs. The psychology grounded in Freud or behaviorism will play host to a cognitive theorist. "New" political scientists will invite lectures on Plato and Burke; old ones will sponsor a treatment of game theory. In their later curricular plans, they may even succumb, in part, to the deviant alternatives.

Finally, let there be intramural competition and controversy about curriculum. Embody competition in the courses of branching pattern described in Prescription 4 and at later levels of the curriculum in distinctly alternative courses. But let the competition be informed—not another regressive instance of opaque electives—by ensuring public debate, discussion, or advocacy of alternatives by their proponents—discussion designed for the information and enlightenment of the student who will choose among them.

THE "COMMUNITY" PRESCRIPTIONS 5

It will be obvious that "community" is not a new topic here. The community I envisage has been abuilding from early in this book—from the first interpretation of a fact of protest behavior as pointing to a specified ill of the collegiate body. This anticipation is inherent to the principles and methods by which curriculums are made and altered: a notion of health is necessarily involved in any diagnosis and prescription, and a defensible conception of health in turn is necessarily grounded in knowledge of the sort of body with which one is working.

It is equally obvious, however, that a body politic, a human association, complicates the biologic metaphor. A human association is not entirely "by nature." It need not be taken wholly as it is, nor its health conceived as merely a statistical norm. It can be altered in some directions and in some degree. Equally, a human association is, in part, "by nature," is not wholly subject to our wishes and the whims of artifice. The character of its material units—persons—makes some changes difficult and invites others. Its circumstances—especially what it suffers and does in transactions with other human associations—set additional limits and elasticities. Its history, as embodied in its internal and external institutional structures and in the memories and habits of its constituent persons, constitute other limits and elasticities. What we must be clear about, then, is not ideals or dreams—the brotherhood, the Gemeinschaft of some protest students and their professional attendants, for example. Nor is it alleged historical-social determinations—Clark Kerr's multiversity as conceived by some, or community-, region- or state-scaled conglomerates as conceived by many others. What we need to be clear about is what we here take to be the movable and the relatively immovable facts of the case; what is possible, therefore (as far as community is concerned), and what among the possibles is desirable.

Community Prescription 1: Society

We take it, in the first place, that a college or university is a society and not a brotherhood. It is constituted of differentiated groups or classes and not one body of peers. There are professors. There are students. There are administrators. There are nonacademic employees. As in any society, these differentiated groups come into being and exist—or ought to exist—for the well-being and effective functioning of the others. If students are to be educated, teachers must teach; and if teachers are to teach, someone else, administrators and nonacademic employees, must supply the necessary conditions of their work—to take only one way around the circle. If professors are to do their work (maintain mastery of the crafts of teaching and mastery of the arts of enquiry in their fields), students must respect their privacies and administrators must find them their needed resources—to take another way around. If administrators are to keep the wheels oiled, obtain needed resources, mend the lanes and fences between the college and its neighbors, respond to the urgent, maintain balance and conversation among the college parts, their limitations of time and energy must be respected and they must be accorded powers commensurate with their responsibilities. (I am moved to take this last way around the circle by a moment's sympathetic pang for what may be the loneliest of collegiate classes.)

Each such group will serve effectively only as its differences from other groups are preserved, for these differences constitute their special competence, their expertise. It follows, then, that legitimate differences of interest exist among the group members of a society, since each role generates its peculiar needs. Hence, as I suggested early,[1] the community of a college as a whole lies in honoring and taking fullest account of the diversities of interest, talent, experience, and habits of thought which constitute its human resources. The satisfactions of community arise, first, from the favors each group receives in virtue of these differences and, second, from the immediate experience of these differences themselves and of their effect on one's own operations. The community proper to a college is, then, a community of collaboration, and the problem of community, for the college as a whole, is not to remove these differences but to use them and enjoy them. (As I shall indicate presently, the same kind of useful differences exist within as well between the constituent groups of the college, though not to the same degree. Hence, here too collaboration as distinct from brotherhood is a desideratum, though not the only one.)

It is true that some societies in some circumstances enjoy moments of incandescence—become virtual

1. Diagnosis 3, pp. 25–28.

brotherhoods as far as the subjective side is concerned. Such moments arise when a society successfully overcomes a surpassing danger or when an artist among them supplies a great celebration of such a victory. These are moments to be treasured. (So much so, indeed, that some have suggested that a society *requires* periodic assault or threat in order to survive.) It is also the case, however, that such moments cannot be sustained. It is beyond the capacity of the persons involved as well as of the society: after ecstasy, exhaustion; after celebration, return to work.

There is another social rhythm between brotherhood and collaboration. The members of the college fan outward in the mornings to collaboration. They return at evening and the weekend with victories to be sung, wounds to be licked, weaknesses to be supported (and, in the case of students, nostalgias to be survived). Some of these occasions are best served by brotherhoods within collegiate classes—student and student, professor and professor. Some are best served by moments of brotherhood across collegiate classes— professor and administrator, student and professor. The latter is emphatically the case for many of the weaknesses, wounds, and nostalgias of students and some of their victories. These are served best, if at all, not by the peer friend or by the official friend or the paid friend (counselor and psychiatrist) but by the professor or one who stands in the professor's stead—at least in the case of an effectively collaborative college. For in the collaborative college, many of these needs for friendship arise from the growing-up involved: the emulation of professorial models, the explorations of competence, and the trials of strength instigated by professors. Only the professor, then, knows well enough what is involved to be trusted by students to give knowing support.

If these friendship needs (student-to-student as well as student-to-professor) are not well served, the college will not function well. Hence it is part of the legitimate business of the college to see that they are served. The times, the place and the circumstances of refreshment, gaiety, domicile, rest, and the sharing of food must facilitate the friendships of student and student—not all meals in the uproar of a cafeteria feeding thousands, not all meetings in fishbowls, but, rather, adequate occasions and places for privacy and intimacy.

The desirability of privacy and intimacy touches a wide range of institutional facilities and operations. It involves the design of student unions—numerous small rooms, small tables in snack bars, nooks and corners, chairs and sofas with high backs. It involves the government of dormitory visiting hours—well into the night and without discrimination as to sex (since many "brotherhoods" will be between boy and girl and since the shadow of childhood bedtimes and imposed coming-home times confer on late hours an evocative power and flavor which we over thirty tend to forget). It involves the availability of community kitchens in dormitories, since the joint preparing of food and the sharing of it constitute a secular communion of the first order. It involves the encouragement—the subsidy, if necessary—of off-campus and distinctly non-campus meeting places. I have in mind not only the inexpensive small restaurant, coffee house, and beer joint but the record shop where snobberies and cults—from Schnabel revivals to hard rock—can arise and recruit, and the secondhand bookshop with dusty aisles for talk and browsing. It involves, wherever possible, the provision of appropriately rundown apartment buildings for upperclass student housing. Such apartments should provide privacy for each sharing student (two, three, four); above all, and whether college-owned or not, they must provide to the student lessee the same rights, powers, and responsibilities over his domicile accorded any lessee in any building. (Such facilities—and the matter of dormitory hours—obviously raise the "problem" of sex. In considering it, we ought to remember that it will be a "problem" for the young with or without apartments and visiting hours.)

We shall examine later the question of the student's faculty friend. Let it suffice for now that the freedoms of reaction professors accord themselves in collaborative transactions with students (not always remote, generic, polite) will go farthest toward rendering the professor appropriately accessible when the student's need is great enough.

Despite their importance, friendships and brotherhoods are only the ancillary business of the college— remedial, supportive. Its central community remains a community of collaboration (indeed, one of the aims of its collaboration is to help wean students from their nostalgias and from too great need for brotherhood), and the precedence of collaboration over brotherhood is one of the immovable facts of collegiate sociality.

There are social movables too, and one especially to our purpose: the groups which constitute a society— and specifically, the groups which constitute the collegiate society—need not exist in a single hierarchy, or in a hierarchy at all, in many circumstances. It is not true that the work of the collegiate community is best performed by a fixed constellation of these groups, for properly speaking it is not work but *works*, different kinds of needs perennially to be met and different kinds of problems perennially to be solved. In different sorts of work, the groups can play different roles to the advantage of the quality of the work.

There are two reasons, indeed, why it is desirable that there be such shifts of role, even at the price of some loss of quality of specific solutions to problems met.[2] First, the long occupation of one role breeds progressive incompetence in the role by blinding its player to the character and the importance of other roles. (Consider any instance you please of a man who has "presided" over one college or university for twenty years—and only "presided"; a man who has taught the same material at the same level for twenty years—and only taught. Consider too the student who has only studied.) Second, time breeds novelty of problems. The placid train of years in which problems have been reasonably well met by a single, traditional constellation will inevitably end in a problem which cries for another constellation when the structure has become calcified by immotility. The most private and isolated maker of administrative decisions is likely to reach a place where faculty discussion, judgment, and sanction are indispensable to an effective administrative action. The most jealous professorial protector of his private "academic freedom" is likely to reach a place where the administrator's knowledge of the character, the quality, and the history of his work is necessary to ensure its continuation. The most bumptious student

2. See Practical Prescription 6, pp. 173–81.

protector of the privacy of his private life is likely to reach a place where a professor's or administrator's informed sanction of that way of life is necessary to its continuation.

Here, then, is a movable which ought to be moved.

(There is some doubt, however, about what rigidities obtain and where. The paranoid protest stereotype of 1965–66 saw students as the slaves or victims of faculty and administration alike. A year later, many student protesters cast faculty in the role of fellow victim, while some faculty members saw themselves as the victims and sought alliance with students as their champions. In one recent case, administrator and students made common cause as ostensible victims of faculty reaction. And if some student protesters have their way, administrators and faculty alike will be enslaved by students. I suggest that none of these, past or future, constitute a good solution to the problem.)

Community Prescription 2: Institution

The college or university is not, of course, an insulated society. It is in constant transaction with other associations. It is not only in but of a neighborhood. It is also of a region and of a nation. As a participant in neighborhood, it owes what every neighbor owes: proper respect for the rights of other neighbors; appropriate service of the needs of neighbors; alliance with neighbors in the solution of common problems. It owes these debts to neighbors, not only out of some abstract morality but because it must live with its neighbors and the well-being of its neighborhood is its well-being too.

Neighborhood, it should be noted, is not a matter

of size or geography but of state or condition. In normal times, it is small: the town; the city precinct. In times of stress, it may be very large, coextensive with the nation. The defining characteristic is not size; it is ambiguity. When a college or university acts as a neighbor it acts out of character, not as a college or university but in virtue of an accidental quality; because it has money or space or facilities or human resources.

To region and nation the college or university is quite another thing. It is part of the national body, the servant of a definite function, not a neighbor but an institution. It is supported in order to serve this function. Its parts and their interactions are the parts and interactions which facilitate this function.

It is clear, I think, that these two groupings of transaction—the neighborly and the institutional—are almost always at odds with one another. A resource put at the disposal of one is withdrawn from the other. And what is clear in the abstract is borne out by the facts: the tension of town and gown is perennial. Only the style changes. In dairy country, a college cannot fire its best economist because he sees an economic place for yellow margarine. In a rigidly middle-class time and place, the college cannot outrage the sensibilities of its neighbors, but it cannot bow to them either. Its institutional function may require an investigation of sex, the reading of a vernacular poem about Jesus, the medical treatment of blacks as well as whites, the professorship of an Indian astronomer, or work on Sunday. In a time of perfervid patriotism, it cannot burn its German historian, scourge its socialist economist out of town, discharge its Cuban mathematical genius; but it cannot flaunt them either. In a time of war or other large disaster, it cannot fail to put its staff and its facilities in the service of urgent need, but at the same time it cannot fail to retain the cadres, the skills, and the other resources which will permit return to its peacetime function. In a time of pressing need, it cannot fail to contribute to that need. Also, however, it cannot be so profligate in its neighborliness that it is crippled in the service of its function.

I take as immovables, then, (a) the coexistence of neighborly and institutional transactions; (b) their tension; (c) the primacy of the institutional function.

What is movable is implied in their tension: the proportion between the two. We have indicated two of the factors which govern deliberate changes in the proportion: the urgency and the acuteness of the neighborly need; what is concurrently needed to carry on or preserve the institutional function. A third factor is involved: the probable duration of the neighborly need. The seeds of the lotus may endure for centuries; the seeds of scholarship will not. Three sorts of brief mortality are involved. Skills grow rusty if unused for long. They die with their possessors if not passed on. And, least often noted, they require a company of like skills in a soil appropriate to their nurture. The seductiveness of the "relevant," the mainstream, the active, is powerful. And amid very many of their voices, the scholars, even if unseduced, cannot hear each other.

A college or university cannot, then, retread its faculty as trainers of naval technicians or as social agents and keep them at this work for long. It can postpone for only for a very short time the preparation of successors. It cannot interpose among its faculty any large number of engineers, whether civil or social, however expert and recondite their expertise may be. Else, the college will be lost or transformed into something else. Whether this is a serious loss depends, of course, on the defensibility of its function.

Community Prescription 3:   Function

There is nothing immovable about the function of an institution or a kind of institution. A maker of buggy whips can become a seller of marmalade. A post office can cease to be a bank. Railway stations can be remodeled into restaurants. Functions will change as the needs of the large society change and as new institutions arise which serve old functions better. The college function we have set forth in these pages—discovery of intellectual competences, disclosure of principles and methods, mastery of arts, and the use of these disciplines in the recovery and extension of knowledge—must then be defended in these terms: whether it serves a durable social need; whether it can serve that need better than can some other institution.

In the context of student protest, a lesser question (not a new one but one implied in the two above) tends to force its way to the front: whether there are not more desirable functions which a college is equipped to serve; specifically, the assertion that it would be better employed in the service of immediate social needs. We have dealt with a part of this question above. Let us deal with the remainder now; it will speak to the large questions.

I can imagine an institution called a college in a place called Gloversville which functions to supply the labor force needed for making gloves. I can imagine a whole chain of colleges in another place which train young people to run restaurants, hotels, truck gardens, insurance agencies, and editorial desks. I can imagine a third, called a university, which supplies secretarial help, mailing addresses, and laboratories for men who solve problems posed to them by industry and government and provide graduate training to others to do the same. I can imagine a fourth which trains its students to serve in ghetto schools, to organize ghetto neighborhoods, to manage, as ghetto agents, the clumsy structures of state and city governments.

I can not only imagine these institutions, I can condone what they do. I do not even mind their calling themselves colleges and universities. I am disturbed by what they do not do. They do not remember tomorrow. They do not maintain the degree of distance, the measure of alienation from today, which is necessary to anticipation of tomorrow. A few paragraphs will indicate what is involved here.

Consider the situation first on the side of enquiry—scholarship and research. It is obvious and almost irrelevant that problems of nation and society are recognized in the light of present knowledge and solved by recourse to that knowledge—knowledge which was sought and formulated before the problems came to be. It is not obvious and not irrelevant that knowledge is a consumable goods—in a specific and urgent sense. Problems are solved by applying new practices and policies. These practices and policies derive from knowledge currently in hand. It is precisely these solutions—these policies and practices—which give rise to the next generation of problems, for new practices divert the old streams of events; some things are different now from what they were; new connections were established and new interactions have occurred. At intervals, then, and by no means distant intervals, problems arise which have a strong tincture of novelty, and that novelty marks the obsolescence of the knowledge which brought them into being. The solution to problems of mass production gave rise to urban crowding. Crowding, in turn, was solved by suburbs, computers and decentralized production. These solutions in turn have given rise to problems of congested highways, impotent city governments, suburban enclaves, and despairing segments of population. These newest problems will be solved—if they are solved—by forms of government not yet tried, new modes of taxation, new ways of effecting human communication and association. And these newest policies and practices will arise in time only if some of yesterday's scholars and researchers were free enough, remote enough, *irrelevant* enough, to the "greater," the patent, the moving problems of their time, to pursue enquiries which were, at that time, equally "irrelevant." And as yesterday, so today and tomorrow.

The "irrelevance" required is, indeed, a very large one. The new formal knowledge required for tomorrow's practical problems will not be achieved if it consists only of accretions to "pure" knowledge in its present form. It is not only more knowledge of the kind we already know which is required but new forms of knowledge, stemming from new kinds of questions and problems, new principles of enquiry, which reach out for new kinds of facts and interpret them in new ways. Hence the adequate freedom, the adequate alienation, is not only freedom and alienation from current problems of social import but also, in some degree, disengagement from the main currents of present research and scholarship.

Consider the situation now on the side of education—recovery and use of meaning.

As we have remarked at length, practical problems are not givens.[3] We are presented with problem situations, not problems. "The" problem is carved from a conglomerate mass which affords many alternative forms. (And this is a practical matter, for the solutions we seek are marked out by the chosen formulation of the problem.) Someone, then, must know about the existence of alternative problem formulations, possess arts of discriminating them and judging them. Others must know the same thing, possess arts for discerning the sense and differences of proffered formulations, with responsible concern for the facts involved and for the structures of meaning which they constitute and, since these tasks are necessarily corporate, all must possess arts of listening and speaking. These needs exist whether we envisage a democracy in town-meeting style, one in the style of delegated powers, or one in the style of disloyal opposition.

Nor do practical problems, even when well winnowed, come to us wearing each its measure of importance on a label, and all resources are limited resources. Hence problems must be given priorities. Again, then, we confront the need for arts: arts of maintaining clarity and distinction in the examination and use of facts (especially, in this case, facts of quantity and proportion); arts of maintaining distinc-

3. See Practical Prescription 5, pp. 166–67.

tion and rigor in arguing from these facts; moral arts
which hold at bay the impulse to be clever, the impulse
to sway; and further moral arts which hold one to the
problem of responsible discrimination when energies
flag.

Proposed solutions to problems pose a different need.
They come to us couched in the language of specialists
even when they come to us at second hand, in accounts
in newspapers, magazines, television. And, if we are
minimally wise, they come to us as competing solutions—not one ecologist or physicist but two—with
different recommendations. How are these proposals
to be comprehended and judged? Not, surely, only by
calling as translator on yet another specialist of the
same kind, for he, too, may have his specialized axe
to grind. In the last analysis, they must be judged by
nonspecialists (or other specialists in the role of non-
specialist)—the persons (or their agents) who must
put into effect a proposed solution, the persons who
must pay for it, and the persons who will undergo its
effects. These judgments will be good or bad as the
judges exercise the appropriate arts of recovery and
take account of the principles and methods of the
specialty which proposes the solution.

The same need is posed by an even more serious
problem: of knowing what specialists to ask for possible
solutions to problems and of knowing how to relate
the offerings of different specialists. Consider, for
example, the solutions to a problem of social need,
offered by a social psychologist, a sociologist, a lawyer,
a political scientist. Each offering is relevant to the
social problem but in a different way. Each specialist
sees the problem and offers solutions in different terms

—the terms appropriate to his field of enquiry, his principles, and his methods. The problem thus posed, of relating each solution to the other, is a problem beyond any one specialty. It can be solved only by exercise of overarching disciplines.

A last and discomforting word on function. We do not eat and sleep merely not to be hungry and not to be tired. The basic needs are merely first needs. We want, not life merely, but a good life—the desperate and the prosperous alike. We want to enjoy ourselves. Hence the need to discover our enjoyable selves: to explore the range of our competences and interests, test them, develop them into resources of enduring satisfaction. Hence the need for an institution which functions to institute and guide this search.

There is a doubly practical point to this function in a world which contains both the prosperous and the desperate. The problems of the desperate will be well solved only if there are solvers, helpers, whose competences are discovered and in good, enjoyable order. The indignity and injury of being helped will be healed only if the helped can, in turn, be helpers. "In turn," indeed, understates the case. The evocation of competences and the mastery of arts should *accompany* the mastery of first needs.

Here, then, is the case as I see it for the existence of institutions whose function is to be "irrelevant" and jealously to guard their competence to serve that function—to prepare for tomorrow's needs by the only means man has for doing so—his intellect. (The case, be it noted, does not ignore immediate needs. The neighborly role will serve them in some small part;

institutions, designed to do so and properly equipped to do so, must be devised to carry the heavier part of the burden; the college and university must contribute to that devising.)

It goes without saying, however, that all colleges and universities need not be of this kind. On the research side, there is need for centers of mainstream research. There is need for "developmental" work—research addressed to the solving of problems which stand between current plans and their realization. There is need for centers to house advisors and consultants. How many research institutions of the "irrelevant" sort envisaged here are desirable, given the size, the technological, and the social complexity of our country? A specific, responsible answer is beyond my competence. I am sure, however, that the number is small—in the range, let us say, between five and fifteen. The defensible number is likely to be nearer fifteen than five because of three special factors. First, they must be small, as universities go in this country. Second, they are vulnerable institutions, very likely to deteriorate or go astray; hence a safety factor is required. Third, they must constitute a diversity, since there are no rules for the game of inventing new rules.

On the educational—the undergraduate—side, the answer is of a different kind. If we are to solve our pressing social problems and enjoy the lives which solution to these problems will confer on us, we need hundreds of the kind of college envisaged. The pressing social problems will not be served only by experts. They will require the service of thousands of capable citizens, the debate of tens of thousands, and the informed assent of hundreds of thousands more. There are community labor needs and people who want to serve them. There are hundreds of simple vocations and hundreds of thousands who would willingly serve in them. There are and should be institutions to serve these functions. But many of the clients of such institutions are also the persons from whom assent, debate, and help are needed, and they too have competences to be uncovered and enjoyed. Hence there should be no divorce of the vocational and liberal functions at this level. (By "liberal" I mean what I have tried to describe—not indoctrinations and not docile "surveys" of this and that.) And this applies as much to the fancy as to the simple vocations— medicine and law, accounting, teaching and business administration, brokering and banking, chemistry and engineering.

It is the case, however, our egalitarian hopes to the contrary notwithstanding, that some people are less accessible than others to such an education. Many, for example, are fearful—afraid to commit themselves, afraid to own ignorance, afraid of being "wrong." Some, indeed, are so fearful that they show panic retreat when confronted with a question which is not answered "in the book." Others are too docile and too anxious to please. Some lack experience—of words, of things, of ideas. Some are constrained by walls of prejudice and dogma built around them from earliest years. Some are inveterately contentious. And some—like some of our protesters—are blinded by the passionate conviction that they already know all they need to know, even when they do not know what it means to know. These ought to be treated as special problems of education, however, before we decide that they are wholly inaccessible.[4]

Community Prescription 4:   Membership

John Dewey long ago pointed out that in a complex society, membership in associations will take the shape of beer glass marks on a polished bar, intersecting ring after intersecting ring after intersecting ring. The ring of labor union members will intersect with the ring of consumers. A member of the College of Obstetrics and Gynecology will also be a member of the Republican party, a neighbor concerned with keeping children off his lawn and a campaigner against the war in Vietnam. In this respect, Dewey has proved to be quite right, and the college association is no exception. Some of its administrators and many of its trustees owe allegiances to business, financial, government, and military associations. Its professorial members are also members of associations of physicists, modern language associations and anthropological societies. Its students move in a hundred different orbits.

Dewey also thought that each such association would form out of the discovered common interest of its members, and that this interest would always constitute the concern and business of the group—that other interests of each member would arise and be served in other associations. In this matter, Dewey has proved to be wrong. Psychiatrists as psychiatrists take stands on presidential candidates. Physicians in conclaves of physicians vote dicta on fiscal legislation. The mem-

4. This entire discussion of function is, I fear, very old hat. However sound its points, it has been said again and again. Perhaps this is why the protest young haven't heard of it.

bers of a co-op supermarket take stands on labor-management feuds. The result in every case is to vitiate in some degree the effectiveness of the group in the conduct of its business, if only, in the mildest cases, because time and energy is taken from that business. In many cases, the effect is far more serious. The association is so torn by faction that little of its own business can be done. The co-op manager is elected because of his political sympathies. A substantial fraction of a chemical society resigns to protest a stand on contraception and disrupts the communications of its researches.

The college campus is also afflicted with this disease. To a small extent (but in a very few cases, conspicuously) trustees and administrators inject their other interests into their functions as college trustees and officers. To a somewhat larger extent, professors disrupt and divide the work of departments or whole faculties by intruding the interests of competing learned societies. To a still larger extent, they are tending to disrupt and divide by raising issues in department and faculty forums which stem from their political and social-class interests. (This is especially true in certain social sciences where it has long been endemic to overlook the fine line between *ex* and *extra* cathedra.) Above all, it is the case with students. They import to the campus their racial, peer-group, and social-class badges and loyalties and are virtually untouched in many cases by their interests as students of a college.

My complaint here is not against the raising of extensive political, social, and moral issues but with the where and when. As to the where, 80 percent of the social psychology department can plump for President de Gaulle so far as I am concerned, and they ought to if they possess scrutinized reasons for such a stand. But should they raise the issue in a departmental meeting and take a stand as social psychologists? As to the when, the distinction of neighbor and institution applies. There can be moral, social, political crises which make neighbors of us all precisely because they threaten the existence of our institutions—Hitlerism, McCarthyism, the witch hunts of the 1930's. Then, every institution must speak and act as neighbors and so speak with all the force it can muster.

In part, these importations of the interests of one group membership into another group are epidemic and of origins so far obscure. In part, however, they mark the failure of colleges and universities to constitute communities, to make their work and function known to their members—and *felt* by them. It is with the members of the community that I am concerned. And it is with the student members that I will mainly be concerned in the remaining pages of this book.

Community Prescription 5: The community so far constructed

The collegiate community envisaged here is first and last, but not always, a collaborative community. (For once, I should like to spell the word in the way which sets forth its fullest meaning: co-laborative.) It is, nevertheless, community: it is a society with a place for students and a society in which they give (to faculty, to institution, to fellow students) as well as receive; it is a society in whose operation students have a voice commensurate with their powers to speak and increasing as their powers increase; it is a community in which students exist and interact in their corporate identity with faculty in their corporate identity *and* where students exist and interact in their persons with faculty as persons, and with each other. It is a society in which there is a visibility of roles and exchange of roles where exchange is proper—so that students discover what it is like to be a professor and professors rediscover what it is like to be a student. It is a human society—not a society of disembodied minds: when professors confront students in the seminar room, they do so as persons who can be annoyed or irritated by students, who can be impatient, tired, distracted, who are concerned for students as well as with them—and by this visible freedom, enable students to be similarly free. (A professor who cannot be talked back to— "good stubbornness"—and a student who will not talk back will not contribute much to this society, since each, by conventional politeness, hides and defends his vulnerabilities to education. Equally, of course, the merely irascible and the merely impudent will not contribute.)

Let us, as reminders, juxtapose some of the devices which embody this community.

First, consider the character of the curriculum as confronted corporately by students.[5] It honors the student by wrestling with the meat of professional thought, not textbook purees for children. The debates of group discussion begin to open these materials to him. Reflexive scrutiny of debate sharpens his competences, brings them toward conscious control, and further honors him by putting attention on his operations— but again, not as they may happen to be but as they

5. Resources 1–4, pp. 51–94.

can become; not child-centered but concerned with learning and maturation. In its concern for articulations, there is concern for the student's world, both outer and inner, not because it happens to be his world but because it and nothing else can provide the base for an enlarging world. By emphasis on principles of enquiry and by engagement in enquiry itself, the curriculum assumes until the case is disproved that the student can operate as a candidate for peerage with producers of professional materials, no parts of them barred as secrets of an inner temple.

Second, consider the relations of student and teacher as individuals in the curricular process. In debate, participation is sought with respect for individual competences, and a good part of diagnosis is devoted to discovering them—but competences latent as well as patent are discriminated. The critical comment of reflexive scrutiny (by students as well as instructors) is addressed to individual predilections and procedures. In enquiry periods and colloquia, attention is entirely on students' own choices of problems and their struggles at formulation. And the alternatives among programs and courses available to students—including alternatives of the student's own invention—speak immediately to individuals, but individuals in the collegiate society, students.

Similar individuation arises in the contrary direction. In his weekly ambit, the student works with four or five professors. The structure of materials, participants, and operations reveals their differences. The exemplary intervals of discussion reveal differences in kinds of professional competence and kinds of sensibility. The critical and stimulative phases of discussion reveal differences of style, not only style in the treatment of ideas and argument but differences of style in the establishment of the professional relation of teacher and student. Of greatest importance, each teacher enters the classroom, not as an actor onto the stage, from an inaccessible region beyond the wings, but bringing visibly with him the marks of his professional life beyond the classroom. His own research is involved in what he teaches. Anecdote and allusion (incidental as well as germane) reveal some of the vicissitudes and some of the triumphs of his work, some of its pains and satisfactions. Wry comment, amused comment, angry comment, convey something of what it feels like to be and do what he is and does. The campus news media (FM radio and newspaper) take some account of his professional comings and goings. And his public engagement with other professors[6]—in curricular and scholarly debate, in query and criticism of reports and lectures, in submitting to what other professors know— reveals still more of him.

Third, consider the relations of *persons* (as distinct from professional individuals) as they arise in the course of collaboration. Students are paired and teamed with one another for conjoint work. Each discovers weaknesses of others and his own. He supports and is supported. Alliances arise—of peers with common interests, of complementary competences, of helpers and helped—and these are identified and abetted by the instructor. With respect to instructor and student, the systematic self-exploration of strengths and weaknesses which takes place in the classroom carries over on

6. See Resource 6, p. 105; Curricular Prescription 10, "The working group" and "The professor's professor," pp. 250–55.

occasion into self-doubts and special masteries which are dealt with in the professorial study (*office* is wrong here) rather than in the classroom. There are also study conferences on papers written and classroom efforts which break through the surface signs of difficulty to interpersonal deficiencies and buried cognitive structures which lie back of them. Pacts arise in which teacher offers and student accepts continuing and special attention to these painful matters as they arise in the course of future work.

Finally, consider the scope suggested for rectifying one of the central indignities of studenthood, its control from afar by others. The student will have a distinctly audible voice in respect to the quality and character of curriculum and instruction.[7] There are means by which courses devised by him can find instructorial service.[8] He will contribute to the substance of examinations and to their "grading."[9] There is scope for the itch to make and do.[10] He will contribute individually to the decisions and operations involved in the day-to-day life of the institution.[11] And there is the unspecified recent suggestion that a fluid hierarchy among the constitutive groups of the college would serve its purposes better than a single one.

Deficiencies of community remain. Some are treated below. On one I am silent: the extracurricular self-government of students. It is a need and a problem beyond my present competence.

7. See Curricular Prescription 10, "The 'confidential guide'," "The valuation session," pp. 247–49.
8. See Curricular Presciption 6. pp. 212–14.
9. See Curricular Presciption 8, pp. 221–24.
10. See Curricular Presciption 5, pp. 209–12.
11. See Practical Prescription 6, pp. 173–81.

Community Prescription 6:   Close collaboration

The remark above, that students are paired and teamed with one another for conjoint work, is a brief reference to suggestions in Resource 4 and Curricular Prescription 1, themselves too brief to carry the full force of what is proposed. It is that we drop the position that every educational step and act should constitute a survival training which each student must run alone. "Is this paper your own work?" "Did you think of this yourself?" "Who helped you on this?"

I suggest, instead, that we maximize occasions for collaboration. Resource 4 suggests that we welcome collaborative enquiries. Curricular Prescription 1 suggests that a substantial proportion of the work of a course be done by teams of two or three, each team being solely responsible for scrutiny of some segment of material and responsible to the group of students as a whole for supplying them with the needed meanings. This pattern should be carried further, for example, to the joint authorship of papers.

The aims here are obvious: to provide occasions for student discovery of the uses of collaboration, to develop the competences and the practical wisdom required for collaboration—including the wisdoms required to protect oneself from one's collaborator.

The justifications of such a procedure are equally obvious. The pioneer who builds his own house, hunts his own game, delivers his own child, is a romantic vestige. We live now in a collaborative world, for the simple reason that the problems we face can rarely be solved by people singly but require a multitude of talents hardly obtainable within the compass of a single skin. For the same reason the notion that education is a survival course and that our task is to judge the student's capacity for sole survival is also obsolescent.

Community Prescription 7:   Metacurriculum

We have suggested numerous devices for increasing the scope of alternatives among which students may find a portion of their education. All these devices deliberately stop short of what some students have demanded. The suggested new alternatives arise from professorial cogitation, from suggestions made by students and developed by instructors, from plans made by students which receive faculty help and assent. None are in the sole power of the student for two good reasons. First, as students they are not solely competent to determine the most desirable curriculum; they are more ignorant of possible alternatives and resources than are their teachers; they are not good judges, alone, of their own competences, interests, needs. Second, it is of the essence of our collaborative community that decisions be made collaboratively, in collaborations across as well as within the collegiate groups.

It is also desirable, however, that short of curriculum in its most formal sense, there be some scope for student-only selection of some of his educative experience. Professors can be stubborn or hidebound or simply old. I suggest, therefore, the provision of funds and facilities for metacurricular operations—retreats, lecture series, extended forums, even short-term "courses," whose targets, topics, and participants will be selected exclusively by students.

These enterprises, however, are not curriculum but metacurriculum. They are the fruits of student decision alone; students, then, are to be solely responsible for them. The invited lecturers are not college lecturers but student lecturers. The visiting "professor" chosen solely by students is not accorded membership in the college faculty. The courses are not for "credit."

Community Prescription 8: The faculty friend

The college we are constructing will be a challenge to students and new in their experience. It will evoke efforts toward a degree and kind of freedom with responsibility untried by most students. It challenges long-accepted and unexamined views of students about their needs, their competences, their likes and dislikes. Some of its curricular standards are demanding and many are new. Perhaps of greatest novelty, its activities of enquiry, mastery, and learning are largely collegial: there is much student collaboration, and the fruits of students' work, whether solitary or collaborative, are largely public, examined by peers and judged by peers.

The college, in short, is engaged in characteral as well as intellectual education: it is concerned with enhancement of certain emotional as well as intellectual resources, those concerned with work and the human conditions of work. It is concerned with the capacity to engage in the familiar and known without crippling boredom; the capacity to suspend reliance on the familiar, to risk the trial of yet untried competences. It is concerned with capacities to receive criticism without being inhibited by the pain and to give criticism without aggression; to suspend work and worry in the interest of refreshment; to survive depressions and control euphorias; to give responsible direction, submit to responsible direction, collaborate as peers.

In the last analysis an emotional capacity, like an intellectual competence, is enhanced only by undertaking and sustaining the actions pertaining to it to the point of perceiving and enjoying the enhanced competence which results. We increase our competence to read a second language by reading it, by noting our increasing competence to read it, enjoying what we have given ourselves increased access to, and experiencing the increased competence as achievement and a new facility. We learn to survive boredoms by working well despite them, by experiencing in succession the boredom itself, its conquest, the completed work as external sign of conquest, and the sense of achievement and growth which supervenes on the conquest.

Competence-enhancing actions are not usually undertaken, however, without help. In the case of an intellectual discipline, the necessary helps are those suggested earlier as resources of curriculum. First, the instructor affords a model of the discipline: the separate acts which compose it, its use as a coherent whole, the satisfaction of possessing it, its fruits. He then provides a kind of operant assistance by the questions he asks which suggest what next to do and what parts of the materials under scrutiny to submit to these acts. He provides support of two kinds: the honorings of the student's efforts, and the articulations which he seeks in the experiences and competences already possessed by the student. He provides advice and criticism. He reassures in three ways: by the gradual withdrawal of guiding questions, by willing delegation to students of some self-teaching and some teaching of others; by his willingness to give his time and sensitivity to the diagnosis of specific needs and difficulties of individual students as preludes to advice and criticism. By visibly functioning as student as well as teacher, he constitutes a model of a second kind: of a man lacking a discipline and undergoing the vicissitudes of mastering it. Finally, by asides in the course of discussion, and by comments on past discussions and lectures, he exemplifies self-criticism, reflexive scrutiny addressed by himself to himself.

With respect to enhancement of affective resources, the same helps are in order: a visibility of character in action; some operant assistance; support; advice and criticism; reassurance; visibility of characteral deficiency confessed and in course of discipline. To a considerable extent (though not entirely), moreover, the occasions and circumstance of their use for affective enhancements are the occasions of intellectual instruction: work in progress, work done, work undone, work aspired to; classroom and professor's study.

Character in action, for example, is made visible in the relations we establish with students, with work, with colleagues. One broad range of charactered relations with students in the classroom is familiar enough, the range of one's receptions and reactions to students' contributions. A proper middle ground between humility and pride is shown by one's reception of disagreements and corrections expressed by students. The steady, continued, patient but unpatronizing pursuit of a misunderstanding which characterizes only a handful of students in the group has something to say to students about duty, about patience, and about the kindness which distinguishes fault from the possessor of the fault. And to the extent that other students are enlisted in the same task, a degree of operant assistance is harnessed to the exemplification. Similar occasions are afforded by one's reception of a student's confession of error following stubborn denial (no glee, no self-righteousness), by errors we ourselves make (catching them, correcting them, being neither shamed nor angered by their discovery), by the onset of felt and visible fatigue in a long session (not pretending to be otherwise, but continuing the work to the extent dictated by the circumstances), by visible mastery of irritations engendered in the course of a discussion or brought to it from an anterior encounter.

Another useful range of relations to students involving character in action is less commonly recognized, relations established in consequence of what I have called provocative testing by students. Provocative behaviors are designed to test the instructor by affording him invitations to behave in ways inappropriate to his role and circumstances. Pretended eagerness, fake interest, test his capacity to distinguish the real and the false and resist the false. Flatteries of him (by calculated reference to his special interests, by flirtatiousness, by inappropriately respectful address) test his ability to recognize flatteries and not rise to their bait. The intrusion of irrelevant questions and information test his readiness to risk disfavor of students in the interest of his duty to the group and its proper subject; so too, the overlong, the unintelligible, the unnecessarily fancy response to a query. Such provocative tests are, in effect, direct demands by students for the display of character and should be fully used for this purpose.

Even operant assistance in the enhancement of affective resources can take place in the classroom. Many students, for example, often act as if ready agreement with another is to put himself in the power of that other: he resists concurrence long after the tendency of the argument is clear, or he withdraws into silence. In such cases, the invitation to devil's advocacy, discussed earlier, constitutes operant assistance. On identifying such a case, the instructor may first afford an example of devil's advocacy by eliciting from some other student expression of a position with which the instructor is known to disagree, then embark on a defense of that position, examine his own defenses, find them weak, and reaffirm his original position cheerfully and with a smile to the student who originally praised the alternative position. Then, on an occasion soon after, he invites the fearful student to undertake a similar advocacy, provides support by joining with him in the advocacy and its criticism, and praises him for his efforts. Similar opportunities are afforded by the student who acts as if ready agreement with others is necessary to abort aggression, by the student unready to risk being mistaken, by the student who displays contempt for other students.

The private conference with a student about his work affords additional and often richer opportunities for initiating enhancements of affective resources, since, on the one hand, the instructor is surrounded by material evidences of his life outside the classroom (books, papers, the unfinished sheet in the typewriter, incoming telephone calls, the memo pad) and, on the other hand, because the complications of the presence of other students are removed and more numerous signs of the present student's needs (the student's paper, his state-

ment of the circumstances and vicissitudes of its production, his reactions to comments on these matters)
are available. The incidental phone call, the unan-
swered letter on the instructor's desk, the intimidating
array of commitments on his calendar, provide occasions for expression of pleasures and pains indicative of
character and of characteral deficiencies in course of
discipline and permit invocations of relations with work
and colleagues as well as with students. Work with the
student on a portion of his paper affords opportunity
for intensive operant assistance. His discussion of its
production will usually provide occasion even for affective advice and criticism—though these means should
always be used sparingly and with great caution: sermons, admonishments, expressed righteousness are
usually insults, not helps.

The helps, or "instruction" aimed at enhancement of
affective capacities, are thus of much the same kind
as those involved in enhancement of intellectual resources, are provided in much the same contexts, and
contribute to one another. They are not, however, administered in the same way. Two systematic differences
distinguish their use. First, the helps toward characteral
enhancement are rarely accorded recognition as such,
and those which take place in the classroom, never.
They take place in connection with intellectual efforts
and in relation to cognitive problems and should be
seen as adjuncts or necessities of their pursuit. (The
same caveat applies, in fact, to the enhancement of
intellectual capacities, though to a lesser degree. One
does not begin a course by saying "Now we are going
to learn how to think—or read, or recover meaning." Enhancements in these respects take place in the course

of solving a problem or grasping and mastering a content; the problems and the content are the targets and should be so seen.)

Second, where the helps toward intellectual competence can be administered by a professor, helps toward characteral competence must be given by a person. The difference is substantial. The professor is constituted of his professional competences and work: his teaching, his scholarship, the expertise which makes them possible, and the subset of characteral competences necessary to effective use of his expertise. The person has other characteral features, some of them weak. He also has daughters, disappointments, pleasures and pains, triumphs, wants, prejudices, pet peeves, and warmth. These additions are necessary to characteral "instruction" because in our culture (and perhaps universally) it is enormously difficult for an adult to recognize characteral deficiencies, even more difficult for a young adult, and still more difficult to receive help toward their correction—even when the recognitions and offerings of helps are subliminal. The minimum condition for the acceptance of such help is that the helper be susceptible to similar failings, preferably that he have a few of his own. How otherwise, character reasons, can the helper know how it feels to lack, and how to help? A mere expert will not do.

The first problem of characteral instruction, then, is to make visible this personal character of the instructor. Much of this is to be done in classroom and conference by the freedoms shown there, by entering the classroom, as remarked earlier, not as an actor from an inaccessible region beyond the stage but as one bearing the visible (and audible) marks of professional and personal life beyond the classroom. It is also usually necessary, however, that the life so marked be made visible to some students on some occasions: the inside of the professor's house; the professor as husband, father, host; the person acting in the moment and without design. It is for this purpose—not for entertainment, for intimacy, or as a haven for students—that glimpses of the teacher's private life should be afforded. Merely occasional glimpses, moreover, are enough.

In addition to the ongoing characteral friendship of classroom and study, there are moments in the lives of students which require a faculty friend in a more homely sense of friendship. These are moments of regret, discouragement, defeat, arising in the student's immediate past. They are also moments of confusion and fear (and hopes) in the face of future needs, especially needs for choice and decision. These are all moments involving the passage to maturity, many of them arising from curricular experience, all of them arising *in* the curricular experience: in doubts of competence, in questions of career, companions, and beloveds, of the risks one runs and the prices one may be asked to pay for one choice as against another. These are problems to be addressed to someone with a claim to maturity, experience, and wisdom with respect to problems and promises entailed in the curricular experiences. Hence the need for the faculty friend as distinct from professional counselor and psychiatrist.

Again, the first problem is to be accessible as such a friend. And again the problem is solved in large part by the accessibilities made evident in classroom, conference, and occasional glimpses of fireside and friends. The appropriate accessibility is *not* provided by becoming a peer of students or a father surrogate. The professor who is indefinitely available, who pours out all his time to students, renounces by these very acts the signs of wisdom and experience which the student seeks in his faculty friend. It is neither mature nor wise to forego a private life. The professor who entertains students, who finds them inexhaustibly entertaining or "interesting," or who panders to them by "being on their side," may, indeed, entertain them and provide them with topics of gossip, but he does not qualify as a faculty friend. As to father surrogateship and inviting expressions of sympathy and affection, the problem is one of threat. Most students are in process of escape from parents, escape from sanctions imposed by affection and the threat of its withdrawal. At this point in students' lives, affection from an elder of any authority is itself a threat.

The effectively accessible faculty friend, then, is one visible as a *man*, visible as one who could be helpful, who probably would help if asked, who *does not want* to help—a man of penetrable reserve.

Community Prescription 9: The Link

The failure of students to find membership in the current collegiate community is due, among other things, to a failure of roots. Three sorts of "roots" are involved. First, students have been deprived of a sense of *lineage*. We have discarded our continuity with a people and persons with a history; with, that is, a record of contribution and achievement accompanied by a recognizable way of life. We have, therefore, no lineage to convey to them. Students, then, are alone in time. They

are shorn of the direction and assurance which comes
from participating in a tested and durable style of life.

Second, college students have been deprived of a
sense of *peerage*. They come from a hundred racial,
ethnic, and cultural origins to find no common basis for
their presence together on the campus. In the absence
of a lineage, there is no estate, nothing of which they
are the collective heirs or beneficiaries. Each, therefore,
is alone in space. They are shorn of the assurance and
support which come from recognizing in a plurality
of similar and collaborating peers evidence that their
commonly possessed style of life is a viable style. They
are further deprived of the stimulus toward adaptation
and development of that style which comes from wit-
nessing the variations which arise in a company of
similar but not identical young people. They refuse,
however, to be so deprived. Hence, they invent a
peerage and one opposed to what little of style they can
see of the style around them.

Third, they have been deprived of *linkage*. They
have no part to play in the lives of the generation
which precedes them. There is no recognizable common life of student and professor, no common goal
toward which each contributes. Above all, there is no
reciprocity. Students receive but cannot give. They
are paying customers or recipients of favors conferred.
Hence, they are shorn of dignity. In consequence,
common goals and interlocking functions are sought
elsewhere.

The suggestions made so far are intended to restore
a lineage and a peerage and one part of linkage—a
common goal. Adequate reciprocity is still required.
To this end, I propose renovation of the ancient and

honorable position of teaching fellow and his participation in curricular roles appropriate to our college.

The development of such teaching fellowships is feasible and appropriate to any of three institutional structures—those which offer only the bachelor's degree, those which have a terminal master's and those which afford training toward the doctorate. They are appropriate whether the curricular organization is entirely one of courses individually taught or one involving staff-taught courses. I shall describe the teaching fellow in the terms most familiar to me: in a university affording graduate work, operating on the quarter system, and with some staff-taught courses.

Consider first who the teaching fellow is and how he is selected. He has lived and worked in the collegiate community. He has been member of a dozen groups concerned for the recovery of meaning and the discovery of how it is done. He has mastered some of the arts of doing it. He has discovered and developed competences, and he takes satisfaction from their use. He has found channels for his own investigating, making, and doing, has been abetted, guided, and rewarded for his efforts. He has prepared and expounded materials for other students' benefit and profited from their expositions. He has done all these things in close connection with professors as well as students and has been witness to the professorial life beyond the classroom. He has done these things for more than three academic years and is embarking on the terminal quarter of his bachelor's residence.

Those students with whom he has worked in the previous two quarters are convened at the invitation of a professor who has worked with them. They know what the call is for, since the nomination of teaching fellows is a regular feature of the curriculum. The faculty member reminds the group of its purpose, requests the nomination of six candidates and leaves the room. The students meet the problem of obtaining consensus, and the special problem of discussing one another in the presence of all, as best they can. When they have completed their work, a spokesman delivers their list to the professor involved.

Each professor who will be involved in the teaching of entering students undertakes this procedure, for there will be at least one teaching fellow for each such faculty member. From the nominees, each faculty member will select the persons whom he thinks most competent and with whom he feels best able to work. These choices are discussed with a chairman or dean for his approval.

The elected fellows are formally notified of their appointment by the same officer of the institution who notifies faculty members of their appointments. He is given a formal contract and his salary is a good one (that fraction of a regular instructorial appointment corresponding to the fractional teaching load which the fellow will carry).

Very soon thereafter, the chairman of the course in which the fellow will work calls a meeting of the staff or, if the course is individually taught, the single professor meets with his fellows. They meet to plan the program for the coming year. They discuss changes in subject matter and modifications of reading lists. Subcommittees are formed, do their work, and make their proposals to the group. All persons present participate as formal equals: the senior professors, the retiring fellows of the previous year, and the new fellows. "Formal equals" means with respect to voice and vote. If the selections have been made well and the meeting appropriately chaired, each man will contribute in the fashion appropriate to his experience. It should not be overlooked, however, that the experience of the new fellow is real and a special one. Of the three groups present, he is in closest touch with experience of the course as a student. Consequently he has a special and important contribution to make to the discussion. These meetings continue through the spring until plans are completed and administrative labors distributed among fellows and professoriat.

Let this description suffice to indicate one facet of the training of the fellow, his participation in curricular planning. I need hardly add that this participation continues throughout the meetings of the coming year.

The second facet of his training consists of teaching *with* the senior professor, teaching *for* him, and, alone, teaching a subgroup which periodically rejoins another subgroup to reconstitute the whole under the aegis of fellow and professor. In the first three weeks of the autumn term, for example, the whole group of some twenty-five students meet for all three of their weekly discussions. The senior professor and the fellow are coteachers, coleaders of the discussion. At some meetings, the senior professor takes the lead, posing the central problem of the day and initiating the line of questioning. The fellow interjects questions of his own, interposes to conduct a supplementary line of questioning, interrupts to point out a matter overlooked by the senior leader, to expand or modify statements made by the senior leader, to object to some aspect of a student response accepted by the senior leader, to voice a criticism, or to draw the senior leader's attention to students whose wish to contribute has been overlooked.

In other cotaught sessions, the roles are reversed, the fellow taking the leading role. In still others, the discussion will take place between fellow and professor, serving thus sometimes as a model of discussion, sometimes to draw the students into the discussion so initiated, and sometimes as a way of airing important differences in interpretation or point of view.

In connection with all these meetings, the coleaders may meet for planning or postmortem, or not, as they see fit.

In the fourth week of the quarter, the pattern of meetings is changed. The whole group meets only once weekly with its coleaders. For the other two meetings, the group is divided into halves, each half meeting with one of the coleaders. This modification serves several purposes. The smaller group permits a different kind of work on the part of students: lengthier and more coherent discourse from each participant, more intimate identification and sustained repair of deficiencies and bad habits. The small groups also foster divergences of emphasis, interest, and point of view which can be used to great advantage in the joint meetings. It affords the fellow time and place for full command over the discussion while providing feedback, by way of the students, through which the senior professor can detect, and, if necessary, rectify the operations of the fellow.

If there are lectures as part of the course, and there should be, the teaching fellows will play a special role. Such lectures will be examplars of research and scholarship brought to bear on the materials being read and discussed by the students. They will be attacks or defenses of one or another doctrine under examination. They will proffer and argue for views deviant from those presented in the texts under examination in the course. The fellows will attend such lectures en bloc; they will take the lead in the question period which follows each lecture and sometimes monopolize the period. They will do so to afford a model of searching and decent questioning. They will do so to enjoy, and to exemplify, student membership in the intellectual community.

Finally, toward the close of the academic year, the senior professor will absent himself for three days or a week to complete a paper, to attend a scholarly meeting, to read a paper at such a meeting, and the fellow will be in sole control.

This is the induction of the fellow and one of his roles. It is clear, I hope, that he is far removed from the teaching assistant, the "TA" of ill fame. He is not a gleaner, following in the wake of the professor. He is a colleague. He does what the professor does and has a voice in determining what is done.

There are other fellowship roles. He will contribute to the content of examinations, will be party to their approval or disapproval; will be one of the "readers" of examinations. Some will have a decent part to play in the research and scholarship of professors. Others will be constituted tutors, playing at least three different roles in the community. Some tutors will be attached to extended courses and announced to its students by reference to the special interest of each tutor. These tutors will be available ad hoc to ordinary students in the ordinary course of events as they wrestle with problems or materials they find especially difficult. The tutor will use his judgment with respect to the kind and amount of help afforded each student; he will meet with the professor and other such tutors of the program to discuss their clients, their efforts, and the conditions of the program which require them. They will occasionally join the class discussions to note the effects of what they do. A second group of tutors will work regularly with students with special handicaps—constituting an additional and especially accessible echelon of regular instruction for such students. And each tutor will contribute briefly to remedial work which may be required. (No tutor will do only remedial work.) Through all these enterprises, the tutor, like all fellows, will function as a member of the appropriate faculty staff.

Consider, finally, a crucial role of the fellow. If we have developed such a community and curriculum as I have described, the students entering our institution will be entering a new world, one whose expectations, obligations, occasions, and actions differ radically from those of home and high school. There is need, then, for mechanisms and agents for his acculturation, links through which he can discover this social structure and find his place in it, persons whom he knows as persons and can reach at need in the first months of his college residence. It is precisely this role for which the fellow is specially suited.

Imagine, then, some of the ways in which he serves this role. Early in the orientation week which precedes classes, he meets his eight or ten young wards. They gather in his room or apartment—with food and drink, of course. They see the pictures on his wall, the books on his shelf, the recordings. They ask questions about them, comment, and, by way of establishing themselves, display a little knowledge, argue a little with one an· other. The fellow gradually turns the questions, comments and debate toward the months which lie ahead, the new adventure. He suggests something of what it will be like; the sorts of books which constitute the readings, the kinds of things done to them, the character of discussion, the many student roles which can be played in discussion. In response to questions, he describes some of the new freedoms which distinguish the collegiate experience from high school—and some of the new responsibilities. He refers in passing to some of the personalities who will be involved—various professors, their special tics, styles, strengths, and weaknesses. These remarks on persons will be variously admiring, affectionate, indifferent, irreverent, ironic. He will speak simply of some of his dislikes among the faculty—a first of the many freedoms which will help free the new students of the distance which otherwise will stand between them and engagement with the curricular challenges, the persons who embody them, and the community, which together constitute the heart of the collegiate experience. Then he returns the conversation to its first condition, comment and debate at large but enlivened by anticipatory dealing with what is to come. The fellow contributes now only occasionally but his comments are pointed to the student speakers: the bents, capabilities, stereotypes and platitudes, insights and early wisdoms they exhibit. These comments are by way of marking the roles and relations which the fellow and his students are to bear to one another in the months to come.

The following night, the young students are to witness what was only talked about the night before and witness it, not as a bland foretaste of their new life, but with the salt of involving their first close link to the community—their fellow. In seventies to eighties the students gather in rooms whose focus is the round, rectangular, or oval table of discussion. The discussants around it are their fellows. The leader of discussion is one of the faculty mentioned the night before. The discussion which follows is in all respects normal. The matter under scrutiny is a text of quality and importance. Some problems dealt with are difficult, some relatively easy. Some stay close to the text, its argument and ideas. Some seek articulations in participants' experience and in the world around. Participant fellows in various moments are variously at ease, discomfited, effective, at a loss, impersonal, personal. Some exchanges take place only between professor and fellow, some from fellow to fellow. Leads proffered by the professor are often followed but sometimes challenged. He voices his own views on occasion and on occasion they are challenged by a fellow, perhaps defended by another. The discussion ends without conclusion.

After the meeting, a post mortem: the fellows in pairs meet and mix their two groups of charges. Fellows introduce students to one another, as often as possible with a comment about one student to another which indicates to both that the fellow has recognized and honored a quality of mind or person which marks the person so described. (The paired meeting, the introductions, the personal asides are of great importance. Like the pointed remarks of the first night's meeting, they begin to lay the ground for one of the fellow's services to his wards—that of affording what help may be needed to induct the newcomer into useful and pleasant relations with other students.)

The post mortem proper begins: the young students want to know why certain questions were asked in the discussion, why others were not asked, what answers were "right" and what made them so. They ask how it felt to be treated in such-and-such a way, why the fellow behaved as he did at a certain moment, why he did not behave otherwise. Each fellow responds as wisely as he knows how. The other fellow may disagree in instances which have room for disagreement. The two fellows debate their differing views—irenically, of course (indicating that the irenic spirit of the discussion chamber is not restricted to the discussion chamber), but with a degree of intimacy and casual wit appropriate to the circumstances. If possible, a young student or two is drawn into each debate, treated in some moments as a peer of the fellows, in other moments in the fashion which characterized the relation of professor and fellows in the earlier discussion—to suggest, of course, the dual role of the young student, a novice, but in a novitiate aimed toward full membership in the collegiate community.

From questions about how it felt and why one behaved as one did, the fellows move the conversation to the suggestion that a "dry run," a mock discussion, be arranged. It is agreed. A book is chosen in a genre familiar to the young students, small enough to be read before the next evening, light enough to promise amusement, with just enough substance to afford discussion. The discussion (little more than a half-hour) is held the next evening, the two fellows functioning as coleaders. The session is taped, then played back and participations noted and discussed (forerunner of reflexive scrutiny of debate).

In the weeks that follow, the fellow continues to see his charges, singly, as they themselves appear, and in meetings of the group—frequently at first, then at longer and longer intervals. In these meetings, the fellow functions as the disinterested and knowledgeable friend—affording support, some advice when asked, comment on the community and its peculiar ways. Since he is not his charges' tutor, he is free to play this role. If he is successful, his charges will seek his aid less and less often, and somewhere between December and April the group will dissolve.

Here, then, is the college in miniature and the first link by which the entering student can discover the college and find his place in it. The fellow, by virtue of his preparation and selection is precisely fitted to his role as link, for he is both novice and initiate, student and teacher, contemporary of students yet privy to councils of the faculty. And as he links, he himself is linked—on the one hand, invested with a memorable role in the durable life of the institution and, through his charges, tied to the life which will go on after his valedictory.